Big Brown

Greg Niemann

4/07

JB JOSSEY-BASS

Big Brown

The Untold Story of UPS

John Wiley & Sons, Inc.

Published by Jossey-Bass
A Wiley Imprint
989 Market Street, San Francisco, CA 94103-1741   www.josseybass.com

Library of Congress Cataloging-in-Publication Data
Niemann, Greg, 1939–
Big Brown : the untold story of UPS / by Greg Niemann.
    p. cm.
  Includes bibliographical references and index.
  ISBN-13: 978-0-7879-9402-0 (cloth)
1. United Parcel Service. 2. Express service—United States. I. Title.
  HE5903.U545N54 2007
  388.3'243-dc22
                                          2006037903

Printed in the United States of America
FIRST EDITION
HB Printing   10 9 8 7 6 5 4 3 2 1

Contents

*This book is dedicated to
my UPS partners everywhere:
past, present, and future.*

*A percentage of every book sold
will go to the Casey Eye Institute
(named after James and George Casey)
in Portland, Oregon.*

Introduction

UPS was half a century old in 1957. In June of that year, I was a seventeen-year-old Californian right out of high school and had already secured morning employment. Still, I complained to a neighbor who always wore a brown uniform that I needed an afternoon job too.

"Why don't you go down to U.P.?" he said.

"Union Pacific?" I queried.

"No, United Parcel. They always need guys to load and unload in the afternoons."

So in June, I became a UPSer, even though I wouldn't be eighteen until July. "Close enough," they said, and I was assigned to load the Arcadia trailer at the old 9th Street Sort in downtown Los Angeles, starting at $1.62 an hour. After a contractual increase and a promotion to router (sorter), I made $2.05 an hour. This was excellent pay at the time, and among my friends, I was the first to break the $2 barrier, making way more than any of them.

In August, the company gave us free cake and pamphlets commemorating the company's fiftieth anniversary. In December we moved into the new state-of-the-art Olympic facility next door, where men in suits were always around checking things out. Another UPSer gave me the heads-up that one of them was company founder Jim Casey.

I sorted for UPS and attended a community college, but quit the company in January 1958, after which I entered the U.S. Army. As soon as I returned to Los Angeles in late 1960, I headed for UPS. By then I was twenty-one, and they hired me as a seasonal driver. On January 17, 1961, I was called back to join Hollywood Center as a regular UPS driver.

From the very beginning, I had heard stories about the company's tireless founder, the guy who'd been pointed out to me a couple of years before. He was a living legend. Jim Casey, the son of Irish immigrants, working from the age of eleven to support a family of five. In 1907, in a basement beneath a Seattle saloon, he conceived the American Messenger Company, which eventually became United Parcel Service.

I drove for five years and two weeks, just barely enough time to get my gold UPS watch for five years' safe driving. In 1966, I entered management and began to edit the local company publication. All the stories I'd heard about the company's origins and history took on new clarity as I met and got closer to the great men who were leading UPS into new territories and increasingly better service, great men including Jim Casey. Though retired and living in New York, he was still a presence. After I got promoted to the region staff, I was fortunate enough to meet him on numerous occasions. His unwavering insistence on strong values kept UPS and its employees on course.

Much later, when I was finishing my career at UPS in the 1990s, books about big American companies and legendary American entrepreneurs were coming out in droves. Yet the story of our incredible company remained untold. UPS—Big Brown—was by then well known and yet a mystery.

I never planned to do a book on UPS, though in my retirement I had written two books on Baja California. A friend, Shirley Miller, who had been married to Jim Casey's nephew, suggested back in 1999 that of anyone, I should be the person to write the UPS story. I mulled it over and realized that the company's centennial loomed in the distance. It's been on my mind ever since, even though I wrote a book about Palm Springs in the meantime.

It happened one step at a time, getting acquainted with Paul Casey and other members of the family and convincing them of my honorable objectives and purpose. It meant trips to Seattle, Washington, and to Candelaria and Goldfield in Nevada. Even in Ireland, I looked up the Casey family ancestral home.

I reestablished contact with numerous UPS retirees through e-mail. I dug up all my old annual reports, old company publications, and any piece of paper that had brown on it. I learned to research on the Internet and delighted in several "ah-ha" moments. As my manuscript shifted from a primarily historical narrative to a more all-encompassing story, I talked to drivers and current managers.

Big Brown: The Untold Story of UPS will be the first business biography written regarding this elusive yet highly successful corporation. I'm proud of these pages—an epic snapshot of American business and culture over the past hundred years—as I'm proud of having worked for such a great company.

You'll read how United Parcel Service grew on the heels of the robber barons and the Wild West gold rush euphoria, by providing delivery service for department stores, then how it evolved into a common carrier. Led by determined men, the company expanded into new cities and states against the background of the Roaring Twenties, the Depression, and the rise of the labor movement. The book shows how the delivery business became "Big Brown" as it burgeoned across our continent through World War II, the postwar suburban years, and the civil rights unrest.

Today, UPS grapples with the need to conserve energy sources. It works to alleviate environmental problems. It maximizes the use of technology in its now-global presence with stunning innovations in package sorting, interstate commerce, and finally, international commerce with its customs brokering, freight forwarding, and supply-chain solutions. UPS no longer just delivers; it now *enables global commerce*. And Jim Casey remains the center of the UPS universe.

The rise of corporatism, reflected in present lobbyist influence, has pulled the shipping giant into Washington, D.C., in its drive to maintain what has always been the company's most pressing agenda—*outstanding service for its customers*. UPS's commitment to keep Americans working with insourcing, its largely employee-owned stock, and the means by which UPS's century-old business model continues to perform in today's global economy are just a few of the book's fascinating themes.

As I put the finishing touches on this book—which actually represents a lifetime of work, not just for me, but for all UPSers— Jim Casey's dream of excellence and unstoppable determination enriches the spirit that now serves nearly 8 million people daily. UPS still upholds Casey's decades-old corporate values to the tune of huge profits, $3.87 billion last year. How could the reading public respond other than marvel over how this occurred? How could the example of UPS's cautious and continual rise not enormously benefit other businesspeople? Marveling and enormous benefit are my hopes behind *Big Brown*.

Note: A lot of the background research for *Big Brown: The Untold UPS Story* is available for interested readers. Several supplemental stories about UPS are printed on the author's Web site. For this more detailed accounting and more historical information, please go to www.gregniemann.com.

1

THE CULT OF THE UPS DRIVER

In every community of America and in more than two hundred countries abroad, brown-garbed drivers in brown vehicles delivering brown packages are a welcome feature of everyday life. They represent the public face of a company that has changed the world, delivery by delivery, for a hundred years.

UPS drivers are strong. They're dependable. They're polite. They're determined. And they nearly always bear an object of desire! No wonder UPS drivers capture our imagination. They meet expectations more than 10,000 times a minute, every day, worldwide. Talk about delivering the goods!

In a world of dashed hopes and diminishing returns, these dutiful UPS drivers are refreshing anomalies. Some would say they are anachronisms. Diligence, dedication, job commitment, and politeness? Hardly the stuff we experience in most service industries today. Yet these old-fashioned values support UPS's impressive century-old success and by no small measure inspire the UPS drivers' cult status.

The Mystique

The drivers, a majority of whom are male, all aged at least twenty-one, are charming but elusive. An irresistible combination. The UPS driver mystique takes effect swiftly. There's the eye contact. The good manners. Maybe the driver gives your pet a treat. Maybe he even endears himself to your children. Then *whoosh*. After the fleeting exchange, you stand there, holding the package, remembering the sincerity and consideration . . . and efficient vigor. Therein lies the UPS mystique.

Moving at a clip can be a UPS driver's best protection. This I know from personal experience. Back when I was a young driver in Hollywood, running off packages all day, I was in the best shape I'd ever been in but was so busy I hardly noticed when people paid attention to me. However, it didn't take me long to figure out that a good-looking administrator in the Capital Records building had a crush on me. When I came in, her coworkers always called her up front to accept, even though it wasn't her job to sign for packages. They were trying to maximize her contact with me. I was flattered, but didn't have time for more than a polite and brief exchange. Plus I was already married. A couple of years later, I ran into her at a UPS company picnic. We chatted and she introduced me to her new husband—another UPS driver! Apparently she caught one for herself.

A crush on a UPS delivery driver certainly isn't hopeless. Several of my fellow drivers met women on their routes whom they eventually married, and many young UPS drivers will tell you of meeting members of the opposite sex during the working day. The *Wall Street Journal* recently ran a story featuring a female runner who ordered new sneakers every week, delivered by UPS, just so she'd be afforded more contact with her brown-collared love target—contact which ultimately resulted in marriage. Another article, this one in the *Seattle Post Intelligencer,* reported that a UPS driver, on his rounds, asked an attractive woman, "Is there anything to pick up today?"

"No."

"Then, how about you?" he rejoined in a greeting that led to marriage.

Infatuation can be a two-way street. My route in the Hollywood Hills years ago had its fair share of attractions. As an example, movie star Ava Gardner's sister lived there, but she rarely received UPS deliveries herself. When her address did get packages, all from numerous top retail stores, I knew that her glamorous sister was visiting. Ava lived in Spain at the time but loved to shop when she came to town. Even in harsh daylight, sans makeup, she was incredibly pretty, with the most seductive eyes. I was smitten with this world-class beauty but she maintained a polite aloofness.

Also in the Hollywood Hills, Jan Sterling, a beautiful and popular actress of the time, came to the door in a slinky dress. Taking the package, she said, "Oh I'm glad you're here." Then she swiveled on her heels and motioned to the zipper of her gown. I did the gentlemanly thing, zipped her up with shaky hands, and continued on my way. UPSers are trained, after all, to provide service.

Mystique aside, UPS drivers have an enterprise behind them that is a lot more compelling than any love fantasy, though to be sure some of them are quite inventive, such as the Internet blog entry featuring an improvised berth of cushion crating and bubble-wrap. I've come to feel that the cult of the UPS driver is actually infatuation with something much bigger than individual drivers or even all the drivers together. It is a cult of UPS's unrelenting commitment to success.

The Rigor

The demands of the job leave no time for socializing. Other truckers and deliverymen may accept a cup of coffee or engage in chitchat. But an urban UPS driver must make approximately two hundred delivery stops in a scheduled day—and make them in a brisk, fast-paced fashion, because beginning the same time daily, thirty or so pickup stops are waiting. The pressure is on to finish, deliver, and unload everything so the package car (never called a truck by UPS) is empty to receive new pickups. This means that even the most appealing customers are outcompeted by commitments, quotas, punctuality, and performance measurements.

Drivers have a lot of autonomy, but at their back is a Byzantine system that evolved over a hundred years along lines conceived by the extremely disciplined and fastidious company founder, Jim Casey. A wiry little man, Casey began at the bottom. He speedily delivered messages and packages in turn-of-the-century Seattle *on foot*. Casey learned about efficiency by doing. Today, optimizing this connection between body and task is the responsibility of UPS's cadre of efficiency experts, most of whom were also drivers. They are just as tireless and never stop honing delivery into a fine art.

From the company's very beginning, UPS has continually improved and refined its methods. Ergonomics professionals analyze and optimize every juncture between work and human being. Anatomy, physiology, and psychology come together to make the task fit the human and the human fit the task, harming neither the human nor the delivery. Add to that beneficial working postures, maximizing power while minimizing excessive force, nutrition, and diminishing vibration and other adverse exposures. Talk about fitness training!

Every motion at UPS is timed, measured, and refined to its ergonomic best, always balancing physical work rate with workload. Engineers, industrial designers, computer specialists, physicians, health and safety practitioners, and trainers strive to decrease stress, errors, and other debilitations. All movements at UPS are subject to efficiency modifications and institutionalized. As the old maxim among what are now many hundreds of UPS industrial engineers goes, "In God we trust; everything else we measure." As a result, UPSers turn out *better* than machines.

Driver training is designed to establish a cognitive match between the trainee and the tasks. Drivers are instructed to park as close to the point of delivery as possible. To minimize accidents, especially backing accidents, the simple rule "Don't Back" is part of their training. Leaving the vehicle, they are expected to grab the keys with their right hand, use the hand rail with their left hand, and then walk at a brisk pace. Upon return they are instructed to hold their keys on their right pinky finger, grab the hand rail with the right hand, enter their package car, buckle their seat with the left hand and insert the ignition key with their right . . . at each stop. It's that precise. The seconds saved become minutes over the day. Since every minute counts when a driver is trying to finish on time, and a few minutes each day mean big dollars, these methods have lasted.

Not just economy of motion and efficiency are quantified. The drivers are measured on safety too. They are gauged by numerous indices—from individual (years of safe driving without a preventable vehicle accident) to group (1,000 collective days of accident-free driving) to district and company-wide (accidents per 100,000 driver hours, and so on). To help reduce accidents, safety committees exist at all levels.

Activities are not just improved and monitored but celebrated. A man who years later became my dispatcher, driver Ray McCue, received the company's first gold watch for five years of safe driving. That was back in 1928. Today, individual safe drivers are still honored annually, and in 2006 there were more than 4,000 active drivers who had driven for twenty-five years or more without an avoidable accident. And eighty-seven of them had over thirty-five years, topped by a Kentucky district feeder driver, Ron Sowder, who had forty-three years without an accident! Today's UPS drivers log more than two billion miles per year and average less than one accident for every million miles driven.

To outsiders the UPS regime has always seemed excessive. In 1947, writer Philip Hamburger described a company so strict that UPS regulations "could easily be mistaken for the house rules of a Tibetan monastery." This rigor, in effect, disciplines the men and women to resist temptation. It also reflects the kind of management that supports those 92,000 UPS drivers.

The Brawn

UPS maintains a commendable female hiring quota. More on this in Chapter Eight. Still, more men apply for driver positions and the majority of the drivers are men.

Why so many men? The extreme physical demands of the job—moving hundreds of packages daily, weighing up to 150 pounds each—tend to attract men. And not just any men. Drivers don't just happen. Usually, UPS novices sweat and heave their way into driver positions via other strenuous entry-level package-handling jobs, such as unloading, preloading, and sorting, most often starting out part time. The long waiting list for driving—up to four or five years—and the exertion these hopefuls do in the meantime separate the wanna-bes from the chosen.

Package handling in the hubs is hard and punishing. It is not for everyone. Recruiters even show videos of package handling to prospects to prepare them. Some handlers quit early on, some even on the first day after experiencing how difficult it really is. Yet, with practice and supervision, they learn how to maneuver more and more weight, which helps prepare them to become drivers.

For those who stick it out, this interlude is a kind of boot camp, indoctrinating employees with UPS's unique corporate culture and expectations, all the while luring them with the considerable bunch of UPS carrots: excellent pay, great health insurance, education leave, tuition assistance, generous vacation allotments, and (since the company went public) the employee stock purchase plan. Regular follow-up with supervisors and the fine example of senior employees combine to inspire (or for some—repel) devotion. By the time employees have moved a few mountains of cardboard-clad merchandise, they have either caught the UPS commitment or they haven't. If they have, that seed of UPS perseverance will spread through their systems until they too "bleed brown blood."

Finally, prospective drivers get to the head of the waiting list. There, they undergo an additional grueling training program that is so effective that government agencies and other companies use it as a model. The indoctrination includes twenty hours of computer-based classroom training and on-road supervisor training, which incorporates "Space and Visibility" training from day one. Following that, they have thirty working days to prove themselves, as a supervisor carefully scrutinizes their performance in three safety-evaluation rides. If they can't meet the demands, they must return to the other job and wait as long as six months before reapplying. This process can be more competitive than law school!

The Goods

People have always bought more than they could carry, and a hundred years ago they had no cars to help them out. Hence, when Jim Casey and his partners began their delivery service, it served only department stores, and the UPS role was to complete the stores' retail transactions.

Today department stores compete with eBay and other online commerce. Many shopping excursions take place in the Internet ether and are de-peopled. More and more, UPS drivers are shoppers' *only* human contact. The drivers' relationship with the packages is again, as it was in the early twentieth century, the closing event in the retail experience.

Back in the 1950s a long-time UPS employee in Los Angeles named Homer Hunt won a slogan contest with his entry "Every Parcel a Guest of Honor." Hokey though this phrase may be, it has endured because it describes the accommodations and services each driver provides during his time with the parcel. UPSers took it to heart.

Every parcel is different and in some way unique. Drivers get to know a package by shape, size, and even odor—as when the distinctive smell from cosmetics permeates a carton—and to associate it with a certain customer. Pulling up to an upholstery shop, a driver might instinctively grab the wrapped roll of fabric, maybe not even checking the label until walking to the shop. Merchandise delivered reflects the route itself. In Hollywood, as an example, I regularly picked up or delivered all kinds of things related to the movie business, including the Academy Awards Oscar statuettes themselves. Drivers can learn a lot about their consignees based on their incoming merchandise. For example, if a company starts receiving more C.O.D. packages than before, it's often a good sign that its owner is having financial difficulties.

The 3.75 *billion* packages UPS delivered worldwide in 2005 represented a substantial section of the world's economy and included a little of everything, from contents obviously critical to those seemingly mundane. The packages have contained time-sensitive serums and other medicines, live animals, firearms, college students' clothing, and junior's baseball cards; the list is endless. With such a large market resting on their efficiency, UPS drivers work to stay comfortable with their cargo. It's a big part of their job.

The Uniform

"There's something about a man in uniform," people say. What is that something? Reliability. Strength. Respect. Safety. These are qualities most people associate with heroes.

When UPS first issued complete uniforms back in the early 1920s most people in uniform were in the military, law enforcement, and medical professions, and uniforms sent a message of assurance. The 1923 UPS driver uniform consisted of shirt and tie, long jacket and cap. The brown color of UPS apparel, first featured in 1925, and of the package cars, was an intentional understatement, designed in deference to UPS's more flashy customers and as a way to project humility, one of Jim Casey's most strongly held values. Sure, brown didn't show dirt, but Casey was also very strict about grooming. UPS washes and mends the uniforms as needed. The bland color was about maintaining a sense of respectful humility.

During World War II, the Korean War, and up into the 1960s, uniformed men traded in authority and popularity, and UPS trousers were still long. When I was a driver, we had to wear thick long pants all year long, even when the temperature inside those package cars would soar over 120 degrees.

In those days the uniform included a captain's hat, with a shiny dark bill and the UPS badge on the peak. It was the kind of headgear worn by fire and police officers and Air Force pilots, rather weighty and uncomfortable after a while. We were obliged to wear them all day, too, or risk getting a pink demerit slip.

Then suddenly the counterculture happened. Young people, protesting against the Vietnam War, segregation, and government authority, looked at uniformed personnel not with respect but with suspicion, adopting a generational style that emphasized individual-ism and informality. While they had no direct influence on corporate decision making, emerging cultural trends that valued comfort over formality began to find their way into corporate America.

UPS driver bow ties went by the wayside in the early 1950s, yet still had to be worn in several Midwest and East Coast locations through the next decade. By the time I became a manager in 1966, no one on the West Coast wore a bow tie; nonetheless, whenever I photographed a driver for national use I had to show him in a bow tie, so I carried a black clip-on tie in my camera case. The UPS headgear was the final point of contention. The hat eventually became optional in 1972—which all but ensured its demise.

Then, by the 1980s, focus group discussions, group meetings, one-on-one "Talk, Listen and Act" sessions, exit interviews, and other ongoing UPS communications revealed that *drivers would like to wear shorts!* It was time for UPS to rethink the haberdashery.

After years of resisting change, the company yielded to the drivers and the famous UPS shorts came into being. In its usual methodical manner, the company selected a few test locations—Sacramento, Tucson, and Hawaii—and supplied some of the drivers with shorts. As a member of management, I interviewed the drivers of one Tucson center who were wearing the "experimental shorts" and learned that they not only loved them, they were fending off questions from the other Tucson drivers, who kept asking when the change would include everyone. Our reports confirmed what was suspected and was already set in motion: *the drivers would wear shorts*. By then, however, I was stuck in a suit and tie every day.

The new uniform recast the UPS driver from a tired, traditional service worker image to one a bit spiffier and more up-beat. Shorts. Polyester. Built-in collar stays. Reinforced stitching, pocket-within-a-pocket for a pen, glued-on gold crest, long shirttails that would stay tucked in. Drivers, whose whole day is an aerobic workout, sometimes roll up their sleeves and wear shorts whether by sleet or by snow or by hail . . . and gratefully.

Many customers have commented that the shorts and the legs that fill them have made driver ogling that much more gratifying. Competition between UPS and FedEx extends to their uniforms. Many drivers and the public too find FedEx's fashion sense a bit flashier than Big Brown's. Still, it's all in what you're after. So what if FedEx drivers have ten mix-n-match options? UPS drivers deliver one-third again as many packages every day, and they generally make more money and enjoy better benefits.

Even though the UPS uniform is, by any measure, staid, UPS cultivates good relations with fashion designers in any way it can. UPS cosponsors the annual New York Fashion Week, selecting ten designers to incorporate *UPS brown* into their collections. Among the inspirations in 2006, svelte models sported thigh-high boots and safari-inspired hot-pant jumpsuits for the gals, and macho work boots and sleeveless shirts for the guys.

Unlike Army-Navy surplus, UPS uniforms are a tightly controlled commodity. The uniform belongs to UPS. Shirts, shorts, even logo-embroidered socks are allocated—five outfits, one for every workday. UPS washes and presses the shirts and shorts, and reclaims the uniforms for replacement when they wear out.

Management guards these items closely because the brown UPS wardrobe has become synonymous with service. They don't risk a uniform's misuse. Selling used uniforms on eBay is against company policy. Worn-out uniforms must be destroyed. Even the American flag, subject of legislation, doesn't have this kind of protection, maybe because the American flag isn't a pass-card to every business and household.

When UPS uniforms are missing, or presumed missing, UPS goes after them like a pack of hounds. A blogger named Darren Barefoot found a shirt at a thrift store and featured it on his Web site. UPS attorneys contacted him immediately and he handed over the shirt. Sometimes errant UPS uniforms set off a national alert. In 2003 a false claim was made that UPS uniforms, valued at $32,000, were missing. What would happen if people posing as trusted UPS drivers gained access to you and your household or business for shady reasons? Sure. Terrorists might want to pose as UPS drivers. After a period of media mayhem, UPS spokespeople debunked the claim. UPS does not condone the sale of its uniforms and continues to investigate any reports of their unauthorized use.

In some instances UPS has allowed law enforcement agencies the use of uniforms, usually with a UPS loss-prevention manager nearby. Say, for example, that acting on a tip or information from another source, the agency has learned that a package contains illegal drugs. Drug enforcement officials in UPS uniform make the delivery and nab the suspect attempting to sign for them. This scenario, and others like it, has happened throughout the country on numerous occasions.

The Service

Jim Casey made sure that service was the fulcrum on which all business decisions swing. If longevity and economics are any measure, the company founder's decision was dead on. "Our real, primary objective is to serve—to render perfect service to our stores and their customers. If we keep that objective constantly in mind, our reward in money can be beyond our fondest dreams," Casey said.

How did the company achieve high service levels in all areas of its operation? The company has high standards and is continually making higher ones. Unrelenting problem solving, innovative technology, new services, and choreographed delivery procedures: all grease the wheels of UPS operation.

Even one package not delivered? That's a service failure. Drivers often find themselves going out of the way to provide utmost service, even if it means incurring extra costs to get one package delivered on time. Management meets regularly with employees to discuss service, to work as a team to solve problems, even with the involvement of hourly employees. Employee groups constantly dissect any service failure at regular *Service Involvement Meetings*.

The meetings are also a forum for recognizing exceptional service stories.

As a result of all this teamwork, monastic-style though it may be, the sum of UPS is greater than the parts. Cult or no cult, no one individual dominates. UPS drivers work as superheroes work, tirelessly and seamlessly. They not only hear but understand and emulate the company mantra intoned by Jim Casey, "Service—the sum of many little things done well." Which raises the question: Who was this guy Casey?

2

THE GREATEST AMERICAN CAPITALIST YOU'VE NEVER HEARD OF

You don't have to be a famous "somebody" to create a global empire. James Emmett Casey, known to everyone as "Jim," moved through his long life as reliably and inconspicuously as a plain brown UPS package car travels between pickups and deliveries. Certainly not with the fanfare we associate with today's high-profile corporate commanders. So what if he lacked charisma? Puffery wasn't necessary to his enterprise because Jim Casey had a profitable approach. UPS's ever-increasing sphere of service depended on a code of ethics as rigorous as a military academy, with some of the best management the world has ever known.

Unflagging Concentration

Casey's definition of good management didn't draw attention to himself, but instead focused on getting results *through other people*. It all came down to that. "Good management is taking a sincere interest in the welfare of the people you work with," he'd counsel. "It is the ability to make individuals feel that you and they *are* the company—not merely employees of it." This vision—his vision of a delivery company made of people—grew in a hundred years from a few foot messengers to a global fleet of tens of thousands of package cars and jet airliners.

Jim Casey was a shy man, anything but flashy. He was diminutive in stature, with sharp features, a long face, and piercing eyes. Fastidious in his person, he was always impeccably groomed and seldom wore anything but an understated dark suit, carefully pressed and of the finest quality. In his day, he could walk down any street in America in his well-polished Oxfords and never be recognized as a master of industry, despite his ever-expanding wealth and influence. A stranger observing Jim Casey might have thought: *This is not a man to be watched. Rather, it is a man who is watching.*

Jim Casey watched the streets carefully. He watched movement. He watched what people sold and what people bought. He was an eternal puzzle solver, his mind constantly preoccupied by every sensory detail involving his core business, packages. He gravitated to them, mesmerized by how they were wrapped and how they were delivered.

The 1972 UPS National Conference, at a resort hotel on San Diego Bay, gives a sense of his singular obsession. During one of my walks between the dining room and conference meeting rooms, I heard someone call out to me. I peered curiously down a short path that ended at the rear door of one of the hotel exits. There, half-hidden in the bushes, was Jim, all on his own, gesturing down at a stack of packages. It was evident that hotel employees had prepared them for Post Office pickup.

"Say, what do you suppose these packages are here for?" the master motivator asked me "I should think *we* should be delivering these packages!" (Meaning UPS and not the U.S. Postal Service.)

"I don't know," I told him, "but I'll find out." I was just there as support for the conference, but I knew I had to do something. While he slowly walked back to the meeting (by then he was eighty years old), I wasted no time in notifying our top customer service people, who put the wheels in motion.

The next day, I told him, "Jim, I'm told UPS will be delivering hotel packages from now on. Thanks to you," I added. What a businessman, I thought. How many of us, top management included, walked past those packages without even noticing them!

An autodidact, he never tired of learning. To keep up on the trends, he read, he listened to the radio, he asked questions. Inquisitive and alert, he didn't hesitate to put himself in situations from which he could learn.

Once on a Puget Sound party boat for a meeting of the Board of Directors and other management, I watched him pumping the skipper for information about the engine. It wasn't an idle query. Jim, then eighty-six years old, really wondered. Not satisfied to relax and enjoy the party, he and a few others climbed down a vertical ladder into the dark recesses of the engine room. Why shouldn't he be curious? After all, engines are a big part of what makes UPS run.

When traveling between meetings Casey would frequently tell his driver to stop when he saw a UPS delivery in progress. Without identifying himself, Casey would ask UPS drivers what they thought of their job. He'd listen carefully and consider their answers seriously. These informal "man on the street" interviews became an invaluable way for him to assess the efficiency of UPS delivery operations in a way that a UPS manager's filtered version could not.

Alda Williamson, who spent thirty-three years at UPS headquarters as the company archivist, worked closely with Jim Casey. Jim's thirst for knowledge was, to her, one of his most impressive traits. "He didn't have much of a formal education, but he learned so much just by listening. When bankers, for example, would have a meeting with UPS managers, Jim would often ask to sit in. The bankers were pleased that the founder was involved, and Jim just sat there and absorbed everything."

Pioneer in People Development

Part of the wisdom Jim absorbed was a keen perception of social justice. Just as he did not regard someone who knew more on a topic than he did as a threat, but rather as someone to learn from, he did not regard people with less than he had to be inferior. Every new person Jim met had value, and the potential of conveying a piece of information or pearl of wisdom that would enhance UPS. And it wasn't just improving UPS that was on his mind; it was applying the financial success of UPS to improve Americans' lives. As he saw it, all people were customers, partners, or employees that he or his business could help.

During the late nineteenth century, before Jim Casey came of age, other business leaders—men like Leland Stanford, John D. Rockefeller, Collis Huntington, and others—had employed cunning and cutthroat tactics to make money, then lived off the spoils. Their methods established the robber baron model for gaining economic power and industrial supremacy. Yet, from Casey's perspective, such opportunism and exploitation seemed at odds with his simple and honest background.

Jim's father, Henry Casey, had immigrated from County Galway as a result of the Great Potato Famine, and his mother, Annie Sheehan Casey, was a first-generation American, daughter of immigrants from County Cork. Both Annie and Henry were industrious and hardworking, but the social fabric within which they struggled was buckling. The family was impoverished, despite their toil and ambition. And so were many, many other families of Jim's acquaintance.

The Pacific Northwest of Jim's early years had a robust social movement, and Seattle, where the Casey family settled, was already known across the country as a haven for left-wing politics. Activists called for the emancipation of the working class from the "slave bondage of capitalism." They wanted the working class in possession of economic power, to control business enterprise without regard to capitalist masters. This is the atmosphere in which Jim Casey matured. Remember, he was always watching. He couldn't have helped but notice the unrest and reasons underlying the working-class argument. Fliers, demonstrations, meetings, and strikes were commonplace in those early years of the twentieth century. For Jim, already in the messenger and delivery business, the working classes were potential customers and employees. It wasn't coincidence that led his company to social responsibility— it was Jim Casey's conscience. Although Jim was conservative and far from radical, the idea of shared responsibility and wealth took hold in him. It became the linchpin of UPS management. He eschewed the path of the industrialists and instead pursued social responsibility and partnership.

Jim Casey knew, instinctively and from experience, that the team would be no stronger than its weakest link, that employees were not just workers but whole people. UPS employees were like an enormous extended family, *his family*.

The "family" commitment continues, twenty-four years after Jim's death. UPS helps with education. The benefits are great. UPSers can count on having their jobs back when they return from military service. The retirement system is set up in such a way as to ensure employees' care in old age. The founder reiterated versions of the following objective over and again:

> I envisage our organization as a means through which each member should be able to achieve a good measure of personal satisfaction and at the same time aid in the advancement of the interests of all the rest of us.

These words were more than pabulum. All aspects of UPS's emerging corporate culture under his watch worked toward these ends. Jim Casey believed in the people who came to work for UPS. He trusted them to do a job, gave them the latitude to do it, respected their opinions, and wanted them to share in the profits. He supplied every reason to become a workaholic, just as he was. His personal values, in effect, became those of the company.

One manager recalled that Jim was never too busy to talk to you. No matter if his desk was piled high with work, he would always put it down and listen to what you had to say. He did not hurry you, but gave full attention to your thoughts and comments and would offer any suggestions he had.

If a driver bumped into Jim Casey at the cafeteria, he would say "Hi, Jim." And Jim might even have answered him by name. Casey wrote in a 1929 UPS policy manual that managers were to be addressed by first name. This policy seems hardly unusual to us today, but at the time it was akin to Bolshevism. Yet although the 1930s were a time of great labor unrest in the United States, UPS weathered through because of a corporate culture based on family-like relationships. These people policies have stood the test of time. Every executive still remains approachable, and people know each other's first names.

Several charities that Casey and his family founded embody the same kind of commitment to people. His giving nature led to the establishment of The UPS Foundation, The Annie E. Casey Foundation, Casey Family Programs, and Casey Family Services, which serve children, youth, and families. The charities focus first on the boys and girls who most need help, as referred by schools, hospitals, the courts, and state agencies. Once selected for care by the Casey charities, these kids receive a wide breadth of services to help them become happy, healthy, productive adults.

Members of his family also established The Marguerite Casey Foundation and Casey Eye Institute. In addition, Jim made private personal donations to worthy causes such as Seattle University throughout his life. He didn't forget the hard times of his youth, and when he died in 1983, most of his money went into these charities. Today, Casey Family Programs alone has about $2 billion in assets, employs a staff of seven hundred, and provides care to more than 500,000 young people.

Thrift and Humility

Despite all this philanthropy, Jim could be parsimonious. He always watched where the money went, a habit left over from his days of supporting a family of five as an eleven-year-old. As an example, in the late 1940s Jim made a friendly suggestion to the president of AT&T, which had a monopoly on America's telephones. Noting that the phone lines weren't much used at night, he suggested that AT&T offer reduced night-time rates. AT&T implemented the idea, and the resulting savings worked well for frugal Jim and for millions of other Americans.

At UPS, he was always quick to hire engineers and consultants to analyze sorting and delivery methods so that every job was performed in the most efficient and economical manner.

For years, the national headquarters for UPS was in the New York hub at 331 E. 38th Street in Manhattan. Among the administrative offices was Jim Casey's office—a small stark room, occupied only by a green metal desk, several chairs, and a coat tree. Except for the few papers he was working on and a metal model of a UPS package car, the desk was always bare. His door was never closed. He often sat in that cubicle poring over reports long after his associates had gone home. In the 1960s, after the company moved across town to 643 West 43rd Street, Casey had an executive office that was a little larger but no more ornate. Again, it was open. Since his office and those of other executives had large glass windows and doors, the area became known as "the fishbowl."

Whether it was because he demanded thrift of other UPSers or whether they too had their eye on the bottom line, his frugality was infectious. Generations of managers have turned off lights when leaving rooms to help cut energy costs—treating the company as if it were their own, because as members of the innovative UPS profit-sharing plan, it does belong to them! For many years offices resembled army barracks or large city hospital corridors. Walls were painted two-tone drab, desks and furniture were designed for durability and function, not comfort. Most office windows had no drapes or curtains at all. Pictures, if any, were usually small photographs, in black and white, of company vehicles or people at work. The floors were linoleum or tile, barren of carpets. In addition to being a demonstration of humility, the minimalism also dispelled any customer questions about the fairness of UPS prices.

No fleet of corporate secretaries for Jim. *All* executives answered their own phones, and none had private secretaries, even the CEO, a practice that still exists. Each department usually had only one clerk. Like Jim, most UPS managers preferred this Spartan business style. They were all owners of the business, and almost without exception they preferred greater profits to splurging on frills. This lack of pretentiousness and its related economy, while toned down somewhat through the years, still prevails at UPS.

Almost his entire adult life Jim Casey lived in hotels, and for over fifty of these years, these hotels were in Manhattan. When the company moved its headquarters to New York City in 1930, Jim Casey took up residence in a single room at the Barclay Hotel on East 48th Street. In the late 1930s, he moved to larger quarters at the Waldorf Towers at Park Avenue and 50th Street. The elegantly furnished hotel rooms and residential suites of the Waldorf Towers have been occupied by some of the world's most illustrious figures, including Mamie Eisenhower, Cole Porter, and Frank Sinatra. With maid service twice a day, it was everything that a tidy, wifeless man might want. Nonetheless, the step up was hard for a person who allowed himself few luxuries. He went from office to office, seeking approval for the move from his associates. "You sure you won't think I'm snooty?" he asked. "You sure it's OK and not too ritzy?" He didn't want his colleagues to think their founder was becoming too self-important.

By that time UPS was well entrenched in seventeen of America's largest cities. The stock Casey offered to employees at $40 per share in 1935 had already more than doubled and was about to split 10:1 by 1947. Jim Casey, reluctant to display pretentiousness at the Waldorf, was already a millionaire, and this was back in the days when a million dollars was an incredible amount of money.

Modestly furnished, Jim's rooms included a Capehart phonograph and some Danish figurines his mother had given him. Over his bed hung an inexpensive etching of a mule. The only other artworks were Western landscapes, to remind him of his young life in a wilder West.

Colleagues asked Jim if he associated with any of the Waldorf's influential patrons. Since he worked long hours at UPS headquarters and the hotel elevator took him directly to his suite, he explained, he had few opportunities to run into them. He somehow omitted the fact that the Duke and Duchess of Windsor were just down the hall. However, he did admit to having shared dinner in the hotel restaurant with Mrs. Douglas MacArthur on a couple of occasions. But no expensive country club memberships or seaside properties for Jim. No ostentation of any type. No one really knows why Jim didn't seek opportunities to rub elbows with the rich and famous. He much preferred the company of his UPS associates. It seems likely, however, that wealth and fame had little place in his longtime, unwavering vision of extending quality package delivery service to every house and business in America.

Deliberation, Not Boldness

By all accounts, Jim Casey was all about business. He relished the daily trials that landed on his desk. He loved them! He didn't want to hear that any challenge was unsolvable, and his managers learned to look for solutions instead of excuses.

Yet he was not the kind of leader to make split-second decisions and rush to conclusions. Jim's feats of derring-do were never rash. They were judiciously deliberated adaptations to the market and the times, all with the objective of expansion. As the twentieth century's new social and business issues unfolded, and sometimes quaked along the way, Casey greeted each potentially cataclysmic event with consideration, quietly strategizing with his partners and managers to turn challenges into opportunities.

The significant achievements that mark UPS history appeared less momentous to the public at the time they emerged, partly because they took so much time, money, and people to think through and realize. UPS delivery innovations and business acquisitions just seemed to happen like the subtle shifting of tectonic plates. We now take for granted, for instance, that UPS is nationwide (and worldwide). Jim Casey didn't make this happen in a wink of the eye. That your grandmother in Vermont can send you a package in New Mexico, faster, more reliably, and less expensively than via the U.S. Postal Service, reflects a network that took almost Casey's entire life to realize. You'll read later about UPS's long slog to acquire the rights to deliver in new regions across the country.

You'll also learn how Jim created his formula for acquisition and dedicated management—partnership; that his response to unionization was good benefits; his solution to buyout was buy back; his answer to civil unrest was equal opportunity and to dissent was immediate communication; his answer for sluggish layers of management was decentralization, and his attitude toward employees was an unwavering belief in and respect for the individual. The methodology behind these adaptations—all "vintage Jim"—provided a model for survivability that moved UPS, even after he passed away, beyond competitors like rival Federal Express, to secure its position as the top delivery company in the world.

A Life Without Distractions

Even though Jim Casey spent most hours of most days around people, nothing remains of him that one could call intimate. No shocking stories. No failed love affairs. No devastating failures. He ate meals out and had only a few close friends, all of them UPS associates. He took in a movie every once in a while, and he occasionally enjoyed a boxing match at Madison Square Garden, but his real high was being on the job. He never married. UPS was his personal life, his eye always on the next business frontier. Money and prestige did not push him. Excellence did. He simply had an insatiable desire to do the best job in delivery and for UPS employees, given whatever circumstances emerged.

Much of the time he got around Manhattan in cabs, which he sometimes hailed with a shrill whistle from two fingers in his mouth, right up until he was bent over with age. For a period in the 1940s Jim owned a Packard, which he drove himself. If he allowed himself a Sunday drive to Westchester or New Jersey he spent his outing recording the travel times it might take him to get to different towns. Back in the office Monday morning, he would check his figures against the official company time allotted for UPS vehicles to make the same run. His mind never shut off from weighing and measuring.

After UPS headquarters moved to Greenwich, Connecticut, in 1975, Jim Casey hired a private secretary (whose name has been lost, I'm sorry to say) who served as his companion and chauffeur, driving his maroon Mercedes-Benz between the two cities. When she couldn't make it, a few times he'd bum a ride back to Manhattan from a fellow UPSer. One such mate was Gene Reilly, at the time a young supervisor from the communications department who drove an old Checker cab painted mustard yellow, with two bullet holes in the door, bad shocks, and cracked windows. The exposed engine fan made a less than reassuring clicking sound. Jim often shared the "cab" with two other communications supervisors, Rheunick Green, a small-statured Jamaican with a strong lilting accent, and Sophia Washkowitz, a grey-haired Russian lady.

Their nervousness at sharing a ride with the big boss dissipated as Jim, by then in his eighties, made every effort to be treated "like one of the boys." As Reilly described these commutes, "He was very interested in our views on the company and how we could make it better. I thought to myself, here is the founder of the company and he is asking us about making it better. That really blew us all away!"

The Park Avenue doorman had some adjusting to do about Jim's unconventional transportation arrangements. The first time he saw the elderly Waldorf tenant arrive in the old mustard-yellow clunker, wedged between a black man and an Eastern European woman, he rushed over, thinking Jim was being abducted. Calming him down, Jim merely said, "Meet some of my associates." No fuss or glitz for Jim.

Other than for business, Jim Casey didn't travel, except for visits to his mother and siblings, usually in Seattle and later, during Christmas, in Palm Springs, California. The eldest of four children, Jim was considered the family patriarch—not a warm, cuddly uncle, but gentle, polite, and considerate. His brother George Casey was a lifelong partner at UPS and, though younger, died twenty-six years earlier than Jim, in 1957. Married to a first cousin, George had no children. Jim was very close to his younger sister Marguerite. She never married either and died in 1987, four years after Jim. His brother Henry Joseph Casey, known as Harry, had no inclination to go into the delivery business. Instead he married, moved to Portland, Oregon, and went to work for Ford Motors. He switched to selling cars and had three children. Harry died in 1992 at the age of 101, the last surviving sibling.

Beyond these few anecdotes, remarkably little is known about this founder of a Fortune 500 company, and moreover a company that's been around for a century and is familiar to all Americans. Even people who worked with Jim Casey for decades knew little or nothing about his private life. It was almost as if Jim Casey had no private life beyond his lifelong commitment to UPS.

It wasn't that Casey had no feelings. Anyone who knew him would tell you that *caring* was at his core. He'd stop, he'd listen, and he'd inquire. Then he would recommend, make a few phone calls, find solutions, make recommendations. It was only that—unlike the rest of us with the normal attachments to friends and family—the context of Jim's caring always had Big Brown as bookends. For this American hero, UPS was the cause, the cure, and the carrot. And that explains the company's astonishing growth and influence under his seventy-six-year watch. Jim Casey the man was subsumed by something greater than himself, a company called UPS, created according to a formula in which the two most important ingredients were people and service.

The Stickler

Jim Casey was neat as a pin. He expected the same of every man and woman who worked for UPS. He lived in a suit; therefore, so did the rest of management. The obsession for tidiness extended to the package cars. Seeing mud on the wheels enraged him, sparked his tightly controlled Irish temper. And it wasn't just spotless clothes and package cars that gleamed. He believed that order and cleanliness should extend through the ranks, right down to UPSers' very souls. Their character should be as impeccable as their stayed collars. Jim had no problem with this ideal and didn't expect anyone who worked for UPS to have a problem with it, either.

He encouraged his staff to look at themselves through the eyes of the customer, saying, "Customers judge us by the visual and mental impression they get. If those impressions are to be favorable, we must have the appearance of doing a good job. Not only does this apply to the physical appearance of plants, cars, and people, it also applies to the impressions created by the work we do and how we do it."

Neatness and dependability relied on alert, sober employees. Jim Casey wasn't a teetotaler. On occasion, he liked his Harvey's Bristol Cream sherry. Yet he established a company policy against drinking alcohol on the job. Of course, drivers have never been allowed to consume alcoholic beverages during the day, and managers reinforce this by setting good examples. Drinking any time during the workday, even at lunch or at any business-related function, continues to be grounds for immediate dismissal, regardless of one's position.

Casey's personal code of neatness was a discipline, a discipline he required of his managers, and through them, the entire UPS enterprise. Cleanliness seemed tied to dependability and in a sense engulfed UPSers' personal affairs, or as he put it: "We demand of all people a high standard of morality. . . . Their private lives should be above reproach." Casey persistently drove home his philosophy.

He wasn't the typical corporate cheerleader. Casey's archived gospel is not so much inspiring as preachy and relentless. What Jim lacked in pithy, dramatic oratory, he made up for with unusual and becoming modesty. Unpretentious, he always referred to other people's good examples, never proclaiming his own. Today's demanding business audiences might scratch their heads and wonder at the difference between this man and Jack Welch or Michael Eisner or Bill Gates or Lee Iacocca or John Chambers. Hardly a shining star, Jim Casey was more a steadily burning flame. Who says that stockholders and employees won't rally around anyone except celebrity CEOs?

He was revered by employees wherever he went throughout the UPS system. They would rush over to shake his hand, hoping to have a photo taken with him. A thirty-year package driver came up to me during one such Los Angeles visit, nodded toward Casey, and said, "He is the reason I've made UPS my lifelong career."

Distill Jim Casey's lifelong message to its essence and you get what we today refer to as core American values. Neatness, humility, frugality, dependability, safety, strong work ethic, integrity, and much more, carved from the corporate culture that Jim Casey established. All principles focused on people and service.

Good Values Were in His Blood

This unassuming ascetic with an iron will based his company and his every move on ethics that he learned as a child, mostly from his Irish mother. Jim Casey's parents, like most Irish of the time, greeted hardship with grit and ingenuity. After meeting and marrying in Chicago, Annie and Henry Casey came west to Mineral County, Nevada—Henry, the dreamer, to seek his fortune, Annie to settle and raise a family.

In the dusty silver-mining town of Candelaria, Nevada, the couple ran a saloon with too few paying customers. To supplement their meager income, Henry prospected for silver. On that high, cold Nevada mountainside, their first child was born on March 29, 1888, and named James Emmett Casey after his grandfather, that first Casey who settled in Clifden, on the rugged Connemara peninsula in County Galway, Ireland.

In 1890, Annie gave birth to Jim's brother Harry and in 1893 to George. Her husband, working long hours in dreadful conditions, contracted the miner's lung disease, *pulmonary phthisis*, and began his slow decline. The Caseys' circumstances were grim, with quickly increasing hardship. Yet Annie's determination and strict code of behavior seemed to embody the proverb, "Necessity is the mother of invention." Seeing Candelaria's opportunities drying up, in 1897 she and her husband decamped with their three sons to boomtown Seattle, Washington, bringing with them the lessons that would provide the foundation for a company that is currently garnering more than $42 billion a year.

3

BIRTH OF A
DELIVERY SERVICE

Life took a dramatic turn for nine-year-old Jim Casey when his family moved from the played-out Nevada mining town of Candelaria to Seattle in 1897. Compared to the bleak high desert, the wet, green Northwest was preternaturally lush. Miles of dark forest surrounded the wharf-side city, with snowy Mount Rainier on the southern horizon.

The Emerald City

Using their savings, the Caseys rented a frame house at 2508 East Union, in a middle-class neighborhood just east of city center. It was not large or luxurious, but adequate and comfortable. Seattle's population was approximately 65,000 in 1897 and 15,000 people lived like the Caseys, near or in downtown. Jim and his younger brothers explored endlessly, immersing themselves in their new surroundings.

Seattle's seven hills gave rise to new adventures by the score. The house was close enough to Seattle's wharf and hub that activity was considerable. The streets were crowded with people from all walks of life. Carriages, open and covered, plowed along the often-rutted streets. Slippery clay soil made the hills tricky to navigate, but moving through muddy terrain was fun for energetic little boys. They combed every part of town, from the fancy mansions on Queen Anne Hill to narrow alleys crowded with makeshift housing and impromptu industries.

Not silver or gold as in Nevada but other rich resources—lumber, coal, and fish—fed the city's economy. Commerce and transportation were additional sources of enterprise profiting from foreign steamers and a transcontinental railway. Young Jim Casey could not have helped but notice the coming and going of shipments—heaps of crates, sacks, and boxes—that made the "Emerald City" America's northernmost gateway to the world.

By the late 1800s, Seattle already had a metropolitan character, crowded by ever-taller brick buildings. Outside the downtown core, the city landscape shifted from large commercial buildings to large houses owned by wealthy businesspeople, city fathers who made sure that the streetcar lines reached up the hills to their properties.

Henry Casey's spirit of adventure and entrepreneurial passion matched the forces that were shaping Seattle. Yet poor health, the ill-fated "miner's lung" developed in Nevada, challenged his ambitions, and his timing was far from propitious. Seattle's economy—indeed, the economy of the nation—was faltering in the mid-1890s. A financial "panic" was eroding jobs and confidence. Steady work eluded Henry and many others. Henry went from job to job, barely making ends meet, coughing and hacking all the while.

Henry continued to set out each morning with determination. His sons were loose in the same city, but without the desperation that dogged their father. Still, Jim was by then old enough to apprehend his parents' mounting anxiety, to understand that his father was not healthy by comparison with other men. The worried atmosphere undoubtedly had effect, as did its contrast with the lush, exciting setting. Prospects of employment seemed almost as scarce as they had been in Nevada.

Klondike Fever!

Then, in the summer of 1897, the steamer *Portland* made its way into Seattle's Elliott Bay, with what the Seattle *Post-Intelligencer* called a "ton of gold" aboard, in a rare case of underreporting. The precious freight from Alaska's Klondike region turned out to be more than double that amount, a yellow cargo that would change

Seattle and change the dynamics of many families, including the Caseys, forever.

News of the gold strike spread throughout the United States, at what we would think of as Internet speed. The mad, frenzied dash was on. Suddenly, crowded railroads and ships were delivering prospectors to Seattle, a contagious tide of "stampeders."

Merchants hastened to supply goods to a growing number of dream seekers who had succumbed to the fever and sought their own bonanza. How-tos, guidebooks, get-rich-quick tales, and other publications fanned the flames of obsession. Outfitters opened their doors, as did mining schools. Services, commodities, and advertising adapted to the new era, right in front of Jim Casey's eyes. For the young and impressionable Jim Casey, this offered an immediate lesson on what it took to succeed. Swift improvisation in the face of fleeting opportunity was a lesson Jim heeded throughout his life.

It was not surprising that 10,000 of Seattle's underemployed townspeople hurried to set out for the Klondike to try their luck, Henry Casey among them. Here was his chance. He hoped his lungs would hold out, that he would return with enough gold to secure his family's future. One can imagine his emotional departure from his family, facing more than a thousand miles of sailing and trekking, the date of his return uncertain. It cannot but have put a burden of responsibility on his eldest son, Jim.

In a single year, 100,000 men and women left for the severe northern climate. Only one in four completed the journey. Many died—from exposure, from starvation, from drowning, from avalanche, from murder. Many simply gave up and turned back.

Seattle was the primary point of departure and ships left the docks almost hourly, its fleet tripling in size between 1897 and 1898. Unfortunately, many vessels of questionable quality were patched up and pressed into service. Seagoing craft of every variety, many ill-equipped to navigate the Inside Passage to Alaska, departed heavily laden, *overladen*, with gear, pack animals, and hopeful prospectors. Some vessels had no compasses. Many had untrained crews. The Inside Passage was fraught with dangers, even for experienced captains.

The treacherous route, often shrouded in fog, contained many out-croppings and submerged rock ledges. Countless ships ran aground during the gold rush north.

No one knows which vessel Henry Casey chose. Like many other ships, the one he was on hit a reef, or rocks, or a huge log, or just ran aground in the fog. It might even have hit another ship. Whatever the mishap, it hobbled to the nearest port. Some shipwrecked miners were able to continue on, but Henry could not and was instead picked up by a southbound ship. Henry Casey returned to Seattle in one piece, his dreams of riches from the Yukon dead. He was dispirited and depressed, and his health con-tinued to deteriorate. Soon, Henry was unable to work at all. As his dreams ended, his son Jim's began to take shape, inspired by thriving Seattle and by necessity.

An Eager Child Laborer

At the end of the nineteenth century, the number of American children in the workforce reached staggering proportions. Over two million children worked in mines, factories, and sweatshops, many in appalling conditions. States and territories passed more than 1,600 child labor laws, but they were hardly enforced. Often the laws did not apply to immigrant families. Most perceived child labor as exploitative, but for the Caseys, there was no alternative. It was critical. With two younger brothers to protect and a mother and an ailing father to support, eleven-year-old Jim Casey had de-veloped a maturity that belied his age. His family was in precarious straits, and it was up to him to solve the problem.

In 1899, Jim shouldered his responsibilities, quit school, and set off to find a job, just as he had watched his father do so many times. Each day he left on foot for center city, twenty-some blocks from home. The streets teemed with horses and wagons, people on foot, bicycles, and cable cars. Dazzled by the electrifying activity there, he combed downtown, always inquiring about work. More than one person suggested that messenger and delivery boy positions were possible for someone so young. Jim checked around and was directed to the Bon Marché, the largest department store in town.

With cap in hand, a nervous but straightforward Jim Casey politely asked the Bon Marché's personnel manager if the store had any work he might do. The manager sized up the diminutive youngster. Almost elfin in appearance, Jim looked even younger than his age. Yet he appeared serious and dependable. His mother had taught him to be friendly and look people straight in the eye with confidence. Those blue-gray eyes, which could twinkle with levity, now bored earnestly into the manager.

Recognizing Jim's courtesy and determination, the manager said, "Our driver could use a helper. It's $2.50 a week. Report tomorrow at 7:45 AM—*sharp*."

The next morning, Jim made his way to the enormous building at the north end of downtown. A manager led the young Casey down to a big room in the department store basement, then gesturing to an elderly man, an Irishman as it turned out, he said, "You go out with him today."

As the pair climbed into a high front seat of a dray, the driver asked, "Well, lad, what do you know about street numbers?"

"Nothing," the young boy admitted.

Then, in a thick brogue, the driver explained the fundamentals of delivery, that even-numbered houses were on one side of the street and odd-numbered houses on the other, and that addresses of houses hidden from view were apt to be fractions. Thus Jim's growing familiarity with Seattle's captivating streets and alleyways became a source of income.

After only three weeks he quit the Bon Marché for a higher-paying job as a delivery boy for a tea store. There, he worked more than ten and a half hours a day, and longer on Saturdays, starting at $3 a week. His younger sister Marguerite was born on September 5, 1900, intensifying the family's financial predicament. So Jim's brother Harry also left school and became a cash boy for the Bon Marché. For a while, the two oldest Caseys supported their entire family on $6 a week. Soon the youngest brother, George, also went to work.

Henry Joseph Casey's respiratory condition—*pulmonary phthisis*, a form of tuberculosis—continued to worsen, and the elder Casey finally died on October 30, 1902. Pulling together as a team, the rest of the family continued to live at 2508 East Union.

By mid-1901, at age thirteen, Jim was making $5 a week—still delivering for the tea shop. He was contemplating attending school again as a seventh grader when he was offered a job as a messenger boy for the American District Telegraph Company (ADTC), on commission. By working afternoons, from 3:30 until 9 P.M. or later, and on weekends, he figured he could pursue his studies and still make almost as much as he had delivering tea. He quit the tea shop.

Tales of the Messenger Trade

ADTC was set up to provide a messenger service for Seattle's Postal Telegraph Company. Since Seattle was a crossroads between Pacific commerce, Alaska, and the nation, messages were abundant. There were strategically placed call boxes throughout Seattle, at businesses, in hotel lobbies, drug stores, and rooming houses. At ADTC headquarters, a busy call-box buzzer alerted the dispatcher. He would send one of the young messengers, or *footpads*, as they were known, to the location. (A contemporary definition of *footpad* is "thief," yet for some reason messenger boys at that time were called by that name.)

There were very few telephones at the time. Hence, delivering written and verbal messages, then returning with the answers, was a big part of Jim's job. He picked up and delivered telegrams, mail, and packages. There was rarely a dull moment.

Jim requested the night shifts, working from 7 P.M. until 7 A.M. The mysteries of the night seemed adventurous and glamorous, particularly to the son of a gold miner and saloonkeeper. Even so, the culture of darkness was another world that was sometimes shocking to a polite, hardworking thirteen-year-old kid. Yet he was determined to treat all of his customers with honesty and courtesy, regardless of who they were.

It wasn't all telegrams. Many of the night calls were drug addicts summoning a messenger to help replenish their stash. For the opium smokers, Jim had to run down toward the waterfront, to Second Avenue where entrepreneurial Chinese distributed the narcotic. Jim intrepidly went into these shadowy exotic corridors to the dealers who, for amounts as small as 25 cents, would place dabs of the pasty drug on a card, then fold it up for delivery. ADTC also supplied the cocaine addicts, or "snowbirds," whom Jim Casey considered the lowest class of dopers. Then there was the booze. Jim became adept at "rushing the growler," a popular euphemism for delivering pails of beer.

On his flat-topped hat he sometimes carried trays of food for delivery from restaurants to homes, hotels, and lodging houses. Routinely, he rushed to notify railroad firemen and engineers of emergency runs or odd-hour shifts. He baby-sat in hotel rooms while parents went to the theater, pumped a church organ during choir practice, collected bail for jailbirds, and even acted as a detective. Who better to shadow people and report back on their comings and goings than an unassuming young messenger who was on the streets anyway?

Jim Casey's first paycheck from ADTC, for a little less than a month's work, was $14.92. Still, the work was allowing him to go to school. The teenager had a great aptitude for learning and dreamed of continuing his education beyond high school. Alas, his educational ambitions were not to materialize. His family simply didn't have enough money, and ADTC needed more time from Jim than he was putting in if he was to keep his position. After only two school terms, he was forced to drop out—in his first semester of high school.

During winters, it rained and rained. Jim was often cold and wet to the skin. Miners down from Alaska and other wealthy people could afford fancy hotels. Jim often looked with envy at them through the slightly fogged windows, as they sat in the big hotel chairs looking out onto the rain from warm lobbies. To the busy and driven young man, life in a hotel seemed the height of achievement.

It is thus no surprise that the future prosperous Jim Casey would end up living exclusively in well-appointed hotels.

Lessons in Partnership

Jim made several friends at ADTC, including one fellow footpad named Claude Ryan, a dapper, curly-haired boy about the same age as Jim who was to play a major role in Jim's future a few years later.

About this time, Jim got it in his head to set up a telephone service. As Claude wasn't interested at the time, two other friends and fellow messengers became his partners. Jim was fifteen years old and had managed to save $30. Telephones were, by 1903, becoming more popular, a likely substitute for call boxes. Jim, already demonstrating a knack for anticipating needs and coming up with solutions, envisioned the importance of the telephone and its future dominance in American industry. In this case, his inspiration proved a few years ahead of its time.

Naming their business City Messenger Service, in November 1903 he and his two partners rented an office at 217 Washington Street, installed a telephone (Phone Number #3043), and waited for it to ring. Business was so slow that one partner got discouraged and left. Jim and Thomas Sweeney, his remaining partner, kept at it for almost two more years.

In 1905 they moved their enterprise to 203 Washington Street, and also opened a second office at 1331 3rd Avenue. Unfortunately, the business was not consistent enough and they spent a lot of time slumped in their chairs reading.

One evening, while reading an article, Jim Casey exclaimed, "Say, listen to this!" It turned out that fortunes were again being made in Nevada, this time in a spot called Goldfield. Memories of playing on slag heaps and dodging open shafts in a dusty mining camp resurfaced. The story tempted Casey. He had spent his early teenage years being responsible and dependable, behaving more like an adult than a child. Not surprisingly, he still harbored a bit of his father's adventurous spirit. This mind-set was, in later years, to serve more often as a virtue than a vice. Casey's enthusiasm, so much more alive than the silent telephone, easily fired up the imagination of his partner, Tom Sweeney.

The two teenagers hunted up a buyer and sold the business to Ralph Lester in November 1905. As a fascinating side-note, that original business begun by Jim Casey and Thomas Sweeney is still operating and recently celebrated its centennial. Lester changed the name to City Messenger & Delivery Service and began delivering furniture. After several name changes and different ownerships, the company is known today as City Moving Systems; it is the largest Northwest agent for United Van Lines.

For their part, young Jim and Thomas were relieved to move on and wasted no time heading off to Nevada in search of their fortune.

Boom Town Messengers

Three years before, two prospectors—Henry Stimler and William Marsh—had followed an Indian named Tom Fisherman to his strike, precipitating a rush to what would become one of the busiest and brightest mining cities in the West. By 1905 Goldfield had burgeoned into Nevada's largest city.

Surrounding the boom town, high plateaus, rocky outcroppings, and broad valleys shimmered with silver sagebrush. Goldfield epitomized the Old West with the coming and going of the country's most opportunistic characters and no small share of legendary figures. Virgil Earp (of O.K. Corral fame) was deputy sheriff and his brother Wyatt worked there for a while. A murderer and former member of Butch Cassidy's gang, "Gunplay" Maxwell, became deputy sheriff under an assumed name, until he was exposed by Sheriff W. A. (Bob) Ingalls, a fearless teetotaler and saloon owner. Ingalls had a big job, keeping peace in this highly volatile setting. Heavy drinking, gambling, and violence were the norm.

The two teenagers stood little chance against so many grizzled, unscrupulous miners. They failed to stake a claim. Luckily, Jim's lofty ambitions were couched in his mother's pragmatism. Through a Nevada friend of Jim's father, the boys met Sheriff Ingalls. After that doors began to open for them, albeit in capricious and dangerous surroundings.

Goldfield already had six hundred telephones, an incredible number given the infancy of the technology. The phones were all connected through one switchboard at a new telephone-telegraph office. The boys' timing was terrific; the office manager needed someone to deliver all the messages that kept pouring in. Jim and Tom set up their own messenger business in the corner of the telephone-telegraph office, and the owner guaranteed them $50 a month.

With plenty of messages to deliver by foot and by bicycle, they welcomed a third partner, John Moritz . According to Jim Casey's recollections, the three learned that service was all they had to offer. Wearing striped pillbox hats and double-breasted jackets with brass buttons, they performed with honesty and worked to the best of their ability in a town where almost anything was likely to happen.

Town boosters were tireless. To generate new investment capital, they staged a major championship prizefight, with the largest purse of the time, $30,000. On September 3, 1906, Joe Gans and "Battling" Nelson fought a marathon forty-two rounds, which is still the longest world title fight in the *Guinness Book of World Records*. The dance halls, saloons, and hotels were electric with activity that week.

The night of the fight there was a call for a messenger boy to go to a hotel. Jim was dispatched, knocked on the hotel room door, and was stunned when the winner Joe Gans personally answered. He invited Jim in and said, "Here kid, have this message sent by telegraph." Jim later told his nephew Paul Casey he wished he'd kept the note Gans gave him. It read, "The dog quit in the 42nd round."

It was an exciting time and amid the crowds that week, the numerous messages and errands had the boys busy running and riding their bicycles all over town. Unfortunately however, the excitement ended in tragedy.

That Saturday night, John Moritz accidentally ran into a vagrant named John Thompson on his bike. Thompson shot and killed Moritz. The cold-blooded murder left the other two boys stricken. They decided to leave Goldfield.

Forerunner to UPS

Jim headed back to Seattle and turned nineteen in March 1907. Stopping by his old place of employment, ADTC, Casey reconnected with his friend Claude Ryan, who was cutting a dashing figure and knew Seattle like the back of his hand.

Again, Casey's timing was great. Seattle was flourishing, but because very few homes had telephones or automobiles, the demand for messenger and delivery services was huge.

"Jim, you're just the fellow I'm looking for," Ryan announced. "No one in town runs a decent delivery business and there's one needed. You and I have the experience. Let's set up our own office and go into business."

An older friend of the Casey family, James Brewster, agreed to lend the young men $100 to launch their new enterprise. Brewster knew young Jim, recognized his hard-working nature and most of all his honesty and sincerity. Brewster's confidence in Jim Casey led to one of America's greatest success stories.

Casey and Ryan launched American Messenger Company on August 28, 1907. From a tiny basement office beneath a saloon run by Ryan's uncle Charlie Jones, with donated furniture and two telephones (one furnished by each of the telephone companies serving Seattle), the two young men threw themselves into the market, hiring and training the best messenger boys they could find. They enlisted a team of six eager, reliable boys. All received a lesson in good grooming and a flat-topped cap with leather visor. On the front of each cap was a badge with the company name and the messenger's identification number. Two bicycles were available as needed.

American Messenger Company rules were few but hard. Only Jim and Claude answered the phones. Messengers were required to be courteous and quick. Only if the destination was too far or unreachable by trolley could the boys use the bikes. The company offered "best service and lowest rates" round the clock, including evenings, Sundays, and holidays.

The company, founded in that six-by-seven-foot basement office, would eventually become United Parcel Service.

4

THE FIRST BIG BROWN

Today, in Seattle's historic Pioneer Square area, gurgling water splashes through a densely green oasis called Waterfall Garden. Hardly anyone knows, unless they stop to peer at the modest sign, that the privately maintained park was opened by Jim Casey in 1977 on the exact site of the subterranean American Messenger Company office, in honor of UPS's birthplace. Yet this thriving garden is an apt tribute to the growth and flow of the company that began there a hundred years ago.

An Environment for Opportunity

The year 1907 was when the United States surpassed France in manufacturing more automobiles than any other country. It was also the year the Industrial Workers of the World (known as the Wobblies) helped the Western Federation of Miners (WFM) strike against a wage cut in Goldfield, Nevada, and the year the Western Union, Postal Telegraph, and Associated Press telegraphers went on strike, as did thousands of sawmill workers and smeltermen. In October 1907 a major financial panic hit the United States because there was not enough cash on hand to meet demand in the burgeoning economy.

These events—from automotive manufacturing to labor organizing to business expansion—were, in effect, the medium in which the American Messenger Company, UPS's progenitor, took root. Though the company began small, with a clientele that frequented nearby saloons and brothels, its horizons seemed endless. Seattle had established itself as the "Metropolis of the North Pacific," and the "Gateway to Alaska and the Orient." Its waterfront was booming with national as well as international trade. Shipments of salmon, lumber, and wheat supplemented the mining economy. Pike Place Market, still a tourist attraction today, opened in early August 1907. The city's sophistication was such that it was selected to host the World's Fair two years later. For entrepreneurs, Seattle had everything to offer.

Four major express companies (Wells Fargo, Adams Express, American Express, and United States Express) were handling interstate shipments in 1907, operating over about a dozen railroads. The express companies shipped contracted mail, goods, and other commodities, but the business of messages, parcels, and intracity deliveries was up for grabs.

Today, if we want answers, we pick up the telephone. If we need ingredients for dinner, we hop in the car. Seattle in the summer of 1907 had two independent telephone companies, but few homes had telephones or automobiles. Nine messenger companies competed for the business of relaying communiqués, delivering and picking up messages, and running miscellaneous errands. And on August 28, 1907, American Messenger Company made a tenth.

Outrunning the Competition

Jim Casey and Claude Ryan were bold young men, both in their late teens. They knew Seattle up one side and down the other. Both had intimate knowledge of the comings and goings of information, people, and goods through the hilly waterfront city. Whereas Jim was unpretentious and thoughtful, Claude was more outgoing. Both were snappy dressers, ambitious and hard working.

To surpass the nine competing messenger companies, Jim and Claude hastened to tack distinctive red-and-white placards all over town:

WANT A

MESSENGER?

Main 1918

Ind. 5074

American Messenger Co.

Messengers—Automobiles—Carriages

"BEST SERVICE AND LOWEST RATES"

Jim and Claude hadn't chosen their motto lightly, and they worked hard to live up to its promise. To achieve the best service and lowest rates, they carefully selected and trained the boys to treat customers and the public with utmost courtesy . . . to look sharp and act sharp.

In dispatching the boys, Claude and Jim, who knew Seattle and the messenger business intimately, briefed them about how best to travel, what was expected, how much money to collect if necessary, and which deliveries required a signature. The messengers walked, ran, used one of the bicycles, or took streetcars or horse drawn-carriages and taxis, if necessary. The company charged anywhere from 15 cents to 65 cents per message, depending on the distance, and an hourly rate of 25 cents. Messengers, if they hustled, could make between $1 and $1.50 a day, good money for a turn-of-the-century kid.

Integrity was also key. If a call came in and a messenger was not immediately available, Jim and Claude never answered "right away," as did many of their competitors. Instead, they would honestly answer that it might be a few minutes, perhaps even a half hour. Customers came to know that American Messenger Company messengers always met the time commitment that Jim or Claude made. The partners' first policy became "never promise more than you can deliver and always deliver what you promise."

Dependability meant twenty-four-hour service, seven days a week. They wanted customers—especially drug stores, hotels, and restaurants—to depend on American Messenger Company at any hour of the day or night. Claude or Jim often slept on the discarded lunch counter they used as a desk, awaiting infrequent middle-of-the-night phone calls.

As Jim had found earlier, the boys had to handle far too many errands that didn't involve messages. They were asked to walk dogs, baby-sit, mind a store while the owner went to lunch, that kind of thing. One posed for an art class. Another took a blind man to a funeral. Sometimes customers asked the boys to play detective, tailing husbands or wives they suspected of cheating. Other calls involved transporting heavy objects on the young boys' backs. Another aggravation was arriving at a call to find out that another messenger had already taken the dispatch, since unscrupulous people sometimes called three or four messenger companies and hired the first one who arrived.

Getting fed up with the nature of some of these errands, the young team cast about for a strategy that would add substance to their business. King Brothers Clothing store, located half a block up the street, signed on with American Messenger Company, allowing the store to offer customers same-day delivery. Few people owned cars, so the service afforded shoppers the luxury of continuing their errands without being encumbered with earlier purchases. The additional volume increased the possibility of delivery consolidation—being able to pack more deliveries into one trip. Packages of clothing purchases arrived at the basement messenger office throughout the day and were dispatched along with messages to the same neighborhood. Effectively, this consolidation generated far greater revenue from a single trip. And retail deliveries suggested a means of getting away from the sometimes irksome and less rewarding message-and-errand business.

After only ten months, the company moved to an office closer to Seattle's retail center, at 115 Marion Street, and a year later to an even bigger office at 123 Marion Street. Jim's younger brother George came aboard in 1911, earning 15 cents an hour to drum up business.

George managed a second location, at 1602 ½ Fourth Avenue, on the other end of the retail area.

This was a period of trial and error. Their increasing volume of delivery business often outran their strategies to cope with logistics and accounting, and they had to learn solutions on the fly. George Casey later commented that they experimented a lot with the operation at first. "We didn't know what rates to charge, what schedules to operate on, how the packages should be sheeted at the store, or even how to record the parcels after getting them." The entire business was learning by doing.

The daily flow of deliveries kept ten regular messengers busy; and occasionally they hired temporary help, especially during the holiday season. When Christmas came around in 1912, seventy-five American Messengers, donning jaunty delivery boy caps, took to Seattle's streets bearing gifts. However, even though business was generally good, it began to plateau. New customers were few, and foot messengers could only cover so much ground—and they were still spending too much time on mundane, low-profit errands.

Partnering Leads to Growth

Jim Casey became obsessed with moving beyond this stasis. He spent many hours pondering ways to become an all-encompassing delivery service that would attract new accounts. Jim and Claude needed to cover Seattle faster and more comprehensively. The founders made a key move that was to establish a protocol for future expansion—partnering up.

Another young man, twenty-year-old Evert "Mac" McCabe, was American Messenger Company's hardest-working competitor. McCabe's company, the Motorcycle Delivery Company, was the first fully motorcycle-based service in the Pacific Northwest. By 1913, McCabe's company had a fleet of about a half-dozen Yale motorcycles serving the Seattle area, each rigged with baskets and saddlebags. Though it was still a "man's world," the truth is that the Motorcycle

Delivery Company was a husband-and-wife team. While outgoing Mac solicited new business throughout Seattle, Garnet Sprague McCabe ran the office operation. Jim and Claude approached Mac first, presenting a vision of acquiring department store deliveries throughout Seattle, which they could achieve by merging their two businesses.

Mac was excited about combining forces, but Garnet was initially cool to the idea and needed some convincing. She had already earned a reputation for being an anxious, controlling woman. Jim Casey met with Garnet personally, explaining the advantages of a merger. Jim must have put forward a persuasive appeal, because the two companies became one, and American Messenger Company moved into McCabe's offices at 4 Union Court in the alley behind the Mecca Bar. They had twenty-five messengers between them and combined revenue of $2,200 a month.

The newly merged messenger company adopted the articles of incorporation filed by American Messenger Company, technically making that company, not the Motorcycle Delivery Company, the founding company. In addition, American Messenger Company had the greater experience, having been in business longer. Together the three new partners—Jim, Claude, and Mac—cast about for a new name that would better identify their plan for the business, which involved focusing on consolidating deliveries for department stores—no more baby-sitting and miscellaneous errands. They decided to call it "Merchants Parcel Delivery." Mac McCabe became the first president. The partners' new slogan was *We Cover Seattle*.

At the time of Merchants Parcel Delivery's inception, people made most of their retail purchases at department stores, and most department stores furnished their own delivery. Jim, Claude, and Mac's strategy was to offer the stores a 1913 version of *cheaper-faster-better* delivery, so they wouldn't have to maintain their own fleets. By consolidating deliveries from several stores, the guys figured they could economize on trips. And customers could receive their purchases at one predictable time, from a single delivery person.

The problem was that one could stack packages only so high on a bicycle or motorcycle. The three entrepreneurs decided to borrow enough money to purchase a new 1913 Model T Ford. After removing the passenger body, they purchased a delivery-van body for about $125 and attached it to the chassis. They painted it bright red, with the words "Merchants Parcel Delivery" on the side. The shiny truck could carry up to fifty packages and was good advertising. By 1915, Merchants Parcel Delivery had four automobiles, five motorcycles, and thirty foot messengers; together they covered sixteen hundred miles each day in Seattle. Merchants Parcel Delivery had become the most successful delivery and messaging company in Seattle, but it needed an infusion of cash to buy more vehicles. Jim talked to bankers and everyone else he could think of.

Establishing a Fleet

Thirteen years older than Jim, Charlie Soderstrom was a seasoned delivery driver and probably the person most knowledgeable about automobiles in Seattle at the time. Everyone had seen him around town, first in a Buick in 1903, next in his Hudson, then in his Stanley Steamer, an early automobile powered by steam. It was obvious that Charlie Soderstrom knew a thing or two about cars. In 1916, Charlie was managing deliveries for a large dry-goods store named the Fraser-Paterson Company. Fraser-Paterson had the best delivery department in Seattle. Soderstrom, a Swede with a good business sense, understood people as well as mechanized equipment. Even though he had his own deliveries to manage, Charlie was impressed with the young men's operation over at Merchants Parcel Delivery. On July 16, 1916, he bought $10,000 worth of stock, becoming a partner in the process.

The new partnership ushered in a new era, with a company equipped to utilize the cutting-edge technology of the time—*the automobile*. Soderstrom's respect for automotive technology created several legacies. The first was a commitment to investing in the latest that technology had to offer. That meant automobiles back in 1916, but the same approach through the years has led UPS to embrace other innovations, right up through electronics, software, and microtechnology.

UPS owes its exceptionally well-maintained delivery fleet to practices established by Soderstrom. UPS vehicles are still maintained in tip-top shape, not only for appearance but for safety and practicality. They are washed several times a week and painted regularly. On scheduled rotations, based on miles driven and time on the road, all vehicles are pulled out of service for inspections, maintenance, and parts replacements, just as they have been from the earliest days. Because the intense Preventive Maintenance Inspections are formalized to address problems before they occur, many UPS vehicles serve the company for half a million miles and more.

We can also credit Charlie for *UPS brown*. In 1916, the partners had heard that bright yellow was an attention getter and were poised to paint their fleet a vibrant canary yellow (like today's DHL delivery trucks). They even discussed painting each vehicle different colors so the public would think their fleet was larger than it was. Charlie Soderstrom was appalled. He intervened, explaining that Seattle's department stores presently saw their own vehicles as a great form of free advertising. They would be reluctant to relinquish their deliveries to a company whose conspicuous vans would compete with their own.

The idea was that the Merchants Parcel Delivery fleet should blend into the background. A carriage painter named Charlie Place told Charlie Soderstrom about recent experiments run by a railroad sleeper-car company named Pullman. They found that a certain shade of brown—*Pullman brown*, it was called—held up best when subjected to rain, sleet, and dust. The Pullman brown color appealed to Jim Casey, and he knew it well as he loved to ride Pullman coaches when he traveled. To Jim and many others the color symbolized the highly respected railroad industry of their day. "Perhaps it will make us equally as famous on the streets of America," Casey ruminated, little knowing just how famous their fledgling company would become. (Over the years, the color changed only slightly to become *UPS brown*.)

Flux and Triumph

The partnership pulled out the stops to better serve its department stores while still maintaining its smaller accounts. Yet its tenth year, 1917, was one of upheaval. "Although the company was born in a basement and reared in an alley, early on we made up our minds that we didn't want to be identified as an 'alley company,' as most other delivery companies had been," Jim said years later. "We decided that we should not allow anybody to outdo us in anything we did." Ambitious, they moved from their alley location to 1326 First Avenue.

At the end of the year, Claude Ryan decided to leave the partnership. His reasons remain murky, but it seems there was a conflict between Ryan and Garnet McCabe, something to do with money. Correspondence from the McCabes' daughter, Ruth McCabe Bertauche, in 1988, affirms that her mother claimed she "caught his hand in the till," but this has never been substantiated by another source. Certainly, Garnet had a reputation for being moody and domineering. Stories hint that there simply wasn't room for the two of them in the office, even though Garnet did not work full time.

That the United States entered the war in Europe in 1917 added to the perturbation at home. Merchants Parcel Delivery lost some manpower to the war effort, including George Casey, who joined the U.S. Navy. George was fortunate to serve his tour of duty in the Seattle area. On the other hand, World War I made it tougher for the department stores to maintain their own delivery fleets, perhaps offering Merchants Parcel Delivery an entrée.

Still, department stores didn't give up their own delivery easily. Management felt that the personal contact with customers was good business, that the publicity value of vans with their name on it circulating in the city helped promote their wares. Merchants Parcel Delivery was unrelenting in its appeals, however.

"We made it clear that we would allow no advertising on our vehicles," Jim Casey recalled. "We also pointed out that we had the safest and best drivers in town. Of course, the best point was that once they got rid of their delivery headaches and let us handle deliveries, they could concentrate on merchandising."

Finally, the prestigious Bon Marché, the department store that had hired Jim Casey for his first job as a young boy, relented and turned its deliveries over to Merchants Parcel Delivery, becoming the company's first major account. Within a short time, Merchants Parcel Delivery was making three daily pickups at the Bon Marché. This was, at long last, a significant turning point. That first major department store kept its delivery fleet for a while "just in case," but store employees were so satisfied they disbanded it two months later.

Once the benefits to the Bon Marché and its customers were realized, the other major department stores enrolled too. Before long, Merchants Parcel Delivery was serving the Bon Marché, the Rhodes Company, and the Fraser-Paterson Company—all the department stores in Seattle, except one. Department store management soon grasped that customers appreciated consolidated delivery because the packages arrived together at a consistent time. It meant that customers no longer had to wait around all day for several different deliveries.

Merchants Parcel Delivery divided the city into sectors and assigned drivers consistent routes; as a result drivers and their customers got to know one another. The drivers' reputation for dependability and the familiarity between driver and customer began to grow. If people weren't home, drivers would make two more attempts before returning the package to the sender. The policies of assigned routes and three delivery attempts survive to present times.

The company moved yet again, first to an old post office at 95 University Street, then in 1919 next door to 85 University Street, where it remained until 1952. As you can imagine, the volume of packages coupled with Seattle's expanding population and commerce presented some logistical challenges. Jim and his partners wanted to design a better system for moving packages. They spent hours, days, even weeks kicking around ideas for sorting and loading packages more efficiently. Finally, they came up with and implemented a new system that Jim Casey devised. It looked like a seashell with concentric circles. To load or unload packages, drivers would back their vehicles up to solid wooden wheels. On the side of the wheel opposite the vehicle, an aisle circled the loading area. There, sorters worked to deposit the packages from and to bins that surrounded the wheel. Variations on the Casey-designed wheel and bin system were used well into the 1960s.

With such demanding logistical challenges, some bosses might have become so caught up in operations that they let go of the big picture entirely. Yet Jim Casey, always inquisitive, kept his eye on the next step. He wondered if there were similar companies elsewhere in the country. If so, how were they set up, how did they operate? Mightn't they be doing something from which Merchants Parcel Delivery could learn? Jim wrote to the Chambers of Commerce of every American city with a population over 100,000, asking for names of local delivery firms. He accumulated the names of a hundred of them, then initiated a communications link that he called the "Parcel Delivery Service Bureau." The bureau was a means of sharing new methods, ideas, or systems that worked in different cities.

Every once in a while, the correspondence disclosed a gem of an idea, which Merchants Parcel Delivery would hurry to implement. For example, a minimum weekly fee for making deliveries that generated a more predictable cash flow was one such idea. Few respondents had much to offer, though, and interestingly most were far from optimistic about the future of their business. Yet, with flourishing department store delivery in Seattle and ever more proficient operations, Jim and his partners remained convinced that they had hit on a good thing, a good thing that could be duplicated in other cities.

5

DETERMINED MEN CAN DO ANYTHING

As businesses expand and adapt, it isn't always apparent how external challenges can dictate their fate. An external event—World War I—had a huge impact on the company that would become UPS. The war, way over in Europe, boosted Merchants Parcel Delivery's success, because its drivers could take over deliveries that department stores could no longer staff. Important to note, however: It wasn't just fate on the company's side; it was preparedness.

The Great War ended. Leaving the U.S. Navy behind, George Casey returned to Merchants Parcel Delivery, taking Claude Ryan's place as partner. From 1919 forward, Jim Casey, George Casey, Evert "Mac" McCabe, and Charles Soderstrom were considered the four founders of UPS.

New City, New Name

The four were in high spirits by December 1918. United in their desire to build upon their successful delivery business model, they made their way to downtown Seattle's Lowman Building, at the corner of First and Cherry Streets. The nine-story Gothic was then a formidable edifice. Intrepid and resolute, the young men strode out of the ornate elevator and down the hall to meet a mature investment banker named Mr. Carstens.

All four believed that their Seattle success was duplicable, and that expansion was the best use of their management talent. In their wildest dreams they probably never imagined their fledgling company would become the world's largest package delivery operation, let alone a global leader in "supply-chain services." That eventuality would, again, depend on externals of an as-yet inconceivable nature. For now, they set their modest sights on the San Francisco Bay Area. Problem was, their profit margin was too slender, and they believed an infusion of capital would be their only means of taking over another market.

Mr. Carstens listened with interest to their ideas and asked a few questions. Then he leaned back in his chair, put his feet up on his desk, and gave what Jim Casey remembered as "the most inspiring talk on the economics of business" that he ever heard. Mr. Carstens told them frankly that he would *not* fund Merchants Parcel Delivery's next venture, but that they should not interpret his resistance as a disincentive. He finished with the words "determined men can do anything."

That comment became an invocation; Jim Casey and the company would use it as a rallying cry time and again. As the years went by, Jim reframed the phrase to his own purpose: "determined men, working together, can do anything."

For the time being, however, the consortium needed to figure out how to apply their proven delivery system to a new market, and without the leg up that the investment banker's money would have provided. As it turned out, lack of capital led to more creative financing approaches, variations of which helped guarantee their fortune in city after city as the future unfolded.

A year before their meeting with the banker, Jim Casey had fortuitously paid a visit to the Motor Parcel Delivery Company, an operation running out of a new building at Fourth and Jefferson Streets in Oakland, California. He'd hit it off with the manager, an energetic and meticulous guy named Con Nelson. Con impressed him greatly. A year later, when Jim heard that Motor Parcel Delivery was about to go into receivership due to money problems, he wasn't surprised to hear that Con Nelson had left the company some months prior. Merchants Parcel Delivery optioned, then purchased the Oakland operation. They had already begun to use financial lessons taught by Mr. Carstens in the purchase of other businesses using little of their own cash up front.

Several immediate challenges presented themselves. Not the least of these was the fact that a small San Francisco company across the bay was also called Merchants Parcel Delivery. Jim, George, Mac, and Charlie sat down to brainstorm a new name for their business. Mac, phone book in hand, read out name after name for inspiration. When he got to United Fruit Company, George blurted, "That's it! That's the name right there. *United*."

With the "United" established, the rest of their new business name came easily.

Jim Casey reflected back over the years of bizarre errands—trays of food, ailing animals, opium, baby-sitting. Having endured more than his share of dubious deliveries, Jim felt strongly that the word "parcel" should be part of their title. At the very least, whatever their drivers carried would be wrapped! Mac suggested "United Parcel Company," but Soderstrom balked, reminding his partners that their business was *service*. We have nothing to sell except service, he said. Thus, all four men had a stake in the name they settled on—United Parcel Service.

On St. Valentine's Day, 1919, the new Oakland operation was incorporated under the name "United Parcel Service" (which would eventually be abbreviated to "UPS"). While titles would never mean much at UPS, Jim Casey became president and Mac McCabe vice president, concentrating his efforts on sales and signing up new contracts. Charlie Soderstrom assumed responsibility for all the company's equipment and vehicles, and George Casey stayed in Seattle, managing that business. (Not until 1925, after the company was operating in several West Coast cities, did the Seattle operation drop the Merchants Parcel Delivery name to become United Parcel Service.)

Before long, United Parcel Service was dominating deliveries in Oakland and a few other East Bay cities, with systems, operations, and drivers that were difficult for the competition to match. Jim tracked down the manager he had so admired, Con Nelson, whom he found managing another Oakland company, Inter-Urban Parcel Delivery. In 1920, United Parcel Service bought Inter-Urban too. With the company came the employees, including Con Nelson. The partners quickly named Con manager of Oakland operations.

The Most Roaring Metropolis of the Twenties

The relative ease with which United Parcel Service had started its delivery service operation in Oakland built confidence among the partners. While waiting for San Francisco stores to make up their minds about contracting with their company for deliveries, they looked south to Los Angeles, by 1922 the fastest-growing city in America. With established oil fields and an emerging movie industry, the sprawling metropolis was quickly outdistancing San Francisco as the most important city on the West Coast. There were numerous department stores in Los Angeles and environs and the potential delivery volume there was staggering in proportion.

The partners repeated what they had done in Oakland. They first conducted a careful survey of the city's delivery companies. Most were serving smaller stores and specialty shops. The largest was owned by Russell Peck, whose company already delivered for one department store and several large specialty shops, store-to-consumer, like United Parcel Service did. It also delivered many packages for Los Angeles wholesalers, business-to-business. But Mr. Peck was finding it increasingly difficult to provide satisfactory service to the numerous and sprawling neighborhoods of Los Angeles. He wanted to retire but didn't want to let down either his customers or his employees.

For the partners at United Parcel Service, it was too good to believe! Even though their Oakland business was just under way, United Parcel Service didn't want to miss this opportunity to acquire the Russell Peck Delivery Company and use it as a nucleus around which to build its Los Angeles expansion, particularly since many of Peck's experienced staff could remain. Among them, Bill

Schlinger and L. D. Hayes became United Parcel Service managers, the former eventually becoming the Western Region (the entire Pacific Coast) manager.

United Parcel Service augmented its new Los Angeles operation by purchasing a smaller company operated by Joe Meiklejohn, then merging the two companies. Rather than paying up front with cash, they funded these acquisitions by pledging what they had, which meant shares of United Parcel Service stock. Though Russell Peck retired, Joe Meiklejohn stayed on with UPS in a management capacity, and with an investment to support, he worked hard to assure the merger's success. (United Parcel Service was to use this strategy numerous times in coming years.)

And what an investment it was! Joe Meiklejohn passed away in 1961. Over the years, his heirs have donated more than $86 million to the Saddleback Memorial Medical Center in Orange County, California. A 2005 contribution of $50 million was the largest single donation to an Orange County hospital ever.

Taking over Mr. Peck's wholesale business was a dramatic change for UPS and a harbinger of things to come. In the early Seattle years, the young messengers had delivered anything to anyone, but by the time the company had become Merchants Parcel Delivery, they no longer delivered business-to-business. Merchants Parcel Delivery specialized in store-to-consumer. Wholesale delivery was completely different from retail delivery and was and is known as "common carrier" service.

Common carrier shipping was regulated by the Interstate Commerce Commission as well as various state commissions. In the decades before deregulation, shippers needed to acquire the rights to pick up and deliver packages business-to-business. The Russell Peck Company had these rights, but only in the Southern California area. United Parcel Service took over the rights with the purchase of the company. This put them in direct competition with the U.S. Post Office. It was not at all like being on contract to deliver a department store's retail sales. In fact, United Parcel Service could not even commingle wholesale deliveries with retail packages, and in some cities later on, including Portland, it had to use different drivers, even when they covered the same neighborhood.

U.S. law stated that common carriers were required to serve any shipper, carrying any package, no matter how small, to all locations within their service territory, no matter how remote. By 1927, United Parcel Service's common carrier service extended 125 miles from downtown L.A. in every direction. That was the extent of it until 1952.

United Parcel Service began Los Angeles operations with thirty-two delivery vehicles dispatched from a building that Mr. Peck had recently purchased. The facility, later demolished to make way for the Harbor Freeway, was located only five hundred feet from UPS's present downtown Los Angeles location at 1201 West Olympic Boulevard. In the interim, however, it didn't take long for growth to demand a larger facility. Just a few months into the City of Angels expansion, the company moved to a 22,500-square-foot building at 420 West Eleventh Street, where it remained national headquarters until 1930.

On West Eleventh in the 1920s, the company got its first automatic car wash, its first conveyor belt (180 feet long), and its first brown uniforms. The first suburban substations (operating centers) were established, beginning with Long Beach and followed by Pasadena (buying owner George Haver's delivery operation using United Parcel Service stock, and asking him to remain as manager), and then Hollywood. Soon United Parcel Service was covering the Pomona Valley, San Fernando Valley, and Orange County. Before long Santa Barbara, Riverside, San Bernardino, and San Diego came on line. The first long-haul service transfers, now called "feeder runs," served those outlying facilities from Eleventh Street. Since packages are "fed" to other smaller facilities, UPS tractor-trailers are not called "semis" or "big rigs"; they're called "feeders."

Keeping packages moving took constant innovation. Jim Casey and engineer Russel Havighorst, who joined the company in 1923, returned from an investigatory tour of Eastern cities in 1927. Inspired by what they saw, they installed new combination bulk and package bins, plus a new conveyor composed of nine separate belts, each feeding a big metal chute—a slide that delivered the packages to a sorting point.

Los Angeles customers of the twenties were in a big hurry, just as everyone is today. Dentists, needing patient dental impression molds right away, were among United Parcel Service's biggest customers. With abundant requests for same-day service, United Parcel Service developed an additional business, a diversification tactic that, because it was so focused on package delivery, it wouldn't repeat again for many years. The company started Red Arrow Bonded Messenger Corporation, launching in March 1925. Red Arrow was not unlike the young men's first business up in Seattle, the American Messenger Company. It offered immediately dispatched, same-day service using messengers on bicycles and motorbikes.

Red Arrow snowballed. Two months later, the Pasadena Red Arrow office opened. Later that year, both Hasty Messenger Service and Page Delivery Service consolidated with Red Arrow. In October 1927 a Hollywood Red Arrow office opened, followed by Portland Red Arrow in 1930 and New York Red Arrow in 1934. Later an office opened in Beverly Hills.

Advertised as the type "you yourself would hire," the messengers were unfailingly courteous, prompt, and neat in appearance. Garbed in dove-gray uniforms and caps, with a distinctive curved red arrow logo, they were welcome everywhere. As the L.A. Junior Chamber of Commerce remarked, they were known for "giving speed when time counts."

Red Arrow filled a same-day void generated by the next-day service of the department store and common carrier accounts. UPS managers themselves used it as a safety net to get misdelivered and other important packages out to customers. Red Arrow was so well known that it inspired mystery writer Raymond Chandler to incorporate the "Green Feather Messenger Service" into his 1942 book *The High Window*.

You can easily appreciate how gratifying this business was. The need was there and United Parcel Service was filling it. Many Red Arrow employees went on to UPS careers, including Harold Oberkotter (UPS Board Chairman and CEO: 1974–1980) and Charlie Buckridge (UPS Management Committee and Board of Directors), both of whom started as bicycle messengers in 1925. Red Arrow Bonded Messenger Service is still a trademark protected by UPS and still listed as a subsidiary organization, even though it diminished in importance when UPS began adding additional premium services, like its 1995 purchase of SonicAir, a same-day delivery service.

In September 1922, Los Angeles area UPS package volume was approximately 2,000 parcels per day. By peak day at Christmastime 1929, that figure reached 29,000, due mostly to expanding service area and signing up new accounts. Los Angeles' original fleet of 32 package cars was, by 1929, 170 in number.

Saturating the Pacific Coast

It wasn't long after United Parcel Service's arrival on the scene in Oakland before big San Francisco department stores took notice and even on occasion used the brown delivery vehicles moving around East Bay to supplement their own fleets. Not until 1925, however, did the city's five largest department stores request a meeting with United Parcel Service's man-about-town and contract maker, Mac McCabe. Following the meeting, the Emporium, the City of Paris, O'Connor-Mottit & Company, and Hale Brothers contracted with United Parcel Service to deliver their goods. The fifth store, the White House at the corner of Sutter and Grant, demurred, and not until 1956 did it turn all of its deliveries over to UPS.

On August 1, 1925, a new San Francisco "plant" (which is what they called each city's major building as contrasted with later terminology—"hub" or "district headquarters") opened to serve the stores . . . despite the fact that the Gough Street building had no doors or electricity on opening day. Founder Jim Casey personally ended up helping a local manager named Tom Barker check the packages in and out of a hotel room while the facility was being completed. The man who had been in charge of deliveries at the Emporium, Jack Davidson, ultimately headed UPS operations in San Francisco.

Two years later, on August 1, 1927, United Parcel Service began operations in yet another Pacific coast city, Portland, Oregon. To make it happen, United Parcel Service consolidated the Portland delivery businesses of Merchants Parcel Delivery (no relation to the partners' earlier Seattle company) and City Messenger and Delivery Company. The Portland operation was an immediate success. That first Christmas season, between December 1 and December 24, 1927, drivers there averaged 410 packages delivered each day.

Unionization

The subject of unionization had not confronted the partners in Seattle, but things were different in the pro-labor Bay Area. By 1919, the International Brotherhood of Teamsters, Chauffeurs, Warehousemen and Helpers of America (known as the Teamsters Union) was entrenched in San Francisco, having first gone on strike against Montgomery Ward in 1905. Since then, the Teamsters had continued to acquire more clout. Eventually their organizers came around to United Parcel Service.

Even though Jim and the others made a habit of communicating with their drivers and were doing a good job addressing their needs, they could see the handwriting on the wall as to the pressure of the union. Jim considered the situation and ultimately convinced his partners to extend an invitation. He told his coworkers, "I think it's possible to be a good United Parcel Service member and union member at the same time."

Jim invited the Teamsters to represent the several dozen United Parcel Service drivers and part-time hourly package-handling employees in Oakland. The relationships from this early proactive position led to future union contracts with many necessary flexible features. These included variable start times, working as directed with minimum work rules, working across job classification, combination jobs, part-time employees for half the workforce, and mandatory overtime as needed.

During the 1930s the United Parcel Service headquarters were in Los Angeles, a notorious anti-union city where the *Los Angeles Times* and the Los Angeles Police Department were already working to put down labor strikes and reforms. Up to this point only the San Francisco Bay Area drivers were unionized, but union organizer Dave Beck (whose success through the West Coast would later lead him to become president of the International Brotherhood of Teamsters) wanted to unionize UPS. He approached the company and was able to successfully negotiate with Jim Casey, resulting in all Southern California UPS drivers and package handlers becoming members of the Teamsters Union.

For many years drivers became unionized by city or local-union jurisdiction. As part of its negotiations, when UPS moved into new areas or hired new people, they agreed to, and did, encourage union membership. This resulted in numerous separate contracts across the country. Finally, in 1979, just four years after UPS extended its service coast to coast, a UPS-Teamsters National Master Agreement was hammered out and remains in effect to this day. The national contract has numerous local riders and supplements that differ for each Teamster local.

Over the last eighty-eight years, the Teamster-UPS relationship has been mostly positive, with some exceptions. Prior to the Master Agreement, a few short-lived work stoppages happened in selected areas, and the feeling was that a stoppage under a National Contract would be so enormous it would never happen.

Then, in August 1997, America suddenly learned how great a role UPS was playing in the economy. A disenchanted former UPS driver named Ron Carey had taken over the Teamsters Union in the nineties and vowed "to get" UPS. Finally, in 1997 he orchestrated a general strike that lasted two weeks and cost the company $750 million and much good will. It had a crippling effect on the country, too, since UPS by then shipped the vast majority of all packages nationwide. Tens of thousands of American businesses—of every size—were paralyzed, as the U.S. Postal Service grappled with parcel business it was unprepared to accommodate.

The strike was an aberration and the actual contract was not even presented to union members for a vote. Carey was expelled from the Teamsters the following year in the wake of a scandal over misuse of union funds.

Through the years, Jim Casey often participated in local contracts and settlements. In one city, one of his managers reflected on how important Jim's influence was in negotiations that were going nowhere and appeared to be headed for an arbitrator. He recalled:

> Hour after hour went by and though we agreed on some issues, at midnight we were still far apart on some major items. Finally, the union people said it seemed useless to continue. We made arrangements for meeting with him [the arbitrator] and the union people started out the door. As they were leaving Jim said, "Now that we've agreed to arbitrate, the air is cleared. Come on back and let's talk for a while and then we'll all go home."
>
> Jim started reviewing the issues one by one and before long, we had agreed on several of them. We kept on talking and finally settled everything about 5 A.M. Jim's patience kept us talking until we had a new contract.

Thanks to successful negotiations between the Teamsters Union and the company through the years, UPS drivers and package handlers enjoy some of the highest wages and most lucrative benefits in the industry. Even the part-time workers are covered with a health and welfare plan. Today, the drivers and package handlers at UPS represent, by far, the greatest number of Teamsters Union members, with over 220,000 union members employed at UPS. Their numbers constitute about one-fifth of the entire Teamster's 1.4 million membership.

Overall, union membership has shrunk through the years. By 2005, only 12.5 percent of all American workers belonged to a union—down from 20.1 percent in 1983. UPS's main competitors, most notably FedEx, remain nonunion, although the Teamsters Union is hard at work, hoping to change that.

Tragedy Hits the Partnership

Charlie Soderstrom, who was slightly older than the other partners, functioned as a company mentor, the United Parcel Service sage. As Jim said, "If we had a problem, we would talk to Charlie about it. Any situation which required the reasoning power, the judgment he possessed, was put on the table in front of him. He could sense whether something should be done or not. . . . We called on Charlie for more or less an outsider's slant on things . . . he could so often see what we couldn't."

Charlie's days as a sounding board were cut short. In late March 1928, he was golfing at the Fox Hills Country Club in Los Angeles, standing in the middle of a fairway when a nearby golfer's tee shot hit solidly on his skull, right above his ear. Though Charlie remained conscious, it was apparent to his playing partner that something was terribly wrong. He rushed him to the hospital.

The impact had caved in part of his skull, and from that area, radial cracks shot out. Surgeons operated immediately and again two years later, a tearful Jim Casey at his side both times. Charlie became a semi-invalid. Though his consulting was still highly regarded, his mental condition deteriorated. United Parcel Service had effectively lost a man who had so contributed to its foundation, in style and in substance.

Yet Charlie's legacy had helped create a business that seemed unstoppable. Back in Seattle, the 1929 Christmas season logged a peak day of 11,000 package deliveries, an increase of 3,000 over the previous year. Company-wide, more than 11 million packages were delivered by United Parcel Service in 1929.

All of this would have been impossible for Jim Casey and his partners had the banker, Mr. Carstens, simply given the four men a wad of cash back in 1919. Forced to innovate, their consolidation program of stock offerings in lieu of cash encouraged the dedication of talented people within the delivery companies they acquired. Rather than a divide-and-conquer mentality, the founders shared with their newfound associates and prospered.

Yet United Parcel Service was about more than successful strategies. It was about a growing sense of belonging, belonging to a business that was helping shape not only the individual lives of its employees but also America itself.

6

JOB FOR A LIFETIME

Many large brick-and-mortar companies are faceless enterprises, their corporate mind-set almost interchangeable with other companies. This was true a century ago and it is even more so today, most noticeably at different companies in the same industry, like automobile manufacturers and the big oil companies. Ford and General Motors. Exxon-Mobil and Arco. Wal-Mart and Kmart. Staples and Office Depot. To all intents and purposes, employment at one is the same as employment at the other. The public views them equally too. Then there is UPS. UPS really has no comparison, even with its closest competitors, FedEx, DHL, and the U.S. Postal Service.

UPS is in many ways an enigma, emerging from decades of quiet diligence to become the high-profile corporate powerhouse it is today. But along the way, UPS has never strayed from its core values, which continue to be the motivation, determination, and drive *of its people*. And these aren't just platitudes; UPS values rest on a corporate culture that still reflects the ideals, personality, and character of its founders. Even in our modern era of mergers and hostile takeovers, that diligent UPS work ethic still prevails.

For a publicly traded company of this size and wealth, the UPS corporate culture is unique—different from other businesses to a degree that could be characterized as archaic and even peculiar. Of course, no one called United Parcel Service's developing character "corporate culture" until the 1980s when the term was actually coined, but that's what it was, even before the Great Depression.

Terry Deal and Allan Kennedy's landmark 1982 book, *Corporate Cultures*, first called our attention to the distinct types of behavior patterns that evolve within companies, with a direct and measurable impact on performance. Businesses, the authors reasoned, are social enterprises with "tribal" habits, well-defined roles for participants, and specialized strategies for determining inclusion, reinforcing identity, and adapting to change. United Parcel Service was a case in point.

Other "tribes" couldn't help but be impressed by UPS's achievements. Hence, many of the company's pioneering strategies, often deemed radical in their own time, have since been imitated and institutionalized at thousands of companies. And many other UPS procedures and practices dating from decades ago now appear quaint to outsiders but remain important components of the company today.

Adherence to what may seem like an excessively methodical method of doing business does not diminish UPSers' autonomy on larger matters. UPS gives individual employees responsibilities that require independent decision making and nearly superhuman performance. Yet these same employees work within controlled regulations and routines that might easily be called "obsessive-compulsive." Somehow UPS achieves a balance between the two extremes. To outsiders the strict regime seems over the top. To UPSers it is the *modus operandi*.

UPSers themselves rarely question the myriad regulations they must abide by, many of which have carried over from the earliest days. Even new hires, carefully screened for their adaptability to a highly disciplined company, quickly acclimatize to the UPS way. Why? Because the procedures work; they work for the employees, they work for customers, and they work for profits. Every UPSer has a clear understanding of what is expected on the job and a sense of pride in meeting these high standards. Added up, these performance expectations and methodologies constitute one of the most singular corporate cultures in the world.

Here, we examine the early motivations behind the philosophies and protocols that make up the UPS corporate culture. You'll see how this conservative, insular culture supported UPS as it reinvented itself time and again in order to survive and keep growing.

Profit Sharing

In 1927, the founders made a decision that very few other companies were making in those days—to share their bounty with employees. They believed their employees deserved a stake in the significant profits that West Coast operations were then generating. The loyalty of former delivery company owners who stayed on as managers inspired this move. Though the founders were primarily political conservatives, they adopted what could be considered even today rather radical pro-labor ideas. To their thinking, a share-and-share-alike philosophy and conservative political leanings were not mutually exclusive. They believed that sharing the wealth in this manner actually helped grow their business. With this in mind, Jim Casey and Evert "Mac" McCabe went to Reno, Nevada, to file documentation creating United Parcel Service of America, Incorporated.

Even then, Nevada was known as a haven for divorces—and also for corporation formation. (Gambling was illegal there from 1910 until 1931, when it was reinstituted to spur the economy.) Registering articles of incorporation there, rather than in California, allowed United Parcel Service to take advantage of Nevada's liberal statute. Upon their return, Jim Casey and Mac McCabe, along with George Casey and Charlie Soderstrom, offered company ownership to fifty-two senior employees, "not because we want your money," they wrote, "but rather because of our desire to acknowledge and reward your loyalty and cooperation."

The offering was an immediate hit. Though three employees declined, forty-nine new stakeholders bought stock and began receiving quarterly dividend checks, the first disbursed in February 1928. Almost immediately, managers began referring to each other as "partners," and they truly were partners in the company's growing success. Most people credit that stock ownership by employees, which continued to expand over the years as new members were added, as the most important factor in the company's ascendancy. It bred enormous loyalty and became a long-standing hallmark of the company.

When presenting the new stock in 1927, Jim Casey remarked, "There is no bigger incentive than for someone to work for himself." The stock offering assured better management—from frugality to employee motivation—which in turn contributed to increased profits. The value of the stock offered was $15 a share, and the company gave the managers five years to pay for it, as proof that they intended to encourage participation. Since UPS stock has split many times in eighty years, that one 1927 share, originally valued at $15, has become 16,000 shares today, each worth $80 (mid-2006 price), for a total value of $1,280,000.

Other privately held companies of the time, such as Cargill, Mars, Koch, Bechtel, and Levi-Strauss, made stock available too, but only among members of the family that owned the company. They did not share profits with their employees. United Parcel Service was a pioneer in employee-ownership, unique in an era of sweatshops and heavy-handed management that often necessitated union intervention. Its employees became the family.

First the founders, then the company's board set the stock price on a quarterly basis and paid a dividend twice yearly (until the company went public in 1999). Most privately held companies have illiquid stock, but UPS stock can be cashed out. Employee stockholders could always, and still can, sell shares back at the earlier board-set price or today's market price. Also, all employees, including hourly, can purchase shares today, but must work for the company for at least one year to be eligible for the company's discounted stock purchase plan. Participating in UPS's profit sharing program remains voluntary, with the exception of all managers and supervisors who receive stock through the Management Incentive Plan.

Management Incentive Plan

Employee ownership was already the heart of United Parcel Service culture by the 1940s, the partnership program having been established twenty years earlier. That managers had enjoyed the opportunity to purchase stock fed company growth. It inspired loyalty and incentive.

United Parcel Service was becoming one of the country's largest privately held employee-owned companies. Employment there, which had carried so many families through the Depression, was coveted. Turnover among full-time employees was negligible . . . just as it is today.

Only a few companies like United Parcel Service decided to "share the wealth" with their employees before World War II. Today's fastest-growing privately held company, Publix Supermarkets, began in 1930 (the first full year of the Great Depression) and right away made employees shareholders. As was the case with United Parcel Service, the Publix stock price was determined periodically by the company. But Publix did not develop a management incentive program. UPS did.

The delivery business's expanding service area made it all the more important to keep great, dedicated managers on board. To ensure that the cream of the crop stayed and kept performing, by the 1940s UPS began to issue shares of stock to managers annually. Through the Management Incentive Plan (MIP) each year managers were awarded a certain amount of shares in appreciation, based on years of service, salary, and job responsibility. United Parcel Service was unique. It was the only company of its size that not only remained private but rewarded its management team with the presentation of stock as an incentive.

According to the plan, when an employee left the company or retired, United Parcel Service had first option to repurchase the shares at a price established each quarter by the company. At the very beginning, this period of redemption after leaving the company was ninety days. It was later extended to ten years, a practice that lasted until the company went public in 1999. That meant that (after a year and a half grace period), the company would call back 10 percent of a retiree's shares each year. A retiree who left with $1 million in stock would have to sell at least $100,000 each year. This situation encouraged retirees to develop good financial planning. (Today UPS is a public company, and employees or retirees can keep their Class A shares, sell them back to UPS at market price, or change them to Class B shares and sell them as they wish on the open market.)

The Management Incentive Plan was never just about getting stock. It was about keeping employees. In the 2004 book *Faith and Fortune*, author Marc Gunther characterized the extended logic behind UPS's Management Incentive Plan, "Stock ownership . . . promotes long-term thinking. Even young UPS managers get a substantial portion of their compensation, perhaps 15 to 20 percent, in stock. Although they can sell at any time, there's a cultural expectation that they will hold their shares for many years and a reward for doing so."

To members of UPS management, the greatest benefit has traditionally been the long view—accumulating wealth in UPS stock over the years. It has never come without a price. Most supervisors and managers become accustomed to long hours, hard work, strict working conditions, and disproportionately low pay compared to managers in other businesses. Most management retirees really earned their palatial estates. For years, new supervisors often made less than some drivers, because drivers enjoyed the bonus system and/or overtime pay. Without overtime, many new salaried supervisors make even less than they did before entering management, especially on a per-hour basis. Since starting management pay was adjusted from drivers' guaranteed wages, I took a cut in pay from what I was earning in driver bonuses when I entered management. Supervisors who worked out their hourly rate by dividing the monthly salary by hours spent on the job per month might see some pretty discouraging numbers.

A new supervisor still does not make much more than a driver unless you count the year-end management incentive. UPS stock is the figurative carrot. Up until 1967, when supervisors were added, only managers enjoyed the incentive plan and 10 percent of the annual profits were divided among them, disbursed according to a formula each December. When supervisors were added, the total profits disbursed went to 15 percent, but the supervisors' allocation was half that of managers, or "one unit," versus the managers' "two units." In the early 1980s an additional stock option plan was made available for higher managers.

Anticipation has always been high each year awaiting the MIP announcement, which would come as a number, such as 1.7 (which was the average for the twenty years from 1970 to 1990). That meant that supervisors would receive, in shares of stock, 1.7 times their individual monthly salary. Someone who made $3,000 at the time would receive $5,100, which (after regular payroll deductions) would be tendered in shares of stock. Managers would receive two units, or twice that. There was also an additional incentive bonus equal to two and a half times the value of one's stock holdings, to a maximum of one month's pay.

It may not have seemed like much, and to a supervisor eking out a living, the temptation to cash it in was constant. Management members have always been strongly discouraged from selling, and district controllers set up local banks to help needy people borrow or "hypothecate" against the stock. Many did at one time or another. The justification for borrowing was that the dividends covered the interest so the loans did not cost anything.

For many years the company paid a whopping 2 percent cash dividend in the spring and an additional 2 percent stock dividend in December. There have always been dividends, and for a public company, UPS's dividends, still at around 2 percent annually, are now considered generous. Many enterprising management members borrowed as much as they reasonably could afford through the years and purchased additional shares, or real estate or other investments, thus hastening their financial independence.

Until the company went public in 1999, the stock price went up significantly each year, most of the time in double digits. (It did dip a bit in 1997 as a result of the strike.) By age fifty-five, most managers have been in the plan for about twenty-five years or so and their initial small stake, added to and accruing each year, makes the majority of them millionaires. After years of a difficult job and with financial independence secured, most retire before age sixty. They also have a pension plan, and later get Social Security, but for most management retirees, their UPS stock and the dividends derived from it are their greatest source of income.

By 1961, UPS leaders wanted *all* employees to acquire a financial stake in the company and initiated the UPS Thrift Plan. Participating Thrift Plan members could have up to $6 a week deducted from their paycheck. The company invested the money and annually contributed to each account. The UPS contribution, when added to the Thrift Plan investment earnings, brought the percentage of total earnings to three times the percentage of UPS profit on delivery income for the year.

Plan earnings for 1972 alone were 22.17 percent. By 1984 an employee who had been in the plan since its 1961 inception had deposited only $7,434 overall, but had earned $59,135 for a Thrift Plan total of $66,569. What was more impressive, at the end of 1987, when 110,000 UPSers had Thrift Plan accounts, a $6-a-week saver who had deposited only $8,370 total since the plan began had a nest egg of $111,609. It was a very viable piece of the action for all long-time participants before other plans took over.

With the advent of the 401(k) savings plan in 1988, UPS provided several options for both the UPS Savings Plan and the Teamsters-UPS National 401(k) Tax Deferred Savings Plan. Today the 401(k) includes a SavingsPLUS plan, which is a UPS Qualified Stock Ownership Plan for all employees and includes company contributions.

When the company went public in 1999, UPS set up the Discounted Employee Stock Purchase Plan (DESPP). When I asked my local California driver, Reggie, if he was buying UPS stock at a 10 percent discount and having it taken out of his pay, he just gave me a broad smile and a big thumbs-up. That option is available to *all* employees with over six months' service. Payroll deductions are available to assist financial planning. As a result, today many drivers are as interested in the vagaries of the stock market as UPS managers are.

In addition, the Dividend Reinvestment program allows all employees the opportunity to reinvest dividends. UPSers can also purchase additional shares without having to pay brokerage commissions and service charges.

On one hand, there was a methodology, the profit-sharing through stocks. The methodology nurtured a philosophy, a commitment. Together, methodology and philosophy made a culture. The partnership concept assured incredible allegiance, a willingness to work hard, and a ready acceptance of the strict set of work standards and ethics.

UPS Policy Book

Once their management team had ownership in the company, the UPS founders felt that a certain conduct was expected of them. They also needed a means of ensuring that autonomous managers still operated within parameters that would result in consistent, high-quality service and profitability.

No sooner had the U.S. stock market crashed in 1929 than United Parcel Service developed its *UPS Policy Book*. This company bible, still an 8" × 10" book of about seventy-five pages detailing more than a hundred policies, has always been hardbound, as rigid as its contents. The *Policy Book* continues to be an important management tool, bestowed upon every new supervisor ceremoniously, with the understanding that supervisors will immerse themselves in its contents and refer to it often. It was decided that *UPS Policy Books* would be carefully numbered and surrendered to the company when the management member left or retired. This distribution plan is now seventy-five years old.

Adherence to the *UPS Policy Book* both instituted and upheld a very conservative company. Many a young supervisor, in asking a policy question of a senior manager, has been chastised with the reproving, "It's in the *Policy Book*." Policies were discussed at meetings and adherence to them was mandatory.

A few policies have been controversial. The most debated one through the years, one that came about to eliminate even a pretense of favoritism nurtured by nepotism—has been the "We Strictly Limit the Employment of Relatives" policy. By the time the *Policy Book* was written, there were several brother hires, including the Oberkotters and Caseys. Mostly these sibling hires were grandfathered in when UPS acquired delivery services as part of its expansion. The practice ended with the clear-cut policy issued in the original *Policy Book*. That meant that family members could not get hired. Period. It actually made it easier for employees whose relatives tried to get help getting jobs (which many did)—they could stop the pressure by just explaining the policy. Many sons and daughters who wanted to become UPSers too had to wait until their parent retired before applying.

A policy against one management person marrying another, established to avoid any potential for favoritism, persisted for many years despite the resulting loss of talented people. It was modified as men and women found each other at work. The company also frowns on rehiring former employees, especially those who had become discontented or whom the company had found dissatisfactory. Since a district-level or higher manager had to approve a former employee being rehired, it rarely happened.

While the *Policy Book*'s purpose is inflexible, it is a working and living guide, updated by input from the entire management team every few years to reflect a changing world. The *UPS Policy Book* spells out its policies quite plainly, from dress codes to much more complicated canons such as decentralization.

Decentralization

The corporate culture grew in a medium of checks and balances. Early on, the founders learned that on-the-spot decisions affecting their delivery operations often had to be made, and employees had to be held accountable for these snap decisions. Executives couldn't be everywhere, so decentralization was the answer. Back in Seattle in 1912 when American Messenger Company (which eventually became UPS) opened its second office, George Casey made his messenger decisions without constantly seeking permission from Jim Casey or Claude Ryan. As the company expanded down the West Coast, local decision making became even more important. Each geographical area had its unique circumstances.

For all these reasons, decentralization of operations was critical to the success of United Parcel Service's expansion. Broad authority freed up managers to serve their customers properly.

Decentralization precepts were put to the test when the company moved its headquarters to New York in 1930. In fact, in anticipating the move in 1929, United Parcel Service developed a functional form of management in which specific managers assumed responsibility for a specific part of the company's activities over the entire system. It was not practical for managers who remained on the West Coast to consult with top management on day-to-day affairs. Here's how the *Policy Book* describes the procedure:

We Decentralize Management
to the Most Effective Degree Possible

To achieve greater efficiency and teamwork, we manage each operation on a personal, on-the-job basis and delegate appropriate decision-making authority. We divide our operations into smaller units to provide closer guidance and support. We have learned that small work groups develop a spirit of teamwork, perform more effectively, and provide greater responsibility for their group's goals.

We divide our operations into regions, our regions into districts, and our districts into divisions and operating areas. The district manager and staff are responsible for our service, cost, and the maintenance and development of our business within the district. The region manager and region staff provide guidance to all districts in their region.

A district might comprise one state, and maybe portions of another or two complete states. Some large states have two or more districts. A region will generally include five to ten districts.

Decentralization coupled with strong common policies worked beautifully, and it has stood the test of time, even with globalization. Along with several international and specialized regions (Europe, Latin America, Asia, Supply Chain, UPS Freight, and others), UPS currently has seven domestic U.S. regions: Northeast, East Central, Southeast, North Central, Southwest, West, and Pacific, plus the Air operation, which constitutes a separate region. As the districts reflect population centers, the West Region is the largest geographically but the sparsest population-wise relative to its size. One of its nine districts (Prairie Mountain) comprises four complete states: Nebraska, the Dakotas, and Montana.

Conversely, the six current Pacific Region districts primarily cover just one state (California). Both regions have about the same number of employees (35,000–40,000). Metro New York is the smallest district geographically, with other districts covering Long Island and upstate New York.

Today, a district might have anywhere from 3,000 to 7,000 employees, and the district manager is, as the UPS Policy Book says, in charge. The manager remains responsible for the district's making a profit and is held accountable for all sorts of production, service, and safety indices—in effect, making decisions that would get mired in the approval process in many other companies while living and breathing policies from the corporate policy bible.

Under the district managers, division managers have a lot of latitude running the six or seven centers in their jurisdiction. Center managers, too, make numerous autonomous decisions. They can shift drivers' routes around to accommodate a shipper wanting a later pickup. Or they can schedule their supervisors' hours to ensure overlapping coverage. Local decision making extends to the hourly ranks. Loaders, for example, know when to leave their posts for a few minutes to help a neighbor who might be getting behind. Drivers constantly make decisions—like returning to a pickup later, or breaking route to deliver a misloaded package—without consulting their supervisor.

Decentralization created autonomy and strengthened responsibility at every echelon. Even today, as an example, many UPS drivers cite their ability to be on their own, making numerous job decisions daily, as a desirable element of their job.

Informality

Some of the culture is procedural. Some is atmospheric. All is designed to make sure employees stay connected and committed. Jim Casey's open office door and later his glass fishbowl office established a precedent for management accessibility at every rank. Employees have always been free to discuss problems or suggestions with virtually anyone in the company without fear of reprisal. Not only are doors open figuratively, in most cases they're literally open as well.

In addition to the open door policy, the *UPS Policy Book* mandates informality in several ways. It includes a We Address Each Other on a First-Name Basis policy. If a driver bumped into Jim Casey at the cafeteria, he would say "Hi, Jim." The same is true of top executives today. Every executive remains approachable, and people know each other's first names. Most staff-level and higher managers got to their positions by adhering to the "people" policies in the guidebook.

In the *UPS Policy Book*, the We Maintain a Spirit of Teamwork policy mentions the informality and cooperative teamwork expected of everyone in the organization: "Every person should feel free to discuss matters with anyone else in our company. However, this informality does not relieve anyone of the obligation to respect delegated lines of authority. Rather, it reflects mutual confidence in the good faith and sound judgment of our associates. Informality enhances the teamwork that is so important in our company."

What makes the demanding UPS culture work is its longtime commitment to communications, both written and oral, and preferably face-to-face. *Better Together* authors Robert D. Putnam and Lewis M. Feldstein note: "For a large, global company that values efficiency almost to the point of obsession, UPS is surprisingly hospitable in face-to-face conversation. Every morning, in every UPS hub and center, drivers gather for a brief pre-work communications meeting, or PCM, before they go out on the road."

A culture that still includes familiar use of first names, frequent face-to-face meetings, and executives who answer their own phones perpetuates informality and approachability. The CEO and top managers of UPS remain accessible—unlike those in other companies of the same size and even smaller.

What seems to some people like a culture of enforced conformity, current CEO Mike Eskew calls "egalitarian." Continuing this line of thought in a recent interview, he said, "We all treat ourselves the same. If you are going to have coffee, you go downstairs and have coffee with people. It's a good chance to walk down to the cafeteria, talk to people, and be together. We don't eat at our desk. We tell our drivers not to drink coffee in the trucks. We answer our own phones. We don't have private dining rooms. We don't have drivers that take us to and from places. We call each other by first names. If you were to go to Atlanta and walk around with me, you'd be surprised. I go downstairs [to the cafeteria], I stand in line like everybody else. People come up to me and say, 'Mike, what are you thinking about these days?'"

UPS Benefits

Traditionally, about 60 percent of every dollar of UPS revenue has gone to its employees on wages and benefits, including vacations, holidays, welfare benefits, social security taxes, and compensation insurance. During growth years this figure has been as high as 69 percent, but has settled to around 57 percent, where it has been four of the last five years. That percentage, higher than most companies, puts teeth behind the UPS adage, "People are our most important asset."

It isn't that UPS has entirely skirted the demoralizing trends that characterize employment at most companies of even a fraction of its size, but it is still a "last best place" for blue-collar workers. In fact, in 2005, UPS hired 3,489 entry-level workers with an average pay of $50,000 to $54,999.

And the company does right by employees compared to other global corporations. As an example, today's drivers, or "service providers" as they are now called, earn top wages for union members— $70,000 and more per year. Drivers get between six and nine weeks paid leave each year. UPS also pays 100 percent of each worker's medical insurance premiums, something of an anomaly in these days of cutbacks. A driver who works twenty-five years or more can receive a pension as high as $30,000 a year.

Even before the 1927 stock offering, United Parcel Service was looking out for its employees' welfare. It started a bonus system in 1924 that paid drivers a little extra for more stops and packages delivered beyond their carefully measured eight-hour workload. That bonus system evolved into a very nice drivers' incentive. Because of opposition from various local unions, this bonus system was not extended universally but has prevailed for years in Southern California and a few other areas. Many drivers have gotten used to the extra money it provides, and continually hustle more packages than required during their eight-hour shifts. Several of us really counted on it in the 1960s.

In the early 1960s, the hourly driver rate was about $3.50, which came out to a little less than $600 a month. In eight hours, I was averaging what were measured to be ten-hour days and was making closer to $750 or $800 a month as I was paid for the ten hours. Imagine my chagrin, and the family cutbacks that followed, when I was offered $600 a month to start in management. But I knew about the opportunities and had been told about the partnership concept and willingly made that initial sacrifice, which was eventually offset by the advantages of stock ownership.

Back in the early 1920s, life insurance was slowly introduced to corporate America—inspired by the World War Veterans Act of 1924 that offered life insurance to veterans. In September 1925, UPS also decided to offer its employees life insurance, becoming a pioneer company to offer this benefit. Only a handful of American companies made life insurance available to their employees, and then only if they paid 100 percent of the premium. United Parcel Service's offering was liberal because the company paid the major portion of the premiums. Initially, fifty-five employees subscribed in Los Angeles and another nineteen in Oakland. By April 1929, when there were fewer than four hundred employees, almost three-quarters were insured. Later on, the company began paying those premiums in their entirety.

The early life insurance offering was but one in a package of benefits that grew to include an excellent health and welfare plan, medical, dental, vision, tuition reimbursement, liberal paid vacations, and holidays and sick days.

A little-touted benefit is the UPS *Employee Discount Program* in which employees and retirees can enjoy discounts on anything from tennis racquets to travel. The company has negotiated contracts with quality suppliers to give employees better deals on Reeboks, Volvos, bank loans, cell phones, hotels, and much much more.

In addition, UPS provides pension plans. Nonunion employees enjoy the UPS Plan, which is generally more lucrative yet less expensive than union plans. UPS Teamsters are bound under collective bargaining agreement to Teamster plans, one of twenty-one multiemployer plans funded by UPS and other companies. Over the last three years UPS contributed over *$1 billion* each year to cover its share of all employees collectively in these twenty-one plans. The UPS multiemployer plan employees are primarily drivers rather than loaders, unloaders, or sorters, since those jobs are typically held by part-timers who participate contractually in a single employer plan.

Multiemployer plans are concentrated in older industries like airlines, auto manufacturers, and trucking. Many trucking companies have gone out of business since trucking was deregulated in 1980. Today's employees move from one company to another more than ever before, accumulating successive pension plans that are lumped into a multiemployer plan. Since many smaller companies go bankrupt or otherwise fold, more stable companies such as UPS are stuck with pension obligations that were accrued outside UPS.

UPS commits to honor the pensions it has already assumed, but wants to be responsible only for its own workers' benefits in the future. For this to happen, the government agency that insures pensions, the Pension Benefit Guaranty Corp. (PBGC), would have to assume benefits unpaid by defunct companies.

PBGC, created by the Employee Retirement Income Security Act of 1974 (ERISA), protects the retirement incomes of 44.1 million American workers in 30,330 private sector defined benefit pension plans. To do so, it collects insurance premiums from employers that sponsor insured pension plans, earns money from investments, and receives funds from pension plans it takes over.

PBGC also pays monthly retirement benefits, up to a guaranteed maximum, to about 683,000 retirees in 3,595 pension plans that have terminated. Including those who have not yet retired and participants in multiemployer plans receiving financial assistance, PBGC is responsible for the current and future pensions of some 1,296,000 people.

The government admits that as a group, multiemployer pension plans are underfunded by $450 billion, and the PBGC has a $22.8 billion deficit. To remedy this growing problem, Congress has been looking into a Pension Reform Act, with support from several lawmakers, including some in Georgia, Kentucky, and Ohio where UPS employees are most numerous.

Finally passed in July 2006, the Pension Reform Act of 2006 puts some teeth into ensuring that employers properly and adequately fund their worker pension plans. UPS hopes this legislation will help the company increase control over its troubled plans. While UPS's multiemployer plans have covered most retirees to date, some drivers have had their work life extended, and the plan's future is tenuous because making good on pension promises made by employers that have gone out of business is extremely costly. Even so, the Teamsters balked when UPS offered buyout solutions back in 1997.

Consider that on average UPS is contributing more than $20,000 per year per full-time employee into the multiemployer funds—by far more than any other American employer and more than UPSers receive as benefits. Contractually, UPS is obligated to make contributions through the remainder of the current 2002–2008 National Master UPS/IBT agreement.

Pensions are already the most important item on the agenda of ongoing union negotiations—for UPS, for drivers who are afraid of losing their pensions, and for the union itself. The problem can't be patched by throwing more money at it. It must be totally rethought and redone. The company and the union felt that the issues were important enough and complex enough that they got a two-year head start on negotiations for the next national contract, due to expire in August 2008, to ensure there is no danger of a disruption in service. The specter of the 1997 strike still looms.

The largest UPS multiemployer plan, Central States Pension Fund, administered by the Teamsters Union, is in serious default and long-time UPS drivers are howling as they watch their retirement benefits being eroded.

Speculation regarding the next UPS-Teamster contract started as early as spring 2006 and drivers have been venting on an unofficial UPS Web site (www.thebrowncafe.com). One driver wrote, "I would probably give up one of my six weeks or option days if my pension problem with Central States could be fixed." Another responded, "They must be screwed over by Central States like I am." Another added, "Give me a lump sum payoff from CS that I can roll into my 401(k)." Several mentioned that instead of a big hourly increase they want the pension situation fixed.

Due to the concern of continuing pensions for all its employees and the viability of various plans, UPS has actively sought to place company management members on the boards of trustees in as many Multiemployer Pension Plans as possible. Currently UPS has fifteen employees serving on six of the twenty-one plans, most added after 1998. Hoping to offer sensible input, the company intends to make sure that the promised pensions become reality. All parties hope that a solution presents itself in the future.

Along with the various pension plans, and the anticipated social security, UPS has strongly encouraged what was to be the third leg of financial planning—individual savings. Through its various stock ownership programs, all employees can have an interest in their company and help ensure their own financial security.

Publications, Awards, and Communication

United Parcel Service was increasingly inventive and conscientious in its goal of nurturing its growing family. In the early days, there were the Breakfast Club meetings, holiday turkeys, and UPS songs with lyrics like *"Over hill, over dale, as they hit that concrete trail, our brown wagons go rolling along"* (Russel Havighorst) and *"It's service we give at every step. On this we all agree. If it's service you want, it's service you'll get. Just come to old U.P."* (Jack Dennis and Bill Buckley). Company picnics, dances, dinners, and other get-togethers were common and regular festivities. Positive feedback became another element in the role the company plays as parent to its widespread family. Awards for safe driving, as mentioned in the first chapter, continue to expand what UPS calls "The Circle of Honor." Today employees are also recognized for longevity, service, sales, and more. And they still get holiday turkeys.

In 1924 the company rolled out its first company newspaper, the *Big Idea*, published in Los Angeles. As UPS pioneer Russel Havighorst wrote me: "The launching of our well-known 'family' newspaper in 1924 afforded our founders a new medium for encouraging that which they had always sought—the development of new ideas for better operations through suggestions by UPSers all over the country. The *Big Idea* gave Jim Casey and Evert McCabe a place to recognize others for constructive ideas." It served as the main written communication tool until the 1990s. New and separate magazines began as territory after territory came on line, eventually over sixty separate publications. I was editor of the *Southern California Big Idea* for several years and later responsible for all the West Coast publications.

The *Big Idea* was a publication for the employees and not a typical mouthpiece of management—although it carried some growth, expansion, and company-wide stories too. A typical issue had a feature (maybe an employee with an interesting hobby or delivering to an interesting place), news (promotions, retirements, upcoming functions, and so on), and lots of safety recognition (with individual and group photos). What made the magazine unique was that almost half of each issue was local news, chit-chat about a center or department, voluntarily written by a driver, clerk, sorter, or mechanic. While my professional colleagues at other companies winced at its abrasive informality, the employees loved it—and flipped to the local news first. Even if they didn't see their own name, they'd have an opportunity to read about someone they knew.

We purposely kept the *Big Idea* as informal as the company was. By the 1990s a new corporate magazine emerged called *InsideUPS*, a slick four-color publication that is as much of a corporate mouthpiece as the *Big Idea* was a folksy magazine. The many versions of the *Big Idea* ceased publication by the mid-1990s.

Today UPSers look to the company's employee Web site, www.upsers.com, for most local news, along with regional and corporate news. The "news when you want it" site recognizes employees for safety, years of service, and more, and also includes features and questions on benefits, pay, pensions, stock plans, 401(k) plans, and retirement. It is still informal compared to other companies' communication channels, though it lacks the chit-chat and local news priorities of the old *Big Idea*. According to numerous employees, it's a well-used Web site.

Communication remains important at UPS. Every workday begins with a Prework Communication Meeting (PCM), a three-minute news or safety flash or other tidbit. Most drivers will tell you that this is where they get their important news.

Employees periodically sit down with their boss to air any gripes as part of the Talk, Listen and Act (TLA) program. TLA gives supervisors an excellent opportunity to know their people better. Senior management members perform follow-up TLA talks at random, just in case someone is uncomfortable about unloading to their immediate boss.

These numerous opportunities for communication face-to-face at UPS include periodic supervisor rides, performance evaluations, job reviews, focus groups, service committees, the informality of the open door, exit interviews, and—to help reduce accidents corporate-wide—a network of 2,400 safety committees primarily made up of hourly employees who hash out potential problems and suggest and implement solutions. These are all viable communication tools.

Promotion from Within

Perhaps second in importance to the partnership concept, the promotion-from-within policy—from entry-level positions to top management—has been a hallmark at UPS ever since Jim Casey trusted his younger brother to run the company's second office. From the early days of expansion and growth, managers were generally given greater and greater responsibility, the opportunity to climb the corporate ladder, make more money, own more stock.

All managers, while personally preparing for a higher job, have always been responsible for mentoring those who worked for them. In 1945 Jim Casey said, "One measure of your success . . . will be the degree to which you build up others who work with you. While building up others you will build up yourself."

Jim Kelly's ascendancy proves the efficacy of the policy. In 1964 James P. Kelly hired on as a delivery driver in New Jersey, while going to night school. By 1968, he'd progressed to supervisor and then to manager, in the meantime earning his degree in management from Rutgers University. By 1979 he was Atlantic district manager, and by 1985 I knew him as labor relations manager in the Pacific Region. He became North Central Region manager and corporate labor relations manager before being named U.S. operations manager in 1990. He joined the Board of Directors in 1991, then in June 1992 became chief operating officer. Two years later he was executive vice president. Finally, in 1997 Jim Kelly became CEO and chairman of the board.

Along with role models and on-the-job training, numerous internal training schools and materials prepare employees for higher-level positions. Managers rarely get fired or demoted to a position with less compensation; they are more likely given other "opportunities" if their performance is not up to par. A district manager with "good numbers" is in line to get a region, while the district manager with the "least best" numbers might be reassigned from the all-important operations job to a less influential staff position, or some sort of special assignment. Getting fired is highly unusual and requires some sort of malfeasance, fraud, impropriety, or other serious transgression.

With few exceptions, the salaried management team is selected from employees earning hourly wages in the same section or division of the company. In recent years, it's been a more formal system that credits current job rating, education (today it usually takes a college degree to get into management), and much more, but in the early days the main criterion was a capacity for hard work. Many people have become successful top managers with only a high school diploma or less.

Before hiring from the outside, UPS promotes loaders and unloaders to package car drivers, and by turn, interested package car drivers to feeder drivers. It makes more sense to promote an employee—someone who is already screened and aware that UPS means hard work and dedication—than to take a risk on a new hire.

Job Commitment

In the fast-paced, noncommittal twenty-first century, some of the culture, like managers' answering their own phones, the strict appearance guidelines and fussy business attire, the tightly measured workplace, abstinence from drinking during the workday even at business functions, and the formal meetings that start precisely on time might seem too demanding or just downright antiquated. A guest at a UPS corporate Monday night management meeting once described it as being as straitlaced as a Quaker meeting.

Nevertheless, UPS—through its corporate culture—has kept core values alive and demonstrated their timelessness and success. UPS offers employees security and a sense of belonging rather than excitement or flashy individualism. Most of it depends on a willingness to become and think like a partner in an organization that has long prided itself on its uniqueness. UPS invests a lot in its workforce and expects a lot in return.

Through the years I'd noticed certain types of people thrive in the demanding UPS culture. Those who adapted the best are those who have already been exposed to discipline: former marines and other servicepeople, Catholic school attendees, and seminarians. Other successful UPSers are those to whom "people skills" come naturally. Drivers are the public face of UPS. Ever met a driver that didn't have great people skills? Overall, they have an outstanding reputation for good rapport with their customers, carrying the affable element of UPS's corporate culture out into communities.

This is not to say that every manager or supervisor at UPS has been a perfect example of the ideal. In every company, there are always bad managers and supervisors. There are those who expend their energies in developing, maintaining, expanding, and protecting their turf. There are those afraid to make a decision. There are those nit-picking micromanagers who can drive people crazy. Some can be insensitive, vainglorious, insipid, and lazy. UPS had, and undoubtedly still has, those types as well. But the tools for success are in place.

This regimented lifestyle is certainly not for everyone, and comes easier to some than to others, but it is a part of life at UPS. An atmosphere of pride pervades UPS. As corny as it sounds as measured by today's opportunism, being part of a "job well done" really is its own reward. The pay, benefits, and security UPS offers all employees is the trade-off for hard work. For the management team, the demanding work ethic becomes a small price to pay as one's personal wealth builds through company ownership.

What is the upshot of employment practices built of self-made men and women? Incredible loyalty. Employment longevity has long been a hallmark at UPS. In the 1930s, people were happy to be working, and United Parcel Service afforded them the security that they couldn't get elsewhere. By the 1940s, with many managers' owning UPS stock, it was rare that one quit the company. It still is. In my years at UPS, there were numerous occasions to honor people who had worked there for twenty-five years, even clerks and administrative assistants. At these events, there were always more than a handful present who had worked more than thirty years!

Even in these times of free agency, employees tend to stay with UPS and turnover is very low, most of all at the management level. Well over 90 percent of the company's top two hundred managers have been with the company more than twenty years. Of today's top twelve executives at UPS, the Management Committee, all are lifers. Eight have thirty years or more service, one has twenty-eight, another twenty. (His company was acquired in 1986.) Only one, the general counsel, has fewer than twenty years. She joined UPS in 1995 but had previously worked on UPS matters. According to one executive, "UPS doesn't often feel the need to recruit elsewhere at the executive level, because of its ingrained succession processes and demanding culture."

Drivers stay over sixteen years on the average—compared to a national job average of four years. The driver job attracts not only traditional blue-collar workers but an increasing number of college graduates looking for better pay and benefits as well as greater job satisfaction. UPS's commitment to technology has helped cut turnover in its IT employees to lower than average and lower than expected for the industry.

As a result of career and company ownership opportunities created for UPS employees, global turnover in the entire full-time workforce of 190,400 is an industry low of 8 percent. It was even lower, but diversification into new business units and more expansion internationally has shifted the numbers. Of the 190,400 full-timers, 95,000 are drivers. UPS expects that 8 percent turnover rate, where 92 percent of its people will be around at least a year, to persist in the future.

Those are the full-time numbers. Part-timers make up 47 percent of the entire UPS workforce. Keeping those part-timers has always been the hardest part of employee retention. The nature of the business requires carriers like UPS to use part-timers. While meeting UPS needs, part-time jobs also meet the needs of thousands of people, like students, retirees, and others who want flexible hours with competitive wages and benefits.

Many of the part-time employees are young, 56 percent of all new part-time hires in the U.S. are college students. Generation Y-ers are, as a group, impatient and uncommitted. Statistically, they rarely look at their first jobs as permanent and may have as many as five jobs in the first five years out of college. The average part-time UPSer is with the company more than three years before seeking full-time UPS employment or pursuing opportunities elsewhere, but that still leaves part-time turnover at 45.3 percent. To keep part-time turnover as low as possible, UPS offers a wide range of tuition assistance programs.

Duration isn't the only indicator of the allure of UPS's corporate culture. It's also in the numbers. In 1947, there were 3,000 employees. When I first hired on in 1957, there were 10,000. Today, UPS is the fourth-largest employer in the United States, and more than 407,000 people worldwide "bleed brown blood," fully half of them for much longer than people stay at other companies.

7

GOING NATIONAL

We take today's broad shipping options for granted, picking and choosing from numerous carriers for our parcels as though that freedom of options was, like oxygen, always available. Even though millions of people today choose UPS, few know that were it not for UPS's gritty resolve, we might still be stuck with the U.S. government-run parcel post monopoly, a service so notoriously inept that the operation has forever been the brunt of frustration and wisecracks. Compare your sociable UPS driver to indifferent government employees and you get a whiff of what life would be like without UPS.

United Parcel Service has always been efficient and economical, but the company's distribution area was at first quite restricted, limited to those delivery areas served by the large department stores of major cities. Outside those areas, people couldn't take advantage of the company's now-famous reliability as they can today because severe federal and state regulation kept that reliability from expanding beyond those retail stores and out of reach. Not until UPS focused its attention on all types of deliveries and obtained the rights to compete did it finally achieve nationwide shipping in 1975. That achievement—which benefited UPS, other companies, and all customers—was extremely hard won.

In the old days, each city and town was an island unto itself. It either had delivery service companies or it didn't. If you wanted to ship a package outside the environs of a particular city, you had to use the U.S. Post Office. Jim Casey's ambition, prompted by his boyhood days eyeing cargo as it arrived on Seattle's wharfs from distant ports, had long been a grand and sensible alternative: nationwide shipping, coast to coast, to every address in the forty-eight continental states. United Parcel Service didn't accomplish this objective in one fell swoop. Rather, the company doggedly pursued it, state by state and in some cases city by city, with applications, formidable paperwork and documentation, meetings with attorneys, and state and federal hearings, with occasional appeals, over a period of sixty-eight years. Over Jim Casey's lifetime. Talk about delayed gratification!

Spoils of War

UPS's history during the Depression is very much caught up with an attempt at air transport, which I will cover in Chapter Nine. For now suffice to say that even during those lean years, the company managed to expand from Seattle, the San Francisco Bay Area, Southern California, and Portland into New York City, Cincinnati, Milwaukee, and Philadelphia. The expansions occurred as UPS literally took over the delivery operations (and in most cases vehicles and personnel as well) for major department stores in those cities.

When the United States joined World War II, economic prosperity returned as factories geared up to fabricate much-needed war materials. Many UPS men went off to war, to Italy, to France, and to remote islands of the Pacific. *Big Idea* publications from the war years were full of letters from these theaters of war, from employees abroad who were letting their coworkers know that they were having a "swell time" chasing Hitler over the horizon.

With the men at war and the factories running at full steam, a new type of employee entered the workforce in large numbers—women. Of course, working was not new to women, especially minority and poor women. Prior to the war 12 million women were already working. They represented a quarter of the American workforce. Most were clerks, domestics, teachers, and nurses. Very few worked in factories or in traditionally male jobs. However, most people still felt that white middle-class women belonged in the home, and this had been especially true during the Depression since women, theoretically or otherwise, might be taking jobs from unemployed men.

The advent of World War II changed everything, and the government lured women into the workforce by creating the fictional "Rosie the Riveter" as the ideal woman worker: loyal, efficient, patriotic, and (perhaps to some women the most important attribute) *pretty*, which is certainly evident in popular films of the time, which featured glamorous starlets working in factories, like Ginger Rogers in the 1943 film *Tender Comrade*. (And the image persisted. Decades later, the 1984 film *Swing Shift* with Goldie Hawn also glamorized the working women of the wartime years.) By the end of World War II, 18 million women were working, 3 million of them in factories.

Noting the man shortage soon after the U.S. declaration of war, some New York City UPS employees wrote a musical comedy called "Romance on Wheels." Intended as a madcap fantasy, it depicted women employed as drivers of UPS package cars, and you can imagine the hilarious Claudette Colbert–like complications that would arise. It happened that the off-Broadway musical, presented at the Henry Hudson Hotel on April 12, 1942, was quite prescient.

Off stage, women soon joined UPS operations as the "brown" version of Rosie the Riveter, filling essential delivery positions left behind by UPSers deployed to the European or Pacific Theater of War. Many women worked nights, sorting or loading package delivery vehicles, and others, as foretold by "Romance on Wheels," drove UPS package cars to deliver purchases to customers. Intrepid Mazie Lanham was the first. She began driving for UPS in Los Angeles in May 1943.

These women were nicknamed "Brown Bettys," not only an homage to UPS's favorite color but a folksy reference to the popular American baked apple dessert. Along with their specially designed uniforms—much like those of their male counterparts, but tailored to fit a female figure—Brown Bettys were considered a novelty at the time, but they got the job done and created a precedent for the accomplishments of women within the fabric of this traditionally male workplace.

At United Parcel Service, the wartime spirit was high despite the sacrifices required of both the business community and civilians. The government issued directives requesting that department stores cut back on delivery services and encouraged customers to carry their packages home. Ever resourceful Jim Casey noted that the mandated department-store delivery cutbacks could spell more consolidated store delivery business for United Parcel Service. And it did. Even though individual stores had fewer deliveries, the company's total package volume actually remained stable in a period of cutbacks and conservation because United Parcel Service was serving more stores.

Fuel and rubber shortages were extreme. The government rationed tires as part of the war effort, and this rationing hit UPS hard. A January 1942 *Big Idea* article reminded drivers that the situation was serious and that the company must economize to help preserve the existing tire supply.

Retail stores immediately agreed to accept deliveries once a day instead of twice, and on April 1, all wholesale deliveries were also cut back to once a day to preserve rubber, fuel, and equipment. By the time federal regulations were issued in May 1942 mandating cutting mileage 25 percent from prior-year levels, UPS was in 100 percent compliance.

Articles in the *Big Idea* encouraged scrap iron drives, victory gardens, and savings bonds. By early 1942 a payroll deduction plan for War Bond purchases was put into effect. Later that year, United Parcel Service received designation as an issuing agent for War Bonds.

Finally, after Japan surrendered on September 2, 1945, the war ended. In its thirty-ninth year (1946) United Parcel Service delivered its billionth package. Business was great. However, if the company hadn't been managed by a cadre of men firmly focused on the future, it might have continued to do what it did well without noticing that the axe was going to fall.

The war effort had changed America, changed United Parcel Service, and changed the delivery business. The postwar years found many people migrating to suburbs, with new homes near large new shopping centers surrounded by vast parking lots. Families purchased more cars, and with second cars, the breadwinner was not the only one behind the wheel. A new American lifestyle evolved.

With more and more people driving their packages home, the retail delivery business that had always defined United Parcel Service leveled off. By the end of the decade, it was clear that a new direction was needed. The company had to reinvent itself once again to survive and prosper during the years following World War II.

As the situation became dire, Jim Casey cautioned management in 1948, "We must be able to move quickly in any direction to meet new conditions of a changing world." He later added, "In several cities, however, we seemed to have reached the peak of volume that can be expected from retail stores alone. In such instances, particularly, it would be a dismal outlook if we could not see beyond."

A Formidable Obstacle

Remember Russell Peck's common carrier business? The rights United Parcel Service had inherited in acquiring his company in Los Angeles in 1922? Common carrier service was broad, including virtually any type of delivery, not just delivering for a retail store to its customers. Common carrier, or wholesale, delivery ferried parcels from one wholesaler to another, from store to store, or from stores and factories directly to consumers. Common carriers were in direct competition with the Post Office and the rights to become a common carrier in new regions were hard to come by because they were highly regulated by both the federal and state governments.

Yet where common carriers existed, they were popular. Western Region manager Bill Schlinger reflected that it was obvious by the war's end that wholesale deliveries in Southern California would continue to grow with the expanding population. The Los Angeles wholesale success suggested new markets.

To accommodate the demand, a new wholesale center (9th Street Central Sort) opened in 1947 and featured the company's first traveling cages. Two cages with bins wound through the building on rollers, one for unloaded packages, and another that traveled along the line of trailers to be loaded. Sorters or "routers" pulled the unloaded packages off one cage and put them into marked and colored sections of the other. Ten years later, my first UPS job was pulling sorted wholesale packages off that original traveling cage and loading them into a "feeder" trailer.

The vision beyond retail store delivery was one that an industrial engineer named E. E. Arison had put in Jim Casey's head thirty-five years before. It made sense to Casey and he later related the nub of Arison's argument: "Think of the scores of millions of additional packages we would handle if we delivered all those going *into* each territory, rather than what goes *out* of the stores we happen to serve." As Casey intoned, "Our horizon is as distant as our mind's eye wishes it to be. . . . The vast field of distribution for wholesalers and manufacturers appears to be wide open for us."

Not that "wide open," though; those new markets could not be had except through the all-but-intransigent Interstate Commerce Commission (ICC). Since 1887, the ICC had tightly regulated the economics and services of carriers engaged in transportation between states. Congress created the ICC, the first regulatory commission in U.S. history, to protect against railroad malpractice, but ICC's jurisdiction extended to trucking companies, bus lines, freight forwarders, water carriers, oil pipelines, transportation brokers, and express agencies too. Except for airlines, any business conveyance that charged money to transport goods or passengers from one state to another was under ICC regulation. The agency's roles included rights, rate making, regulation, and resolving labor disputes in interstate transport. The ICC represented a formidable challenge to UPS's expansion plans, allied as the ICC was with UPS's biggest competitor, the U.S. Post Office Department.

The company had had only one previous brush with the department. In the early days of Merchants Parcel Delivery, Mac

McCabe had arranged with the U.S. Post Office Department to deliver its special-delivery letters and parcels in Seattle. This was the first and only such arrangement in the country, slipping in despite the Parcel Post Act of 1912, which locked out other shippers. Merchants Parcel Delivery enjoyed this contract in Seattle, delivering about 125,000 pieces per year, for a couple of years—until the government decided to operate its own vehicles.

Add to ICC impediments a considerable wad of red tape, courtesy of state commerce regulators. The Public Utilities Commission (PUC) in California (as in other states) wielded enormous power over all aspects of transportation, and still does. Another prime example of difficult bureaucracy is the omnipotent Railroad Commission of Texas, which was to present UPS's final stumbling block in achieving complete nationwide service: shipping packages from place to place within Texas.

The company made the momentous decision to pursue wholesale package delivery despite the challenges, to expand United Parcel Service's "common carrier" services to deliver packages from any customer, whether private or commercial, to any other. Having made the commitment to bring better delivery service to more and more communities, United Parcel Service's highly disciplined employees had renewed verve, ready to take the company to greater success. They were extremely motivated, because it was *their* company and because they knew customers would happily use the service. They tenaciously began to pursue the rights necessary for a national delivery network.

A New Horizon

Later United Parcel Service would take on the ICC one city, state, or multistate area at a time. For the time being, however, management wanted to see if the existing California service could serve as a foundation. In 1952, the company applied to the state of California for a certificate allowing common carrier service in the San Francisco Bay Area and also for transferring packages between the Bay Area and Los Angeles.

Even though United Parcel Service was well established in both California cities, the company was unable to move packages between them. This meant that if Los Angeles parents wanted to send some personal items to their daughter at the University of California in Berkeley they had no choice but to go to the Post Office. In the Bay Area itself, United Parcel Service could not deliver anything other than from its retail store clients. So a San Francisco company that wanted to send some printed office supplies to its Oakland subsidiary also had to go to the Post Office.

The demand was there, but Big Brown couldn't get bigger, couldn't operate over wide enough areas to satisfy it, without the proper certification. It wasn't easy. A mere extension of its operating authority in California precipitated a series of legal battles before regulatory commissions and in the courts. The United Parcel Service regulatory department became a steely, indomitable group and, with assistance from outside legal counsel, fired the first volleys in the battles for additional rights.

California's PUC granted package-transfer rights in 1953, and the company immediately began moving packages between California's two largest metropolitan areas, San Francisco and Los Angeles.

Later, the PUC granted *overnight* common carrier service rights between the two California cities, and in 1956 that service commenced. To anyone but a bureaucrat, it must seem silly, but *overnight* common carrier service rights between the two California cities required a separate application.

The raging success of this new delivery channel strained delivery facilities to the max in a very short time. By early 1957 Southern California wholesale packages had reached a peak daily average of 76,000, all of which went through 9th Street Sort in Los Angeles, a system designed for 25,000 packages.

Growth assured, United Parcel Service invested in the new Olympic Hub on the property adjacent to the Sort. When the Olympic Hub opened in late 1957, it was a state-of-the-art package sorting facility. It also included the district and region offices and six package delivery centers. The hub provided a welcome relief as common carrier package volume in Los Angeles had more than tripled in the decade from 1947 to 1957.

Today, a customer who wants to know the status of a package needs only log onto the UPS Web site and check on it. This wasn't always so easy. Imagine keeping track of the volume without the aid of computers. All packages, both wholesale and retail, were "sheeted" or logged in a general stop-for-stop order on multiple-carbon delivery records (eighty-line legal sheets once suggested by Jim Casey) by UPS "nightloaders" (today called "preloaders"). In some locations the drivers themselves logged the packages. All information was abbreviated to identify shippers, street names, and so on.

The driver took a copy to follow for the route and the carbon was kept in the package delivery center. Customer inquiries went directly to the center, where harried supervisors or dispatchers did their best to determine if indeed a package for the customer was out for delivery that day. "Yes," they might respond, "I show one package from . . . it looks like, "Heflond Inds." for your address today. Yes, he should be there, probably late this morning."

We still provided retail deliveries, especially for exclusive stores. A unique retail delivery chore that UPS drivers from the 1950s and 1960s remember was the "Fur Call," known as the "F/C." Major upscale department stores, such as Saks Fifth Avenue and I. Magnin in California, kept their customers' furs under refrigeration each summer. So each spring, drivers in affluent residential neighborhoods would pick up furs that they would later redeliver in the fall. Each Fur Call required a large box the size of a suitcase made of heavy steamer-trunk material secured by buckles. Drivers were trained in handling "m'lady's fur." We carefully folded the garment fur side in, attached the stub to the buttonhole (never the button), and wrapped the item in the tissue paper supplied in each box, provided a receipt, tipped our hat, and left leaving the customer the feeling that her valuable fur was in good hands.

So some retail work persisted, but the common carrier vision went beyond California and was national in scope; thus permit applications were being filed by United Parcel Service all over the country. From 1952 until 1980 the company waged legal battles before regulatory commissions and courts across the nation to secure additional permissions to expand delivery service. Early applications requested only small expansions of territory, either just a particular city or perhaps an entire metropolitan area. Then, emboldened by growing operational success and depending upon regulatory jurisdictions, the company began to request more and larger areas, whole states, and even multistate regions in a single application.

Like Aesop's tortoise, United Parcel Service was sure and steady, plodding toward its objective of providing delivery service all over America, moving forward with perseverance and a humility that bordered on stealth. Big Brown was slowly but inevitably taking over the country.

The wisdom of establishing a national delivery network piece by piece, rather than applying simultaneous and massive infusions of capital, is no better illustrated than by the disastrous experiences of many dot-com companies during the 1990s. Many of these failed start-ups made the mistake of ignoring the low-tech realities of matching customer demand with the astronomical costs of building distribution infrastructure from scratch. Online grocery shopping, spearheaded by Webvan, Streamline, Homegrocer, and Shoplink, failed miserably in the 1990s partially due to miscalculation of the costs of their food distribution centers. Only today are traditional grocery chains venturing into the online grocery market, applying the UPS model of utilizing their existing delivery networks, which serve their brick-and-mortar stores, to slowly expand into this emerging market.

During a span of nearly thirty years UPS pursued over a hundred applications for common carrier operating authority. In 1953 Chicago became the first city outside California where UPS offered common carrier delivery service. Four years later, United Parcel Service was able to expand those common carrier rights to five states within a 150-mile radius of Chicago.

As of 1956, however, all cities introduced to common carrier service were cities where United Parcel Service had already established a flourishing retail delivery business. This approach had its limitations—many metropolitan cities, like Boston, had no existing fleets of Big Brown package cars. Rather than take over the delivery operations of a regional retail store, United Parcel Service elected to start from scratch in building common carrier service in Boston. They purchased new UPS package cars, hired drivers, and initiated delivery routes. Boston, an amazing success, moved 10,000 packages a day within six months of launch.

Boston became a model for hundreds of new openings all over the country. This was it. There was no turning back. Common carrier package delivery transformed the company, defined it, with retail deliveries becoming an increasingly smaller percentage of the business volume.

Little by little, the government yielded common carrier rights to the boys in brown, and the company jumped at each opportunity. Each extension created new customers who came to appreciate and rely on the confidence of having pickups at the same time every day, the dependable service, the three delivery attempts, and the return policy. Except for the U.S. Post Office Department, as it was then known, nobody except United Parcel Service delivered single packages to remote residences. The company went everywhere, not just downtown to downtown. People began to rely on United Parcel Service for out-of-the-way deliveries.

The *Big Idea* regularly featured stories of unusual and remote deliveries. As editor, I participated in my fair share, riding with drivers on time-consuming ferries to places such as Washington's Vashon Island, to Hawaii's Ford Island, and South Padre Island off the Texas coast. I spent a full day with a Navajo UPS driver delivering just a handful of packages across Arizona's vast Navajo Reservation. I also rode to the remote North Rim of the Grand Canyon with a driver and his one package for the lodge there. Those stories and many others like them were instrumental in helping our executives convince the commissions that we did, indeed, go everywhere.

Obviously, the decision to pursue common carrier service was hard to implement, but it was a clear winner. Years of hard work were reshaping the delivery company and it was time to update its image. In 1961, the company replaced the old shield trademark—in service since 1937 and sporting the words "The Delivery System for Stores of Quality." The new logo was also a shield, but on top was a simple rectangle neatly tied with string to symbolize a package, and below it the sans serif letters "UPS."

The emblem, designed by Paul Rand (who also did the logos for CBS, Westinghouse, and IBM), announced a new era. This transition tracked with other old-line companies that were starting to pare down their wordy slogans to create a modern iconic branding for their companies. Atlantic Richfield Company became ARCO in 1966. International Business Machines and General Electric were more commonly referred to by their stock-trading names, IBM and GE. It made sense to modernize the now-venerable United Parcel Service too, by calling it "UPS."

Changing of the Guard

The logo, name, and delivery areas weren't the only big changes. Six months before the company's fiftieth anniversary in 1957, George Casey passed away at the age of sixty-four. Of the four founders, only Jim Casey was left.

Five years later, in 1962, Jim Casey, by then seventy-four years old, relinquished responsibility to George Dempster Smith. George Smith, whom Jim had hand-picked, assumed the titles of chief executive, Chairman of the Board, and member of the Executive Committee, roles in which he had been acting in many ways anyway. In fact, some consider him a fifth founder. Jim Casey didn't retire. He lived another twenty-one years and remained active in the business almost until the end, going to the office daily, traveling with the Board of Directors, and presenting at management conferences. (As it turned out, he outlived Smith, who died in 1972. At Smith's funeral in Glendale, California, Jim's booming voice held the audience with feeling. With a deep, strong resonance, a contrast to his frail eighty-four-year-old appearance, he gave a brief message, then held his head down and said simply, "Goodbye, George.")

The company had grown beyond the control of an inner circle of visionaries into an aggressive and very competent system that employed about 30,000 employees by 1967, triple the 1957 total. The nationalization process had turned UPS into a sort of machine, one that never lost its sight on the coast-to-coast coverage envisioned by Jim Casey.

Every service expansion was hard-earned and in many cases came about only after UPS lawyers and executives presented mountains of evidence and hours of testimony, after customers pleaded for service, after local officials made personal appeals. Sometimes letter-writing campaigns by employees and customers were necessary to spur legislators to prompt bureaucrats into action. Some argued that the rights might have come quicker with a little grease—in the form of payments to decision makers. Yet that wasn't the UPS way; its leaders put out no notes or markers to repay because they didn't want to compromise the integrity upon which the company was founded.

Characteristically, UPS did its best to keep a low profile. No splashy media campaigns. No saber rattling. The thinking was that the company would get further using polite persistence in battling sluggish and imperious bureaucracy. And the company continued to expand.

By 1965, the company's East Region alone was serving ten complete states, parts of three others, and Washington, D.C. In the Midwest Region, UPS was shipping to and from all or parts of fourteen states. On the West Coast, UPS provided service in most of California, Oregon, and Washington.

President Eisenhower's interstate highways, which were expanding across the country, gave UPS a boost, creating smooth corridors for the movement of packages from one metropolitan area to another. Applications were on file that year for all-points delivery and pickup service on the West Coast, service to the remainder of the partial states in the East, a large area of the Southeast, and intrastate service within Texas.

With each application that was filed, the company swung into action to help make the presentation at hearings before the ICC:

regulatory people had to document and redocument exactly what UPS wanted to do; industrial engineers determined the needs in personnel, vehicles, and facilities; customer service people gathered customers who would serve as witnesses. Many trees' worth of paper went into each presentation.

As soon as the ICC assigned examiners to conduct the hearings, the company sales job would commence. Usually, key people at each hearing were the CEO, the CFO, and the communications manager. Paul Oberkotter attended so many hearings as CEO that it became sort of like his road show. Like the actor Hal Holbrook performing as Mark Twain, he continued testifying for many years at ICC hearings and issues before the Postal Rate Commission even after he was no longer CEO.

Like battlefield commissions, promotions came easily at United Parcel Service during those years of rapid growth. The regulatory commissions posed very real opposition that required strategies and tactics not unlike a military campaign. A new group of leaders emerged to assume positions in the company's advancing fronts.

Both CEOs George Lamb (1980–1984) and Jack Rogers (1984–1989) were part of the corporate planning teams and with the expansions, continued to assume greater and greater operational responsibility. They both contributed directly to the "browning of America," and later extended that browning to distant lands.

All the new leaders either knew personally or were inspired by the far-sighted founder Jim Casey. Even the clerks, loaders, sorters, mechanics, and drivers looked to Jim Casey as a model. I learned this firsthand as I observed him interacting with the employees. UPSers found Jim Casey's homilies, indeed even his presence, an almost beatific direction finder.

Unworthy Opponent

Until other competitors entered the package-delivery fray, United Parcel Service rates were lower than the U.S. Post Office Department in all categories. This was the case despite that fact that government's parcel post was running at a loss and needed to subsidize package delivery to keep the rates as low as they were. Its rates did not reflect costs.

That United Parcel Service's main competition subsidized costs, paid no taxes, and did not have to show a profit is testimony to the superior UPS service during the growth decades. The company wasn't bothered by the U.S. Post Office Department's tactics. The partners were too busy opening new districts. In 1960, common carrier service spread to several New England states, throughout New York and New Jersey, and it was extended to more California areas.

As UPS expanded with greater and greater competence, the Post Office Department was becoming mired in ever-deeper and stickier ineptitude. Despite precipitous increases in the volume of correspondence and packages, the Post Office Department delivered mail the same way it had delivered mail from the beginning, with very little systematization and even less innovation. The agency added sorting by five-digit zip codes in 1963, but even that didn't help. Meanwhile, mismanagement impaired postal function from the top down and across the country, slowing and even stopping deliveries in some instances. In 1966, postal employees in Chicago threw up their hands over the avalanche of mail and mail delivery was virtually suspended.

At a hearing in 1967, Congressman Tom Steed, chairman of the House Appropriations Subcommittee on Treasury-Post Office, pointedly asked Postmaster General Lawrence O'Brien:

> Would this be a fair summary—that at the present time, as manager of the Post Office Department, you have no control over your workload; over the rates or revenue; over the pay rates of the employees that you employ; you have very little control over the conditions of the service of these employees; you have virtually no control, by the nature of it, of your physical facilities; and you have only a limited control, at best, over the transportation facilities that you are compelled to use—all of which adds up to a staggering amount of "no control" in terms of the duties you have to perform?

The Post Office Department's admitted incompetence made it easier for UPS to make a case for expansion into new territories. Moreover, shippers who didn't want to risk mishandled delivery of their parcels and merchandise could, in a growing number of locations, choose the UPS option.

Even the Postal Service Act of 1969, which replaced the U.S. Post Office Department with the self-supporting government-owned corporation known as the U.S. Postal Service, did not result in a worthy competitor. It did create a behemoth. Remember that UPS is the fourth-largest employer in the United States. Guess who is third? The U.S. Postal Service, second after the U.S. Department of Defense and Wal-Mart. In sum, the U.S. Postal Service has more employees, more resources, fewer constraints, and a monopoly on first-class mail.

The Postal Service also had friends in Congress and periodically one of them would attempt to slip through some legislation benefiting the sluggish department. That's why UPS maintained a handful of public affairs people (read "lobbyists") in Washington, D.C. Every time they'd spot legislation likely to make life harder for UPS, the company would develop a game plan and UPS would fight the proposed legislation with the tenacity of a grizzly defending her cubs.

On a couple of occasions I went to Washington as part of a team to combat some particularly pernicious legislation. Or to support one that would help. In July 1975, we were supporting an amendment of the Hanley Bill that would limit the subsidy for zone-rated mail matter. While our public affairs people garnered support from the Post Office and Civil Service Committee members, we were busy cranking out speeches for them should they go to bat for the amendment. The effort was unbelievably orchestrated. First, we received the congressman's name, his detailed bio, and the number of minutes he could speak. Then, we would tailor-write the speech, hoping to reflect his constituency. Hey, if they agreed to two minutes of support, they shouldn't have to write their speeches too.

UPS not only had its own friends in Congress back then, it continues to develop strong relationships with legislators and elected leaders everywhere.

The Postal Service still sees itself as neck-and-neck with Big Brown. To compete directly against private companies, both large and small, the U.S. Postal Service continues using its monopoly to subsidize lower prices on parcel post. It pays for the shortfall by raising the price of the first class stamp. For example, in 1999, raising the price of the first-class stamp to 33 cents, together with other rate increases, generated an extra $1.6 billion in annual revenue. Today, each penny increase in the stamp generates about $1 *billion* for the Postal Service.

According to former UPS CEO Jim Kelly in a 1999 *Journal of Commerce* report, "The ability to use monopoly profits to subsidize new products isn't the Postal Service's only advantage. As a government agency, it pays no federal, state or local taxes, is exempt from zoning laws, pays no parking tickets or vehicle licensing fees and has access to cheap government credit. In international delivery, it gets special Customs treatment. These are all significant benefits that no private company enjoys."

Meeting the Demand

Keeping up with the U.S. Post Office Department during the growth years wasn't difficult. But how did United Parcel Service keep up with itself? Each opening and service expansion was a major undertaking. Observing and documenting several of these openings throughout the West, I never ceased to be amazed. The resourcefulness, the determination, and the innovation were palpable!

Like generals preparing for war, UPS managers projected, prepared, and executed on many fronts at once. Industrial engineers planned the openings based on months of projections (number of packages expected, number of people needed, where facilities should be located, and so on). Every function was busy: Facilities—enough temporary warehouse space secured for vehicles and belts and the like. Check. Temporary hotel room space for offices, training, and other needs. Check. Personnel supervisors set to interview and hire drivers, loaders, sorters, car washers, mechanics, clerks, and others. Check. Training supervisors ready to indoctrinate new hires with UPS methods and safety. Check. Teams of sales and customer service people set to fan out and sign up accounts. Check. Enough vehicles borrowed from nearby districts or rented. Check. Management people from around the country cleared to train and assist with the opening. Check. And so it went.

It was a group effort of an amazing corporation-wide magnitude. It affected even those managers and supervisors not sent to the new areas, since they often had to fill in for their missing partners.

At almost every new location, we started with rented trucks, improvised sorting locations, and an unpredictable tempest of unknowns. Remember—years before, even Jim Casey personally sorted packages in a hotel room when UPS opened in San Francisco. In Utah, for example, one group of drivers used a restaurant parking lot to sort and exchange packages as snow flurries coated them with powder. In Hilo, Hawaii, we launched service with virtually no packages to deliver. I accompanied a new driver halfway around the Big Island just to deliver one package. In Anchorage, training drivers in winter darkness on icy streets was a hurdle. No matter how carefully they were planned and how many staff were sent, openings were usually arduous and sometimes hair-raising! Yet despite all the challenges, service in these locations persisted and became routine.

In 1965 alone, the company added 1,970 vehicles to swell its delivery fleet to 15,000. It expanded into thirty-five new buildings across the country, including new hubs in Landover, Maryland, and in Philadelphia, St. Louis, and Los Angeles. We usually leased buildings while UPS engineers worked with outside contractors to build a specific modern UPS facility. Hubs, like the five mentioned here, are larger buildings that include trailer unloading and loading docks, sorting facilities, and several package delivery centers. In almost all

cases, we purchased large lots to accommodate future growth—
growth that almost always occurred sooner than projections had
anticipated.

Euphoric States

The Los Angeles hub that opened in 1965 to help provide relief for
the Olympic Hub was a 330,000-square-foot facility spread out over
sixteen acres at 3000 East Washington Boulevard. At first it was
called the "Washington Hub," but because interoffice mail kept
ending up in Washington state, they changed it to the "Soto Hub,"
named after a nearby cross street.

The Los Angeles hub opened just in time too; on January 17,
1966, West Coast UPS service extended to cover 350,000 square
miles. Shippers could send packages via UPS to any location in
California, Oregon, and Washington, plus the most populous portions of Idaho, Nevada, and Arizona. At the same time, the company obtained intrastate rights for deliveries anywhere within
California and Washington.

Intrastate rights in Oregon did not come until 1971, so in the
meantime, one couldn't ship a package from Portland to Salem. It
confused the customers and created an onerous situation for the
company. We couldn't commingle Oregon retail packages and incoming interstate packages. UPS had to have separate retail and
wholesale drivers in Portland, often driving roughly the same routes.
This negated the company's successful principle of consolidation.

Rights granted in 1966 also extended Arizona service from the
Mexican border north through Tucson, Phoenix, Prescott, and
Flagstaff. The Las Vegas area of Nevada became part of the Southern California operation, while Reno and Carson City began to be
served out of Northern California. In Idaho, Boise, Lewiston,
Moscow, and Coeur d'Alene also received United Parcel Service
coverage.

During 1966, the company received rights to six southeast
states, and Georgia, Tennessee, the Carolinas, Alabama, and Florida

commenced service by early 1967. This was the first time a whole region had gone "brown" at one time. All told, this meant that United Parcel Service had expanded into a million square miles in twenty-eight states in just five years.

Each year saw numerous successes, some major, some local, yet all contributing to eventual nationwide service. With each victory, large or small, a bell in the national (now corporate) office rang to celebrate a UPS expansion (as it still does). When rights to any area were granted, the CEO has always ceremoniously rung the bell. The loud gonging reverberating throughout the office reminds employees that their company is on the move. Today the bell still peals—for example, Mike Eskew rang it when UPS bought Overnite Freight in 2005.

Many years, 1969 for example, saw some setbacks, but there was enough bell ringing to provide a constant and welcome diversion. There was the linkup between the thirteen-state East region and the combined nine full and three partial states of the Midwest and Western regions. Still some areas lagged. ICC hearings were completed on nine prairie states with approval recommended, but reopened for further consideration.

Meanwhile, real estate acquisitions and construction were unstoppable. In 1969 alone, UPS completed and occupied forty-two new facilities. That year, UPS purchased forty-four parcels of land, encompassing almost seven million square feet, in twenty states. Twelve of those parcels were developed during the year. The company signed thirty new leases in 1969 and renewed twenty-five others. It wasn't always acquisition. The burgeoning size meant selling several obsolete properties.

Intrastate-wise, 1969 was also busy. That year UPS received rights for the southwest part of Nebraska, all of Vermont, Alabama, Maine, and Florida, with minor exceptions. UPS applied for rights to provide intrastate service for the entire states of Arkansas and Iowa. In Texas, the company appealed a recommendation to deny its application for statewide intrastate service. In Virginia, early in 1970 the state legislature unanimously adopted legislation creating a special category of parcel carrier that opened the way for UPS to apply for intrastate rights in that state.

The steamroller continued, and each year's activities echoed those of the one before it, as can be noted in real estate activities alone. As an example, during 1972, a "bigger brown" completed and occupied twenty-seven new facilities, constructed to UPS specifications. Ten more were under construction. That year UPS purchased twenty parcels of land, encompassing more than 3.6 million square feet. During 1976, twenty-two new buildings were completed and occupied, five of which were major hubs. UPS purchased twenty-two parcels of land in thirteen states consisting of nearly 6 million square feet.

UPS continually bought real estate to create permanent homes to replace what had often been makeshift quarters. Today, there are over a thousand facilities in more than 120 countries, occupying 35 million square feet.

The Golden Link

The largest United Parcel Service territorial expansion in the United States came in 1971 when the company received ICC authority to serve nine central and prairie states, from the Gulf of Mexico to the Dakotas. A hundred years before, the "Beehive State" had been the missing link in the railroads' coast-to-coast service until Utah got its tracks in 1869. That piece was still waiting for United Parcel Service, too. Finally, in 1975, the ICC granted UPS the authority to begin interstate service to and from Montana and Utah, to extend to statewide the partial service in Arizona, Idaho, and Nevada, and to connect these five states with those both to the west and the east. That made forty-eight states. The coast-to-coast Golden Link was forged!

Hawaii went brown in 1975 too when the company bought Mercury Parcel Delivery. It took five more years for service to spread to all points on the Hawaiian Islands. Alaska joined in 1977. The last interstate restrictions in the lower forty-eight states dissolved in

1980, allowing the company to deliver packages to and from all points in the United States.

The only service holdout was Texas. While the rest of the country was enjoying full service, one couldn't send a package from Houston to Dallas using UPS. It took twenty-one years (1965–1986) before the Texas courts finally intervened and overruled the Railroad Commission of Texas, which did not want to allow an outside company equal footing with the numerous small Texas delivery companies. On several occasions the UPS application was shot down and at the last hearing three hundred witnesses took more than fifteen months to present the UPS case. UPS had earlier gotten itself fully entrenched in Texas with facilities used only for interstate shipments, and waited. In 1986 it was granted intrastate service by the courts. Texas UPS was finally able to put on more people and use those facilities fully.

After all those years of toil for UPS, of taking new territories like Sisyphus pushing the boulder uphill, the federal government finally deregulated interstate commerce. Just as United Parcel Service was mapping its final districts in the United States, the Motor Carrier Act of 1980 opened up the trucking industry to new carriers. There were 18,000 truckers that year, and only a handful had the authority to operate nationally. By 1990, there were 45,000, 20,000 of which had national operating authority.

UPS had won the hard-fought battle, but company management and employees had no time to rest on their laurels. Now the upstarts swarmed in to wrest that shipping dollar from UPS—freight companies, railroads, the U.S. Postal Service, and others. Competition was good for consumers because it offered shippers more choice. It allowed manufacturers to reduce inventories and move their products more quickly. That situation also created opportunities for UPS years later, when the company began to offer supply-chain services to help customers move their products to consumers when they needed them.

In the interim, United Parcel Service's extraordinary commitment to the pursuit of common carrier deliveries resulted in deregulated shipping, numerous delivery choices, and also the improved reliability with which most all delivery companies operate, because there isn't one competitor that hasn't learned from and emulated UPS, which created the standard for the industry.

As UPS saturated America, real estate costs in the northeast soared. The southern Connecticut area, where UPS headquarters had been since 1975, had become one of the most expensive locales in the United States during the 1980s. The corporate offices employed about a thousand people at the time, but found it hard to attract entry-level workers. The need to commute long distances from affordable housing was especially hard for those who held lower-paying jobs. Once the decision was made to leave the Northeast, the company looked at numerous locations and finally narrowed it down to a handful, including Dallas and Atlanta. Atlanta with its large airport won out. UPS headquarters have been in Atlanta since 1991.

8

ADVANCING SOCIAL RESPONSIBILITY

By any measure, one fundamental key explains UPS's long record of achievement: *People*. Even today, twenty-four years after Jim Casey's death, that focus, that attention to the needs of people continues to run strong. And in good measure, it is due in large part to a management style now a century old. Jim Casey created and led a company of leaders that both advanced the interests of individuals and enabled them to achieve personal satisfaction while contributing to the company's success. As you've read, UPS managers and supervisors still refer to each other as "partners," still speak of "our company." Turnover is low. Time has proven Casey's belief that sincere interest in the welfare of coworkers is the best form of management.

Yet much has changed over the last hundred years. Today's partners are not yesterday's partners. Achieving coworker welfare has become a bigger, more multifaceted task. It's not enough to assure an employee of great benefits and a lifetime of professional promotion. Now, a socially responsible company also pays for that employee's education and perhaps the employee's children's education, extends opportunities to disadvantaged children who might become tomorrow's employees, and labors to improve the environment for the sake of the company and for the sake of the planet. To remain socially responsible, UPS has had to stay alert, flexible, resourceful. Because the social fabric of the company has been dynamic—in response to both internal and external events—it has many times had to adjust to new social demands.

A company of "determined *men*" had to become "determined *people*," and not just white people but multiethnic people. A company that hires many young people made a commitment to support better education and higher education. A company that uses vast quantities of fossil fuel today invests in greener technologies. Last year, in addition to numerous other donations, the company that earned nearly $4.3 billion gave away about 1 percent of that amount, $40 million, to hunger, literacy, and voluntarism through its charitable foundation.

As is ever more obvious, social responsibility goes much beyond awareness. It is about action. UPS has excelled at responding sagaciously to change, and even to *shaping* change. The best way to explain how it does so is to look at social topics, one at a time.

Determined People

Jim Casey's company was a typical American business in the first half of the twentieth century—*white and male*. By long-standing tradition many companies did not hire minorities and UPS was one of them.

UPS found it easier to go along with the majority of white America, and its managers indulged in stereotyping minorities rather than hiring them. Jim Casey was not exempt. According to author Philip Hamburger in 1947's "Ah, Packages!" Jim Casey was once standing on a platform above a conveyer belt full of packages when his eyes blazed with exhilaration, "'Packages for everybody!' he said suddenly, beginning his colloquy. 'Packages for Chinatown—a difficult area. Drivers have trouble remembering who they left the package with—everybody looks alike! Packages for Harlem—hardly any charge accounts in Harlem! Packages for the West Side—democratic neighborhood. Give packages the kind of welcome packages deserve! Packages for Greenwich Village—*very* odd packages!'" This outburst was not about biases, it was about Casey's love for packages.

Stereotyping of that sort was common in 1947 America, in speech and even on the printed pages of major magazines. Casey was typical of his time, but his sensitivity to America's shifting trends would soon change his attitude and change his company.

Jim Casey, George Casey, and Charlie Soderstrom, from left to right, in Los Angeles during 1920s with early UPS feeder vehicle and personal auto. (Photo courtesy of Jim Casey collection, in care of Paul Casey.)

American Messenger Company advertisement, 1907. (Image from the collection of Greg Niemann.)

Jim Casey at American Messenger Company office in 1909, with his two telephones. (Photo courtesy of Jim Casey collection, in care of Paul Casey.)

George Casey waiting for phone calls at second office of American Messenger Company, while messenger boys wait to be dispatched, circa 1912. (Photo courtesy of the Jim Casey collection, care of Paul Casey.)

Claude Ryan (seated) and Jim Casey in American Messenger Company office at 123 Marion Street in 1911. (Photo courtesy of Jim Casey collection, in care of Paul Casey.)

The four UPS founders: Evert McCabe, Charlie Soderstrom, Jim Casey, and George Casey, from left to right, taken in Los Angeles in the 1920s. (Photo courtesy of Jim Casey collection, in care of Paul Casey.)

Motorcycle fleet of Merchants Parcel Delivery in Seattle, 1913. (Photo courtesy of Jim Casey collection, in care of Paul Casey.)

Early UPS Sort in Oakland, California; Evert McCabe at top of slide. (Greg Niemann collection, courtesy of Joe McTigue.)

Goldfield, Nevada, 1906: Jim Casey (age eighteen) is the young messenger at the far right, in the doorway. (Photo courtesy Goldfield Historical Society, Jon Aurich Collection.)

Seattle UPSers in front of Merchants Parcel Delivery on University Street, in 1922. The Seattle operation did not change its name to UPS until 1925. (Photo courtesy of Jim Casey collection, in care of Paul Casey.)

UPS logo from 1961 to 2003. (Image from Greg Niemann collection.)

Greg Niemann, UPS driver in Los Angeles, early 1961. Note old logo, which said "The Delivery System for Stores of Quality." (Greg Niemann collection.)

UPS air operation in 1929. (Greg Niemann collection, courtesy of Joe McTigue.)

Casey family: Jim, Annie, and George seated. Harry and Marguerite standing.
(Photo courtesy of Jim Casey collection, in care of Paul Casey.)

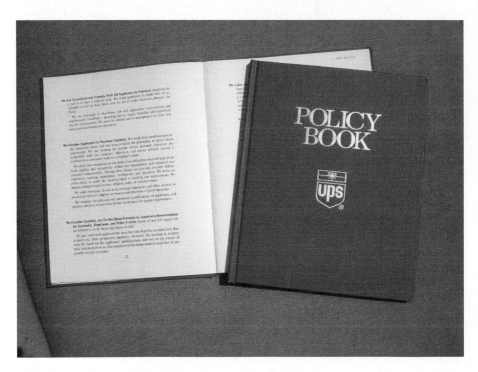

UPS Policy Book, 1992. (Greg Niemann collection.)

Los Angeles UPS drivers in 1925 with new uniforms. (Greg Niemann collection, courtesy of Joe McTigue.)

Jim Casey and Greg Niemann, in 1977. (Greg Niemann collection.)

Brothers George, Jim, and Harry Casey, from left to right, revisit site of original Seattle basement office of American Messenger Company in 1957. (Photo courtesy of Paul Casey, Harry Casey's son.)

Model T Fords were used for deliveries as early as 1913.

Merchants Parcel Delivery vehicle using Model T chassis, circa 1913. (Greg Niemann collection.)

U.S. Secretary of Labor Elaine L. Chao, Paul Casey, and UPS CEO Mike Eskew at Jim Casey's 2002 induction into the Labor Hall of Fame. (Photo courtesy of Paul Casey.)

Hollywood UPS Center drivers, 1961. Greg Niemann (front row, fourth from left) and company's first five-year safe driver Ray McCue (front row, second from right). (Greg Niemann collection.)

UPS advertisement, early 1920s. (Greg Niemann collection.)

Civil unrest grew during the 1950s and by the early 1960s many civil rights advocates took to the streets. America would never be the same.

Jim Casey and the others on the Management Committee, including George Smith (who took over the company in 1962), began consulting outsiders in 1961 on how best to face and embrace the new order. One such consultant, Walter G. Hooke, who had many years in labor relations and personnel, also had numerous connections in the minority community. Through Hooke, UPS established a relationship with the National Urban League as early as 1962. The League, based in New York City, was already one of the most visible advocates on behalf of black Americans. Today it is the oldest and largest community-based organization of its kind in the nation.

UPS, through its new contacts, began to hire a few minority drivers. But the company was not fully committed. It wasn't easy being one of the first black drivers. I was a driver in Los Angeles at the time. The first one hired among the five centers in our building in 1963 was so light-skinned that there was rampant speculation as to whether he was black or not. Some fellow drivers went out of their way to assist the first few black drivers, to make them feel at home. Others, raised in a different era and threatened by change, refused to so much as speak to them. One old manager, lamenting the influx of these new drivers, told several of us that his hands were tied, and that when he went to Personnel to interview a prospective driver, he just hoped he'd be white. It took a lot of adapting and adjusting on all levels to turn acceptance into the norm.

In today's America, it is difficult to imagine how institutionalized discrimination was until the 1960s. Most companies considered hiring blacks a risk, particularly companies with a public face like UPS. Management worried, just as did management at other businesses, what the public would think! In fact, I did have a customer complain when a black driver filled in for me on my day off, and several others made comments about it. Hiring minorities would be a very dramatic change, with unpredictable ramifications; it would take federal pressure to bring about real change.

President John F. Kennedy promised civil rights reform in a summertime address in 1963. His words—"The rights of every man are diminished when the rights of one man are threatened"— spoke volumes about the need for a new sort of social responsibility, not just in business but universally. Nearly a century after the Civil War, repressed groups were increasingly volatile. The sixties were like a pressure cooker on an ever higher flame. President Kennedy's assassination turned up the heat on civil rights and the women's movement.

Congress passed several antidiscrimination laws, the first of which was the Equal Pay Act of 1963. The act protected men and women who perform substantially equal work in the same establishment from sex-based wage discrimination. While employers were mulling over what to do about the revolution that law required, Congress passed an even greater jolt to the existing paradigm, the far-reaching Civil Rights Act of 1964 (Title VII).

Title VII got serious. It prohibited employment discrimination not only based on race (as it was originally conceived), but also based on religion, sex, or national origin. Despite an eighty-three-day filibuster in the Senate led by segregationists, both houses of Congress ultimately voted overwhelmingly in favor of the Act, and President Lyndon Johnson signed the bill into law. More acts followed. To protect individuals who are forty years of age or older, the Age Discrimination in Employment Act passed in 1967, followed by laws that prohibit discrimination against qualified individuals with disabilities.

Minority group demonstrations against East Coast companies, including UPS, increased. The company's leaders knew they had to do something immediately. In 1965 Walter Hooke joined the East Region personnel department. A hire to such a high position, directly from the outside, was almost unprecedented. It was a big step, but Hooke became what UPS most needed—a dedicated catalyst for change.

In 1966, at Hooke's request, the company produced its *Impartial Employment and Promotion Guide* and issued copies to all managers and supervisors. The guide was not only updated regularly but all members of the management team were scheduled to attend meetings to review each policy. In 1968 UPS appointed Walter Hooke to the UPS functional group as national personnel manager. He wasn't the most well-liked guy early on, and many managers thought he was going too far.

The laws were there, but few corporations knew how to effect the radical changes that were necessary. As part of the Civil Rights Act, the government formed the Equal Employment Opportunity Commission (EEOC) to enforce its new legislation. Enforcement powers were weak until President Johnson appointed William H. Brown III as its chairman in 1969. To show that the government meant business, Brown, a black Philadelphia attorney, took on a behemoth—AT&T—that (like most American companies) notably favored white males. Brown won a landmark decision against the huge company. The case was settled in early 1973 with a very expensive consent decree. It was a wake-up call to American industry.

Clearly, hiring a few minorities at entry-level positions, as UPS and many other companies had begun doing, was not going to pass muster. Corporations hastened to change their ways substantively and fast, as much to avoid litigation and bad publicity as for any other reason. To help effect the change at UPS, in 1972 the Board of Directors promoted liberal operations manager James P. McLaughlin to chief operating officer and UPS president.

Across America, the EEOC began looking at percentages of minorities at every echelon. The agency examined applicant flow compared to actual hires, whether the number of minority applicants actually reflected the surrounding community population, and whether companies were aggressively seeking minority applications. Lip service to Title VII wasn't enough. The EEOC was looking for demonstrable commitment.

Despite many managers' reservations about Hooke and his changes, EEOC cases proved Hooke right. Hooke and McLaughlin, whose new title gave him more meaningful clout, were the cops who pushed for compliance. Under their pressure and with the strong support of the Management Committee, UPS realized that it had to adopt new hiring practices with the same kind of fervor that it devoted to expansion. UPS management decided to seek out William Brown for his advice. In 1973 Brown reentered private practice, joining the Schnader, Harrison, Segal, and Lewis law firm in Philadelphia, which was UPS's primary counsel (Bernie Segal had served on the UPS Board of Directors for years). Shrewdly, UPS had Brown assigned as counsel, developed a strong relationship, and in 1982, invited him to serve on the UPS Board of Directors. Mr. Brown was the first minority to do so.

The upper brass came to the conclusion that they needed to hold operations accountable to a different sort of high standard. Managers throughout the company participated in diversity training, which better prepared them for the changing company. Special slide presentations, booklets, the *Impartial Employment and Promotion Guide*, *Big Idea* articles, group sessions, and meetings all relayed the newly diversified face of the company.

Some management members didn't like it and grumbled to themselves or to others who shared their thinking, but they were so committed to their jobs and to the company that they went along with the program. In those early years, with many it was a *changed acceptance*, but not necessarily a *changed attitude*. UPS sent district managers who were committed, whose attitudes had changed, to areas where the management team was most reluctant. Top personnel people, including a few newly hired and developed for the challenge, helped interpret policy, ensure compliance, and change attitudes.

Yet the ball was rolling, and hiring and promoting practices at UPS had forever changed. UPS consulted numerous other experts in the field for advice, including the National Association for the Advancement of Colored People (NAACP), the Urban League, and the Congress of Racial Equality (CORE).

In 1968, UPS initiated an extensive Urban Internship program to create managers more in tune with society's challenging issues. As of 2006, 1,360 mid- and upper-level managers have spent three-

and four-week assignments in various inner-city locations. Living for weeks out of their offices and away from their families, they experience issues such as homelessness, drug addiction, and poverty firsthand. Immersed in impoverished situations, they work as volunteers side by side with those less fortunate.

Participating in what is now called the Community Internship program, fifteen to twenty managers each year spend time in diverse locations such as the Henry Street Settlement in New York, the Mexican American Cultural Center in San Antonio, Texas, and San Francisco's Chinatown. The interns, as they are called in this unique and long-lasting corporate program, actually perform a lot of hands-on work including distributing food to indigents, teaching sportsmanship to inner-city kids, and even washing dishes. Jeans and sports shirts replace the suit and tie for three weeks, and a better understanding of those less fortunate replaces former biases and mind-sets.

In its relationships with outside organizations, UPS often offers expertise instead of just throwing money at organization budgets. In May 1973, CORE requested UPS aid through national personnel manager Walter Hooke. When Walter understood that the goal was getting some brochures and flyers written, he said that he had someone in mind who could do just that. I was thereby dispatched to CORE headquarters in the heart of Harlem, New York, at 135th Street and Lennox Avenue, where I worked for three weeks on the special writing assignment.

CORE made me a temporary member of the staff, and I reported to Doris Innis, wife of CORE's executive director, Roy Innis. I was the only white face in the building. CORE staff playfully called me their "house honkey," but I plugged away at what they wanted and experienced my own indoctrination in my own inner-city internship program.

Long-standing biases weren't just racial, of course. The inclusion of "sex" was a last-minute addition to the Civil Rights Act of 1964 (Title VII), spearheaded by the National Woman's Party, who lobbied for it in Congress. Creating equal opportunities for women in traditionally male jobs had remained challenging, particularly in states that had their own restrictive laws, ostensibly to *protect* female workers and children.

The laws fell into three categories: Thirty-five states and the District of Columbia limited the hours that women were permitted to work on a daily or weekly basis. Ten states and Puerto Rico limited the weights that women could lift. And six states and Puerto Rico had laws prohibiting women from working at night.

In 1970 the National Women's Party and the National Organization for Women pushed for the Equal Rights Amendment, a proposed amendment to the U.S. Constitution that would have guaranteed equal rights under the law for Americans regardless of sex. As part of that appeal, both organizations argued in a Senate hearing that the "protective" legislation of the states harmed rather than helped working women by reducing their opportunities to acquire higher-paying jobs. Congress struck down the state-restrictive laws giving companies across America greater latitude. However, the Equal Rights Amendment never went into effect because, although it passed in Congress, it expired in 1982 with support from only thirty-five states—three short of the thirty-eight necessary for ratification.

Amendment or no amendment, women had no reason to back down. The feminist movement surged forward and American business reacted right down to its lexicon. "Flight attendants" replaced "stewardesses." "Fire fighters" replaced "firemen." "Police officers" replaced "policemen." "Chairpersons" or just "chairs" replaced "chairmen." And so forth. Society changed in fact and in nomenclature.

Lawsuits proliferated. To stay out of the crosshairs, companies strove for political correctness across the board. Even though UPS had had its share of female employees during World War II, the Brown Bettys had disappeared from the workforce immediately after the war ended. Hence, UPS too found itself having to make another important and difficult adjustment. Just as UPS had aggressively added minorities to the payroll, so too did it pursue women—and for more than clerical work. Soon there were female loaders, sorters, drivers, frontline supervisors, and managers throughout the operations, including district and region managers and members of the venerated Management Committee. The company also hired women pilots, including Emily Warner (who had been the first permanent female pilot for a U.S. airline) as captain of a Boeing 737 brown-tail.

Again, while it's easy to change a policy in print, and even to change the makeup of the company, changing attitudes is a lot harder. Many white males felt as if their world was being turned upside down, and it was all moving too fast. However, for minorities and women, change undoubtedly seemed too slow.

Nevertheless, change happened because the management team was proactive in diversity. Transition was spearheaded by *example*, the best teacher of all, as the company put teeth into its policies with programs as well as new hiring and promotion practices. Diversity became a way of life at UPS, inseparable from the evolving corporate culture. Obviously, UPS's adage, "determined men can do anything," had to change. By the late seventies most of the references to "men" in the UPS archives had been struck and replaced with "people" or other nonsexist terms. From then on, it was "determined people can do anything." And they did.

Forty years later, UPS employees act much the same, but they look much different. The company is definitely no longer all male and no longer all white. Black Americans, Hispanics, Asian-Pacific Americans, and other minorities account for over a third of the employees and approximately half of the new hires. Minorities hold 27 percent of the managerial positions. In the United States, women make up 21 percent of the UPS workforce. Twenty-seven percent of all U.S. managers and 25 percent of all supervisors are women. There are two women on the Board of Directors and a third just retired. Two other women are on the UPS Management Committee, one a minority.

Today's diversity programs at UPS include Workplace Flexibility, Women's Leadership Development, and Supplier Diversity. Under Workplace Flexibility, the Family Transfer Request allows full-time employees to request transfers because of a spouse or domestic partner's job transfer or military obligation, marriage, child custody, or family health issues. Full-time workers can go part time for up to twelve months for child care, elder care, or other family medical issues. The revised rehire policy allows certain employees to be rehired based on their reason for leaving and need.

The Parental Leave Request is liberal, allowing care for a newborn or newly adopted child. It applies to eligible mothers, fathers, and domestic partners, and allows UPSers to schedule vacation time, take consecutive discretionary days, or request unpaid leave through the Family and Medical Leave Act (FMLA). FMLA allows up to twelve weeks of unpaid but protected leave.

Despite the programs, women in management still leave UPS at a greater rate than their male counterparts, and at a greater rate than they are replaced. The Women's Leadership Development program addresses these issues and was created to ensure a supportive environment for women on the UPS management team.

Formally launched in 1992, the UPS Supplier Diversity program extends business opportunities to small and minority- and women-owned businesses. For instance, in spring 2006, UPS announced expanding its Worldport Hub in Louisville, Kentucky, by 1.1 million square feet. This was great news for many area contractors because UPS included a promise that 20 percent of the construction work would be set aside for minority- and women-owned businesses.

Over the years UPS has won numerous awards for its cultural diversity. Since 1999 *Fortune* magazine has listed UPS as one of the "50 Best Companies for Minorities," and 2006 was the seventh straight year. *Hispanic* magazine and *DiversityInc* have both singled out UPS for honors and the National Urban League presented UPS with its Corporate Leadership Award. *Black Enterprise* magazine lists UPS among its top forty companies for supplier, workforce, management, and board of directors diversity. Highlighted statistics include the 70,000 black Americans on UPS's U.S. workforce.

UPS works hard to counteract workplace biases as they manifest. In July 2006, UPS was recognized by the national Human Rights Campaign for implementing pro-gay policies, ranging from domestic partner benefits to protection from discrimination based on sexual orientation.

Education, UPS Style

As a teen, Jim Casey longed to go to school and graduate from college. He was determined to learn as much as he could about science and mathematics, history, and writing. Although his academic ambitions were cut short by necessity, his real education never stopped. An autodidact, Jim had a curious nature that was as stimulated by the amazing innovations that heralded the twentieth century as it was by high technology in later years. In 1957, he received an honorary degree from Seattle University. Commemorating many years of learning and achievement, this could not have been more deserved. In conferring the degree, the Very Reverend A. A. Lemieux, S.J., said of Casey, "His greatest accomplishment lies in the men that he has trained, chiefly by example, but also by precept. He has taught them that a friendly, selfless devotion to people is the most direct avenue to business success."

Despite being self-taught, or perhaps because of it, Jim Casey took a long view of what it takes for any child to learn, but particularly for children from poor families. Early on, he decided that he wanted to help children in difficult circumstances.

The UPS Foundation was established in 1951 to develop and champion innovative solutions to social problems. The foundation first focused on higher education, through endowments with organizations, colleges, and universities.

In 1963, it established the James E. Casey Scholarship for UPS employees' children who were about to enter college. As Casey himself said, "Good management is taking a sincere interest in the welfare of the people you work with. It is the ability to make individuals feel that you and they *are* the company—not merely employees of it." Twenty years later, in 1983, the George D. Smith Scholarship (named after Jim Casey's successor) extended education benefits to employees' children who were entering trade schools. An outside firm awards these scholarships. It is true that the majority of recipients are children of UPS managers and supervisors—but since so many package handlers and drivers are young, people in these groups have fewer children of college age to apply.

In 1988, The UPS Foundation launched the Literacy Initiative, a multiyear effort that has contributed over $9 million in support of four hundred local literacy programs in 120 communities across the United States.

UPS's commitment to education goes beyond philanthropy, though. Remember this is a company that began with messenger boys—hard-working, motivated teenagers. The personnel profile is still heavily weighted toward young people, though these days none are younger than eighteen years old. The bulk of UPS's package handlers, which number in the thousands, are between the ages of eighteen and twenty-five and most of them are students.

UPS encourages them to go to college through its Earn and Learn program. In the last seven years, UPS has spent over $47 million on tuition assistance and helped more than 30,000 student employees attend college. The kids don't have to stay with UPS, but the hope is that they'll want to take advantage of the "promotion from within" policy and start taking those upward steps on the UPS corporate ladder.

Casey's words, "I envisage our organization as a means through which each member should be able to achieve a good measure of personal satisfaction and at the same time aid in the advancement of the interests of all the rest of us," spoken so long ago, require new action to remain vital today.

Thus, UPS now spends about $300 million a year on employee training programs. At fifty-one UPS locations across the country, UPS's Earn and Learn program will donate $3,000 per calendar year to a full-time employee's college education, with a lifetime maximum of $15,000. For part-time management employees, the benefits are $4,000 per calendar year with a lifetime maximum of $20,000. In addition to tuition assistance, part-time employees are eligible for forgivable student loans of $2,000 per calendar year with an $8,000 lifetime maximum. How's that for supportive?

Obviously, this is a good deal for students. It also works for UPS, because it keeps its hubs staffed. In Louisville, the demand is especially high. About three-fourths of the approximately 7,500 part-time workers who unload, sort, or load packages at Worldport are students. Most work the graveyard shift. They can get Earn and Learn help paying their tuition—or they can have all their tuition paid if they go to Metropolitan College. Metropolitan, established for UPS workers, is a program of the University of Louisville and Jefferson Community and Technical College.

These education programs are consistent with UPS's decades-old corporate culture. To be eligible for free education at Metropolitan College, students must work part-time at UPS Louisville, between 10 P.M. and 4 A.M. UPS pays half the tuition and the state pays the other half. Students work at night, then sleep and attend classes during the day, so UPS works with the universities for special class schedules and dorm arrangements. Nearly 3,000 Metropolitan College students work at UPS Louisville.

Brown Is the New Green

Excessive use of fuel is a major concern to UPS, both financially and as a matter of global and political conscience. In this regard, UPS is constantly seeking ways to trim its fuel usage. The company can only pass so much along to consumers in the form of surcharges.

Just by using railroads to transport some packages the company reduces fuel consumption by up to a third. Called TOFCs (which stands for "trailers on flatcars"), UPS trailers are piggybacked around the country by rail, saving fuel, manpower, and delivery vehicle wear and tear. UPS is one of the largest railroad customers in the United States. When it does use its tractor-trailers for ground transportation, UPS realizes significant fuel savings by using double feeder trailers instead of single ones.

Charlie Soderstrom would be proud of what excellent maintenance can do. The company estimates that its regular and thorough Preventive Maintenance Inspections save more than 330,000 quarts of oil each year.

Doing everything by the numbers, the company closely monitors its fuel, using a gallons-per-package rate on a fleetwide basis and committing to decrease that number. As an example, the automotive staff is hoping to bring it down from about 0.1015 to 0.1008 as I write this book. UPS deals with several different oil companies to keep its thirst for fuel sated. The company buys in bulk and locks in fleet prices on a periodic basis.

UPS is no newcomer to alternative energy, though certainly the incentive is ever higher. The company used electric delivery vehicles in New York and Los Angeles as early as the 1940s. In the 1970s UPS teamed with major oil companies in attempts to develop more efficient gasoline engines. While slight improvements were made, the results were not revolutionary.

More recently, UPS has conducted its own experiments with alternative fuels to power its massive fleet and improve automotive emissions. The UPS fleet added fifty new hybrid vehicles in June 2006 and now has more than fifteen hundred vehicles powered by alternative fuel. Those hybrids are now in their third generation. Studies suggest that they will save 35 percent in fuel economy over the vehicles they replace. Additionally, UPS operates 989 compressed natural gas vehicles in the United States and another dozen in Europe and Brazil. It also has 687 vehicles running on propane, 623 in Canada and 64 in Mexico City. And though you can't see it from the street, a white roof panel on UPS package cars helps reduce interior temperatures, a welcome relief to drivers since package cars are not air conditioned.

Skyrocketing fuel costs are keeping UPS at the drawing board. The U.S. Environmental Protection Agency (EPA) developed a first-ever "hybrid hydroelectric" diesel urban delivery vehicle working in a partnership with UPS, the U.S. Army, and International Truck and Engine Corp. Beginning in mid-2006, UPS is testing the first models, which are expected to boost fuel efficiency by 60–70 percent in stop-and-go city traffic, and reduce carbon dioxide emissions by 40 percent. According to Stephen L. Johnson, EPA administrator, "EPA and our partners are not just delivering packages with this truck—we are delivering environmental benefits to the American people."

Not only is the company cutting down on fuel usage, it is demonstrating its corporate responsibility by controlling emissions. UPS added 4,100 low-emission vehicles in 2006, raising its fleet to over 12,000 such vehicles. UPS was also the first commercial fleet in the United States to deploy hydrogen fuel cell technology. Those few experimental vehicles, which emit only water, have been driven thousands of miles since 2004.

Conserving fuel by cutting mileage has long been a company practice. Strategies for so doing have kept industrial engineers busy for years. It was when FedEx became a serious challenger in the 1980s that UPS went from its fabled time-management studies, which measured miles and shaved minutes or even seconds, to high tech. Since then, few industries, maybe *no* industries, have exploited digital technology better than the delivery industry.

In 1986 UPS purchased Roadnet Technologies, one of its first subsidiaries. (Roadnet had developed PC-based routing and scheduling systems, used primarily to assist food and beverage distributors in making timely deliveries.) Through Roadnet, UPS acquired the means to computerize its deliveries. A computer picked up where the guys with clipboards left off, scrutinizing all possible delivery sequences, taking into account all sorts of variables including preferred routes, drivers' start times, time windows, and even the number and sizes of available vehicles.

The Roadnet purchase represented a pivotal point in the "teching" of UPS. It led to more acquisitions and ultimately provided the backbone for UPS Logistics, which I'll talk about in Chapter Eleven. Shortly after Roadnet, UPS also purchased II Morrow, an Oregon-based technology firm whose 167 employees had developed all sorts of vehicle tracking systems. Those two initial firms gave

UPS a three-year jump in developing its technology; half of Road-net's and two-thirds of II Morrow's work was initially focused on UPS projects.

Today, new package-flow technology uses digital information from scanned UPS labels to plan routes that require the fewest miles. In addition, if traffic is backed up, adjustments are made to prevent drivers from making left turns, detouring them several blocks if necessary. Drivers idling in left-turn lanes for extended periods can waste fuel, time, and money. Plus, left turns are not as safe. With the computer programs and GPS (Global Positioning System) technology knowing where every package is and where it's going, the computer actually plots which streets the driver should drive on.

To give you an idea of how economizing these package-flow innovations are, in Sacramento, California, this new technology shaves a quarter million miles each year (out of 4.5 million), saving about 30,000 gallons of fuel. Once the package-flow technology is fully implemented, it is expected to cut 100 million miles annually, saving almost 14 million gallons of fuel. I'll talk more about package-flow technology in Chapter Eleven as well.

The company asks customers "What can Brown do for you?"—and it asks itself "What can green do for Brown?" Looking into wind, solar, and biomass (energy from the gasses of organic matter), UPS has been making strides in its quest for "green power." The facility in Palm Springs, California, has been powered by solar panels for several years. Many UPS offices around the country go into "sleep" mode daily to conserve power. Fourteen UPS facilities get 10 percent of their power from biomass. The supplier, 3 Phases Energy Services, converts landfill gas, human and animal waste, or agricultural waste to energy. According to UPS spokesman Mike Herr, as quoted on the UPS Pressroom site, "This commitment, which will prevent the release of 2.4 million pounds of carbon dioxide, a leading cause of global warming, has the equivalent environmental impact of removing 213 cars from the road for a year. This carbon reduction is equal to the carbon absorption capacity of 330 acres of trees."

In striving to be as efficient as possible, UPS's industrial engineering department contributes to energy efficiency by streamlining operations. As an example, today more than thirty engineers are assigned to a technology laboratory in Atlanta, continually looking outside the box—the shipping box, that is. They test packages, the robotic labeling of them, how to better handle odd-shaped ones, and even how to scan and sort them better using lasers and multidimension readers. By making shipping easier, these technologies economize on electricity and fuel.

Efficient energy use not only benefits the bottom line, it also helps cut costs for consumers and works toward reducing global warming. When a company as large as UPS, and as fuel-dependent, makes extensive use of sustainable methodologies, it pressures others in the transportation industry to do likewise—and contributes to UPS's reputation as a socially responsible corporate citizen.

Do Unto Others

Jim Casey never forgot the tough years of his childhood, and he always wanted to do something to help children in difficult circumstances. Drawing on the experience of his past and the values his family embraced, he and his three siblings, Harry, George, and Marguerite, got together in 1948 and formed a foundation to help disadvantaged youth, especially those who had been separated from their parents. They named it after their mother, Annie E. Casey, whose love and wisdom kept the family afloat in the early years.

The Casey siblings later established additional charities, and all four of them would be extremely proud of the work done in their family's name if they were alive to see it. When Jim Casey relinquished his CEO obligations at UPS in the sixties, he had time to improve the programmatic focus of the foundation. "Let's not just hone in on kids and families who need us most and help them. Let's save them!" he exclaimed.

Even though he had no children of his own, Casey had a special dedication to young people, particularly those having a hard time. In 1966 his interest in long-term foster care led him to establish the Casey Family Programs, now an independently operating foundation in Seattle with a current endowment of $2 billion.

Foundation case workers seek out children who need help, usually boys and girls who have had at least six previous foster homes. The average age is thirteen. They are referred to the foundation by schools, hospitals, the courts, and state agencies. Once children are selected for care, the Casey Foundation will provide whatever it takes to make them grow into happy, healthy, productive adults.

The foundation's main interest is children at risk and family preservation, but it is also looking at other problems, such as child abuse and neglect, teenage pregnancy, and underperforming schools.

As of the year 2005, Casey Family Programs has provided long-term foster care to more than 2,150 children in more than a dozen western states and three tribal Indian nations. The charity's programs have led to collaborations with foster parents, counties, states, and American Indian and Alaska native tribes. Direct services have improved the lives of more than 500,000 young people in out-of-home care across the United States. The foundation's goal is to increase this number to 100,000 per year. Over the years total grants have now exceeded $120 million.

Jim Casey's sister, Marguerite, served for years on the board of the Casey Family Programs. Never married and childless, she nevertheless had a lifelong interest in family well-being. In 2001, Casey Family Programs established the Marguerite Casey Foundation in Seattle in her honor. The foundation's goal is to strengthen communities through strategic grant making, helping families become more resilient and less dependent on public systems. During 2004 the Marguerite Casey Foundation made grants totaling over $28 million. One of the grants, $1.5 million, went to the Associated Community Organization for Reform Now, a grassroots effort aimed at working with and educating low-income individuals and families about possible tax credits and assisting them with preparing their income tax returns. The Marguerite Casey Foundation is also a big contributor to the Public Broadcasting System.

Jim and George Casey's brother Harry was instrumental in setting up the James and George Casey Eye Institute (CEI) in Portland. The institute opened in 1991, the year before Harry died at the age of 101. The institute is the only free-standing academic eye research center west of Salt Lake City and north of San Francisco. Engaged in ophthalmology research, specialist medical education, and advanced medical care and surgery, CEI has an impressive history that includes numerous milestones. Two of the seven genes currently known to cause glaucoma were discovered at CEI. In addition, CEI surgeons developed Oregon's first corneal transplant service, and their researchers pioneered microsurgery by building the world's first microscope for ocular surgery. Harry's son Paul Casey works closely with the enormous institute (120,000 square feet on the Oregon Health and Science University campus in Portland, Oregon). Paul Casey's daughter Maureen volunteers with the Casey Eye Institute on a marketing outreach program.

Since 2000, UPS has been the nation's largest corporate giver to the United Way. Nearly 237,000 UPS employees contributed $49.4 million in 2005, with the company adding $8 million for a total $57.4 million. UPS's Employee Gift-Matching program, which is just what it says, has made dollar-for-dollar matches to worthy organizations since 1963. UPS's Region/District Grant program, established in the 1980s, gives employees the opportunity to identify community-based organizations and recommend funding. For several years in the early 1990s I chaired the Pacific Region program. Each year, our seven districts would winnow their selections to one needy organization. We chose the one we felt most worthy, giving that organization $100,000. The second most worthy received $50,000, while the five others each got $10,000. Organizing that program and attending those check presentations were some of the most gratifying moments of my career. The programs these charities support promote a Casey-style determination. They carry Casey's legacy forward, promulgating skills that will equip people to lead.

In addition to his charitable work through foundations, Jim Casey also distributed unsolicited checks to the needy, independent of charities. In the old television show from the fifties, *The Millionaire*, an unnamed and unseen zillionaire assigns an underling to give a check to a complete stranger. Not unlike *The Millionaire*, Casey used region managers, region personnel managers, and others to help locate needy people and make sizable donations. I once helped get background information for Jim Casey on a prospective recipient in a Portland, Oregon, suburb. The beneficiary was, I heard, overwhelmingly thrilled with the presentation.

Globalization has expanded the scope of UPS philanthropy. For example, following the devastating Southeast Asia tsunami in December 2004, UPS provided $3 million in aid, including in-kind services, cash grants, and employee gift-matching.

UPS China has shouldered commitments to help impoverished community schools in the Hubei province. Donations include hundreds of thousands of dollars, a scholarship fund, computers, and musical instruments. Operation Blessing supports the elderly in Beijing. In addition to the company's charitable works, UPS employees and family members extend themselves to disabled and orphaned Chinese children.

There remains nothing like the home-grown commitment to local tragedy . . . and UPS is local all over the United States. When Hurricane Katrina hit in late August 2005, UPS immediately mobilized, first to move more than 4 million pounds of medicine, food, and emergency supplies to aid Katrina victims. Second, it hastened to improvise means of reestablishing the communications system upon which so much American transport depends. UPS staff reconfigured routers and switches, bypassing inoperable local phone networks. In some cases, dedicated UPS employees saved data to CDs and personally drove them to neighboring facilities that still had network access, so they could plug them into the main system. UPS was ultimately able to deliver more than a million packages using these alternate methods.

It's easy to see why UPS is so often rated "most admired" for social contributions. Like everything else it does, UPS is unrelenting, not just as a corporation and the foundations it sponsors but also as a group of dedicated individuals.

9

THE WORLD'S NINTH-LARGEST AIRLINE

UPS ground delivery was like a robust pair of lungs. The company lived and breathed this service, ever ready for the marathon bursts of energy that expansion into new markets demanded. Given a certain amount of perseverance, UPS has always been up to the task of couriering parcels across roads and streets within virtually any community. As efficient as army ants, UPS managers and employees optimized procedures in one delivery location, then adapted and cloned them in new locations as brown package cars found their way across America. And like an ant colony, UPS had a collective mind—its corporate culture, which infused all individuals with incredible motivation, keeping feet on the ground, eyes focused, and noses on the trail of quality service.

So earthbound was this enterprise, it wasn't easy for UPS to get off the ground. Twice, a half-century apart, airfreight brought the company almost to its knees. First, United Parcel Service's inopportune 1929 merger (built around a UPS subsidiary, United Air Express) almost erased the company from the face of the earth. And second, FedEx's stupendous introduction of overnight air delivery service caught UPS off guard and threatened its avenues for expansion.

Lessons in rebounding are evident in the recovery strategies the company implemented in response to these near-disasters. One can hear aphorisms along the lines of "when the going gets tough, the tough get going." That UPS now cuts as prodigious a swath in the air as on the ground—running the world's ninth-largest air fleet—is a testimony to the company's resilience and triumph.

That fine pair of lungs learned to function well at high altitudes, the hard way.

Jim Casey's practical temperament defined UPS for most of the twentieth century. The determined leader knew how to move parcels on wheels, but he was wary of wings. As a fifteen-year-old in December 1903, he had bought a paper from a passing newsboy from the doorway of his City Messenger Service. At the time, what struck him about the article on the Wright brothers' flight at Kitty Hawk, North Carolina, was not its technological implications but the unusual brevity of the article, which he took to mean that the editor simply couldn't believe the story was true. Few could. Air travel was still in the realm of Jules Verne's science fiction.

Later, like everyone else, Casey was astounded by World War I aviation successes and the rate of innovation. He knew that the U.S. Post Office Department had in 1918 initiated an intercity air mail route and established a transcontinental route. He knew that the Post Office had begun contracting with private airlines to transport mail in 1925. Nevertheless, the company's promise of *dependable* delivery seemed at odds with such a still-dangerous and undependable conveyance. Plus, to provide true advantages over other long-range transportation options, airplanes' speed and range needed to improve. The nerve-shattering vibration, the deafening engine noise, the air sickness and painful ear pressure during takeoffs and landings, the usually fatal accidents . . . these were just a few of the reasons flight just didn't tempt him.

Not so his partner Evert "Mac" McCabe. McCabe was totally infatuated with air travel. In personality, he had much in common with the impatient adventurers that were the aviators of the time. McCabe had tried to become a pilot during World War I, but Uncle Sam turned him down because he was married. Flying was that perilous and McCabe was that crazy about flying. When United Parcel Service began operations in Los Angeles, his love affair with planes intensified. Southern California, with its grand flying weather, was a Mecca for aviation enthusiasts. It attracted both aviation industrialists like Howard Hughes and Donald Douglas and stunt pilots like Pancho Barnes and Roscoe Turner.

For McCabe, temptations were everywhere. He eagerly sought out those who were making a name for themselves in the air business, always with a United Parcel Service of the skies in mind. He met and befriended Jack Frye, who flew one of the earliest and safest airplanes from the war, a Fokker. Mac also compared notes with another aviation buff named Monte Abrams, and in 1926 the pair explored possible West Coast landing sites.

Like a child badgering his parents, McCabe ceaselessly tried to sow a grain of enthusiasm in his partners. Jim Casey and the others weren't immune to suggestion. After all, the company was a partnership. He and Claude had been drawn to Mac in part for his visionary spirit. Casey recalled that McCabe "arranged for me, Dee Hayes and himself to meet with Donald Douglas, founder of the Douglas Aircraft Corporation, at his plant in Santa Monica, California. It was a most interesting session, but at the close when a Colonel Nelson suggested we all take a flight with him in his army plane, I said no. Mac and Dee were all for it. Well, when Mac took off in that plane I thought his imagination had carried him too far. He would certainly crash. He didn't."

Yet McCabe wasn't alone in his passion. The whole country followed Charles Lindbergh's historic transatlantic flight in 1927. When Lindbergh's sleek monoplane, *Spirit of St. Louis,* touched down at Le Bourget Airport in Paris, it seemed to the entire world as if the sky was quite literally the limit.

Talk about air express was beginning to surface. At McCabe's suggestion, the company sent surveys out to businesses to weigh the interest in and need for an air service. The results were very encouraging. Finally, in 1929, United Parcel Service formed United Air Express and hired Mac's mentor Monte Abrams as traffic manager. They contracted with three air companies, including pilot Jack Frye's Standard Air Lines, to deliver parcels by air. (Jack Frye later became president of Transcontinental Western Airlines, which developed into Trans World Airlines, better known as TWA.)

Standard Air Lines flew Fokkers between Los Angeles and El Paso, with stops in Phoenix and Tucson. Maddux Air Lines, using Ford Stout tri-motor all-metal monoplanes, operated between Los

Angeles, San Diego, San Francisco, Oakland, the Imperial Valley, and Phoenix. The northern route, with Union Air Lines delivering between Portland, San Francisco, and Seattle, was due to open some weeks later.

At the airports, United Air Express delivered packages to carriers and picked up packages for delivery. In cities with no United Parcel Service ground delivery, local companies were hired. The partners' same high service standards applied. According to Jim Casey, Mac once spotted a package that had missed a flight to Phoenix. He immediately contacted Jack Frye. The company spent $250—an enormous amount of money in that era—for Frye's extra trip to Arizona with one package!

United Air Express was up and operating before the northern route opened, but express service overall was slow to catch on. Airplanes were still a novelty and many people looked upon the emerging industry as an aberration. It was pricier, and in many people's minds, shipping by air was only an emergency option. The inaugural flight of the northern route gave the company a P.R. opportunity that wasn't lost to McCabe, who by then knew an impressive range of celebrities. Using his natural gifts as an impresario, McCabe organized a gala event at the Los Angeles Airfield on February 15, 1929. Flamboyant actors such as Douglas Fairbanks, Mary Pickford, Wallace Beery, William B. Mayo, and many others of that epoch's glitterati helped attract media representatives keen to report as the plane departed to the north with packages.

United Air Express, the first package delivery company in the United States to offer air service, captured national attention, especially after that February 1929 gala opening. People in the aviation industry, with pocketbooks fattened by a heady decade of prosperity, smelled opportunity.

Meanwhile, the UPS founders had already determined a need for their delivery service in New York City and desperately wanted to begin service on the East Coast as soon as possible. Just as Jim Casey and his partner Evert McCabe were laying out long-distance plans for possible expansion of retail store deliveries into New York

City, an offer came to them that seemed like it was dropped from the heavens.

It was tendered by the high-flying Curtiss Aeroplane and Motor Company, which would soon change its name after a July 1929 merger with Wright Aeronautical and other companies to the Curtiss-Wright Corporation. The offer to UPS came through the investment banking firm Bancamerica-Blair Corporation (not affiliated with today's Bank of America), which represented Curtiss-Wright and a few other aviation firms. The group envisioned a huge air express company, with UPS providing the ground service.

On July 5, 1929, Curtiss merged with Wright Aeronautical and ten other companies. On August 22nd of that same year, Curtiss-Wright Corporation was listed on the New York Stock Exchange, where it still trades today. The brilliant financial mind of company president Clement Melville Keys created an upbeat mood as he had just brought Curtiss-Wright from near bankruptcy to being the largest aviation company in the country, with $75 million in assets.

Deal Worth Millions

Tantalized by a means of financing expansion into New York City through what had become the Bancamerica-Blair offer of a buyout, and ebullient that their fledgling air service would become a major entity, Jim Casey and Evert McCabe flew to New York in 1929, with attorney Fred Athearn in tow. There, McCabe realized a personal dream when he met Charles Lindbergh. According to McCabe's daughter, Ruth McCabe Bertauche, her father described "Lucky Lindy" as "a very modest and personable young man." The trip itself was less than lucky.

No country bumpkin, Fred Athearn had written the State of California's Laws of Incorporation. Athearn represented his clients' interests very well and helped structure a deal that worked to their advantage. After negotiations, all parties signed a contract under which the Bancamerica-Blair holding company bought United Parcel Service for $2 million and 600,000 shares of Curtiss Aeroplane (later Curtiss-Wright) stock. Using the $2 million primarily for expansion, United Parcel Service was also able to give its stockholders (employees) cash, along with Curtiss Airlines shares, for their holdings.

According to the agreement, the three still active UPS partners (Evert McCabe, Jim Casey, and his brother George Casey) would remain with the company to oversee the planned ground expansion. They were guaranteed management control for a five-year period, drawing the considerably high salaries of $25,000 each per year. The terms of the deal anticipated and assumed that they would remain indefinitely after the initial five-year period.

To the Caseys and McCabe, the future possibilities were staggering. The financial backing was more than they could have saved in years. "Without the added capital secured at that time, we could not have expanded from the Pacific Coast directly to New York in 1930, and in one jump become the largest retail delivery system in the world," Casey later explained.

As stipulated in the sales agreement, in the fall of 1929, Jim Casey and Evert McCabe went to New York. In anticipation of the move east, Casey and McCabe rented temporary office space in the exquisite new art deco Chanin Building, where they laid the groundwork for opening their first eastern operation. They sent for several key people, including accountant George D. Smith to set up the books and Jack Davidson to help set up the delivery operations.

Right away, Casey had misgivings. Regret and worry moved in to occupy his mind. He and his partners had given up control of everything they had built over the previous decade. More important, Casey doubted that the new guard would honor the commitment to his loyal employees, upon which rested United Parcel Service's successes. These men had become stockholders expecting to share in company profits over coming decades, and an abrupt payoff and stock in another company was certainly not what they'd been expecting.

The quick payoff seemed at odds with everything Casey, his partners, and the company had represented when they made United Parcel Service stock available two years earlier. Then, just as abruptly as the offer to merge had fallen into their laps, so too did the solution to undo it.

No one suspected the ballooning economy would suddenly burst. The historic October 1929 crash of the New York Stock Exchange was shattering. Its profound effect on the U.S. economy for years to come is legend. It changed businesses. It changed attitudes. It changed lives. Overnight and indiscriminately, from one coast to the other, there was no one who was not affected somehow, many dramatically. At UPS, the crash and the Great Depression that ensued would be a double-edged sword, both taking and giving.

Financial institutions were hard-hit, and the holding company Bancamerica-Blair was not exempt. The grandiose plans of its member airline firms hoping for an air-UPS delivery system fizzled. With the advent of catastrophic inflation, interest in air deliveries waned. Most of the rich individuals and industries who could have afforded air delivery were in ruins. The rest of the country was barely surviving. Volume was too low to sustain the air service. McCabe's brainchild, United Air Express, ceased operations after only about a year.

Yet the financial disaster, while forcing a good idea that was before its time onto the shelf, created an opportunity for United Parcel Service to reinvent itself, because—like a lot of businesses—Bancamerica-Blair was looking to divest itself of some of its holdings.

Casey, through professional consultants, was able to strike a deal with Bancamerica-Blair. UPS retained the $2 million, and the investment company returned the United Parcel Service stock, but the intrepid delivery company had to assume responsibility for all outstanding obligations. One of these was the expensive lease at 331 East 38th Street in New York, which was to serve as UPS headquarters for many years. Also in 1930 UPS formed United Parcel Service of America, Inc., a Delaware corporation, and that year again made UPS stock available for senior employees in all job categories. Casey breathed easier.

The divestiture didn't happen overnight, and it took four fretful years and a lot of hustling before all the UPS stock was returned to UPS employees in exchange for the Curtiss Airways stock they signed back. UPS stock was again offered to the employees. Their independence was preserved. Jim Casey recalled, "We learned in those four years lessons that never should be forgotten."

As Jim Casey commented many years later, "Employee-ownership is credited by the people inside and outside the company with having done more than any other thing toward making our company and our people so notably successful financially and otherwise."

A Shocking Death to Absorb

When United Parcel Service made the decision to headquarter in New York City, key executives moved to Manhattan and brought their families with them. In 1930, Paul and Harold Oberkotter joined the upper echelons in the Big Apple, their wives and children in tow. Garnet and Mac McCabe had four children away at school, and she joined her husband in New York.

Given the dismal economic environment and the scope of what they hoped to accomplish and the financial upheaval to overcome, the team went to work feverishly. It was the worst time to start a business, but they started anyway. Mac ran all over New York and Newark persuading department stores to give United Parcel Service a chance. Mac even persuaded West Coast department-store customers to write laudatory letters about the delivery service to their East Coast counterparts.

United Parcel Service hammered away at merchants who were interested in the new service but reluctant to relinquish their own delivery fleets. One by one, UPS slowly added stores, assumed their deliveries (in most cases taking over their facilities and vehicles), and hired their delivery people. The Oberkotters set up new systems and accounts and eight other top managers were called to New York to assist in July 1930: Willard Bixby, Ted Johnson, Bert Barnes, Bert Meyer, Joe Meiklejohn, Jesse Whitt, Bert Geary, and Earle Small. From then on, the company's headquarters were on the East Coast. On August 18, 1930, UPS brown took to the streets in New York City.

Sadly, in 1931 the McCabes' eldest son, Gene, died at the age of twenty-two. Garnet McCabe was heartbroken. She had great difficulty accepting the loss and became obsessed, withdrawn, and increasingly unstable. Meanwhile, her husband, "The Man with the Smile," dealt with his loss by distraction, in the form of hustling new business for the company, a time-tested and valid strategy that was nonetheless lost on poor Garnet.

Before long, United Parcel Service in New York was delivering for thirty-seven stores, with 159 delivery vehicles covering a radius of fifty miles from Manhattan. Big Brown's consolidated delivery vans replaced many smaller delivery fleets, for department stores that could no longer afford them or wanted to focus on their own merchandising. Newspapers reported that, with United Parcel Service's presence, traffic actually *improved* in the Big Apple.

Then, on January 12, 1933, at two in the morning, United Parcel Service suffered another inconceivable loss. The grief-stricken Garnet murdered her husband in their posh Woodstock Towers apartment. Evert McCabe lay dead, shot point-blank in the left side of his head. Garnet stood by with a photo of their son Gene and tears streaming down her cheeks. Two notes, written by Garnet, were nearby—one asking why her husband didn't talk about Gene, the other hinting that she would kill herself. Police arrested the sobbing woman on the spot; she was arraigned before the grand jury, and an alienist (an old term for a psychiatrist specializing in the legal aspects of mental illness) determined her to be mentally unstable. A first degree murder indictment was returned against Mrs. McCabe but held in abeyance when she was committed to the Matteawan State Hospital for the criminally insane, where she remained until she was discharged on her own recognizance on July 27, 1936. Her sister had petitioned the court, insisting that Garnet McCabe had regained her reason.

Following the murder, everyone in the company was stunned. United Parcel Service had lost its most charming idea man, and a man to whom an idea meant action. Funeral services for Evert "Mac" McCabe took place at Universal Funeral Chapel on Lexington Avenue, Monday, January 16, 1933, and internment was a private affair with family, a few close friends, and a very saddened Jim Casey.

UPSers at the time were certainly profoundly aware of the loss of one of their key leaders, but as years went by, the incident was just not mentioned. Those few managers who knew about the murder didn't deny it happened. Still, the subject was so rarely commented on that facts became hazy; it became part of the company's unofficial folklore.

Mac McCabe's death deeply affected Jim Casey. Their relationship had been close, and he was well aware of the unique strengths this flamboyant VP brought to the UPS enterprise. Casey said, "When Mac decided something should be done, he didn't stop to think of the reasons why it might not be possible to do. He didn't count on failure—in fact, he completely ignored the possibility of failure. . . . As long as United Parcel Service has men who are overly optimistic, men who are dreamers, practical or impractical, men who put their imagination into play, and men who believe in people, there will always be an Evert McCabe."

And McCabe's hard work paid off. The number of UPS employees more than tripled between 1930 and 1934, from four hundred to more than fourteen hundred. Cincinnati, Milwaukee, and Philadelphia came on line. In May 1935—at the heart of the Great Depression—Jim Casey wrote another letter offering more UPS stock, at $40 per share, to employees with two or more years of service. As most of the shares came from the McCabe estate, and were the only ones available, they were quickly snapped up.

Still McCabe's biggest idea—air service—was shelved and would remain so for more than twenty years after his death.

Blue Label Air

In 1953, United Parcel Service got back into the air business it had abandoned twenty-three years before. More and more customers wanted to ship packages rapidly from one city to another, and once again, UPS looked to the skies. By this time, Jim Casey had lost his resistance to air transportation. He and his colleagues set up what they called United Parcel Service—Air.

United Parcel Service—Air began as a two-day air service between major cities on the West Coast, as well as selected cities in the Midwest and on the East Coast, most notably Chicago, Detroit, and New York.

In explaining his support for the air service, Jim Casey concluded a talk on competition with parcel post the following year (1954) by saying, "I am sure we can compete fully as well in rates, and better, as to speed, over longer distances. I believe the time is near when our ground and air services will be combined, without distinction, under a zone-rate system, and that we will then make regular deliveries across the continent, using airplanes for the long-line hauls."

The name United Parcel Service—Air was later changed to UPS Blue Label Air and a small rectangular blue label was placed on all such air packages as an identifier.

UPS Blue Label Air packages flew in the cargo holds of regularly scheduled domestic airlines, packed into airline hampers that were configured to fit in the bellies of the planes. The service was not labor-intensive since each city in the system needed only one air manager to confirm that airline staff loaded and unloaded from the proper planes (United Airlines, American Airlines, and the rest). Add a few clerks and some drivers to move the packages to and from the UPS hubs to the airports, and you had a two-day air service with the front end delivered by UPS package cars.

By 1957 nine U.S. cities were linked by Blue Label Air service, and new cities were periodically added. Blue Label service continued to grow modestly until by 1980 it was available in the larger metropolitan areas of all forty-eight contiguous states and the island of Oahu, Hawaii.

One might think that with a half-century of air experimentation, UPS should have been a little more aggressive, applying to air service the precepts that had worked so well on the ground. Some managers did advocate a more ambitious approach, but because the

Board of Directors was far from receptive, no serious planning ever got under way. In those days, top management was made up of very conservative men whose acumen was in making systems, keeping ledgers, and providing top-notch service. There wasn't a daredevil among them.

Jim Casey was the son of an unfulfilled dreamer. When UPS's Icarus-like reach for the skies failed in 1929 and almost the company with it, it was Casey who had been obliged to pick up the pieces. He seemed to want people in charge around him who wouldn't push the company to any new brink. He handpicked George D. Smith, CEO from 1962 to 1972, because Casey felt the company needed someone to help it "stay the course" in expanding the territories. Paul Oberkotter followed Smith (1972–1973) before Paul's brother Harold Oberkotter took over (1973–1980). All three were lifetime UPSers with accounting backgrounds, financially astute, and deeply committed to the welfare of the people who made up the company. Nary a boat-rocking rebel among them.

In truth, air service simply wasn't the company's focus during these years. The company was, in the late 1960s and early 1970s, in the midst of major common carrier expansion throughout the continental United States. United Parcel Service's prize at the time was new cities, new districts, new regions. The tasks at hand for Smith, the Oberkotters, and their management teams were thorny enough without looking over their shoulders or trying something totally different. Their attention was directed at UPS's main competition, the U.S. Post Office, not at a twenty-seven-year-old retired U.S. Marine Corps pilot with fourteen jets and a dream.

Then FedEx Happened

Because they were keeping their collective noses to the ground, UPS managers were caught napping in the early 1970s as FedEx exploded into the air business, setting itself up as an airline that delivered packages, overnight ones at that. There was UPS, only minimally in the air business, primarily a package-delivery company that used the air for second-day deliveries.

Former marine pilot Fred Smith and his FedEx (at the time always called Federal Express) was, by any measure, sheer genius. That FedEx was established in 1973 as an airline, not a ground delivery company, is an important legal distinction, because the company was exempt from onerous common carrier regulations. Airlines fall under a different regulatory body (the Federal Aviation Administration—FAA), not the ICC that regulated trucking companies including UPS, and even though FedEx also had trucks, its corporate structure exempted it from ICC regulation.

And FedEx didn't intend to start up city by city as UPS always had. The concept was hatched nationwide, with its one hub, from the very beginning. Smith designed it to work systemically, the way a clearinghouse does. It copied how UPS was using its ground hubs, a concept the passenger airlines also emulated to set up their hub-and-spoke airport layout systems. For example, UPS packages from all over a metropolitan area arrive at a central hub in each city. There they are sorted and dispatched to destinations all over the place. Similarly but on a much larger scale, all FedEx packages, no matter where they came from and no matter where they were bound, flew into one hub—Memphis, Tennessee—from the get-go. Flying and sorting at night, when air traffic was lighter, facilitated one-day delivery. With these modifications, FedEx revolutionized air delivery, and when UPS leadership got serious about next-day air, they did the same thing.

But this wouldn't happen for *eight more years*. The vast delivery market that had taken UPS sixty-five years to accumulate was suddenly jarred by this upstart, Federal Express, a company no one had even heard of. Most UPSers took the ostrich approach, ignoring the new company. Some denigrated it, saying, for instance: *How are they going to deliver them on the ground? Their network's too small. People don't need that much delivered overnight. Costs are too high. They'll probably go under.*

But many UPS managers were not in denial. My boss at the time (a former marine pilot himself) watched the new company carefully and predicted success. As former pilots rarely relinquish their love for the skies, he had been advocating a UPS air service for years.

However, he and thousands of other UPSers were very busy celebrating the periodic service expansions. They were caught up in following through with all the staffing and planning demanded of opening new territories. We rarely mentioned the new competition. In fact, UPS annual reports of the late 1970s and even 1980 made no mention of FedEx, still decrying the U.S. Postal Service as the number one competitor.

While UPS continued staking new territory, fanning forward across America on wheels, FedEx worked out its kinks and got even further ahead in the air-transport business. It added planes, people, and, what was more important, a comprehensive ground network.

FedEx was one of the factors that actually helped bring about the deregulation of the airlines. (The bill passed in 1978. Cargo deregulation occurred in 1979 and passenger deregulation in 1980.) The company had entered the air cargo business by using the Civil Aeronautics Board (CAB) exemption for small planes. With the business literally soaring, Fred Smith discovered he had to use two small planes to cover some of his busiest routes. The CAB turned down his request to operate one larger jet instead of two small ones for those segments. Not one to be denied, Smith launched a massive postcard write-in campaign to Congress to tie in cargo with their ongoing deregulation hearings.

Politically powerful Flying Tigers had to be placated first, however, because initially they were skeptical about what cargo deregulation would do for them. As it turns out, it did plenty. Air cargo deregulation went into effect on January 1, 1979, a year ahead of passenger service, and with both FedEx and Flying Tigers grandfathered into the new system, the two companies made a killing before others, including Airborne, Emery, DHL, and UPS, entered the market. To show its gratitude, FedEx later gobbled up the old Flying Tigers.

Then the Motor Carrier Act of 1980 deregulated the trucking industry. This meant that United Parcel Service had competition on the ground as well as in the air. The company scrambled. Before it even attempted to take on FedEx, it extended its brown tentacles, for the first time, into the foreign market, which I'll look at more carefully in the next chapter.

The Motor Carrier Act of 1980 also removed all regulatory restrictions against the ground movement of packages that were transported partly by air. In other words, ground service that operated in conjunction with Blue Label Air service had been restricted in a ten-state area, but no longer was. With the restrictions removed, in 1980 UPS hastened to expand its Blue Label Air (two-day) service to all forty-eight states.

Finally in 1981—with CEO George Lamb, who'd started as an operations manager instead of an accountant, at the helm—UPS made a decision to get into the air business in a big way. George Lamb was a former Army Air Corps gunner who, paradoxically, didn't like to fly. (On several occasions I picked him up at various West Coast train stations.) Yet he knew that the future was in the air.

George had come to UPS as a clerk, while he waited to pass the bar exam. He passed, but stayed and went on to orchestrate the company's growth during its major expansion across the United States. As he assumed a string of higher positions, he changed UPS from a loose patchwork of local operations to a tightly knit national network. He not only insisted on the highest standards of service and integrity, he motivated employees to take pride in their work. The company needed new direction, and the Board of Directors summoned the well-respected George Lamb to give it.

While there was isolated idle chatter among employees about Federal Express, even up to the time George Lamb took over as CEO, the only acknowledged competition was the U.S. Post Office. This very real and ongoing battle was so ingrained in every UPSer's brain that there was hardly room for another ogre.

Hence most UPSers did not realize that the company was going to give FedEx a run for the money until after the fact. Without mentioning any competitor, a series of small announcements added up to the obvious—UPS was about to be a big player in air express delivery.

Starting an Airline

UPS entered the overnight air delivery business one toe at a time. It bought its first airplane in 1981 and began using several smaller air companies, like Evergreen and Orion, to provide the pilots and supporting airline services. In 1982 UPS selected Louisville International Airport to be the center of its air operations and began to set up a Memphis-like hub on 550 acres between the existing airport's two parallel runways.

Even this didn't happen overnight, but more in the methodical "making a list, checking it twice" UPS way. But the process didn't fail them. By 1985 UPS Next Day Air service was available in all forty-eight states and Puerto Rico. Alaska and Hawaii were added later. That same year, UPS began its intercontinental service as it commenced flying packages and documents between the United States and six European countries.

Blue Label Air service morphed into UPS 2nd Day Air, giving shippers a less expensive alternative for important packages that didn't have to be there overnight. It wasn't until 1988, when the FAA granted UPS authorization to operate its own aircraft, that UPS was able to take direct control over all its air operations. Immediately UPS Airlines was born.

Over the next year, UPS Airlines was the fastest-growing airline in FAA history. It purchased aircraft from Boeing, other aircraft manufacturers, and other airlines, hired pilots and air-support loaders, sorters, and other personnel, while it accumulated all of the necessary technology and support systems. By the end of 1989, UPS owned 110 airplanes, including seven 747s, and leased an additional 247 airplanes.

For stodgy old UPS, building an airline so quickly and from scratch was not without problems. The ingrained culture prized (and still prizes) company loyalty, years of service, and promotion from within—biases other companies regard as arcane. Imagine this group welcoming pilots and associated flight personnel into the company. These men and women weren't going to start out as part-time sorters, see if they could conform, and then work their way up. They hired on as extremely well-paid specialists, right from the start.

Air-industry deregulation delivered flight personnel right into UPS's old-fashioned world. It forced several major airlines to reduce flights and cut routes. Pilots in search of more secure jobs came to UPS. They knew they'd make less than they had as passenger pilots, but the long-term security and benefits at UPS were persuasive. Most signed on not because they fully embraced UPS culture but out of a sort of resignation—and the fact that they could continue to fly.

To dyed-in-the-wool UPSers, who had worked their way up from the bottom over a period of years and often decades, the sudden infusion of flyboys and gals was nervous-making and even dispiriting. It seemed to some as if the company had passed a portion of the reins over to a bunch of free-spirited iconoclasts. Mac McCabe would've adored the comparatively untrammeled flight folk, and maybe even helped them acclimatize, but the new direction made many UPSers feel insecure.

This challenge of having to embrace outsiders and somehow get them to embrace UPS would also manifest itself when the company needed to hire other specialists, most notably in information services. The "outsider dilemma" was obvious, *glaring* even, so much so that management gave it a name and discussed the burdens that incorporating outsiders presented at meetings of the UPS Management Committee.

Some UPS managers have always adopted the generalist theory, the idea that anybody at UPS could change jobs with anyone else. Of course, they didn't have to train someone with limited writing skills to edit a company publication, as I did. The theory that all employees were UPSers first and specialists second worked overall for years, and is still the case in most of the traditional parts of the company. But it was finally put to rest with the advent of skilled outsiders, most notably with UPS Airlines.

Interestingly, outsiders or not, pilots still gravitate to air cargo today. Just as before, the jobs appeal to some professionals because they are a lot more stable than the other airlines, even if passenger pilots make better wages. UPS and FedEx accounted for 28 percent of all U.S. pilot hirings during 2005. UPS added 300 pilots that year and another 150 in 2006, bringing its total to about 2,850. Plans are for an additional 150 UPS pilots to be hired in 2007.

In 2006 UPS pilots ratified their contract, which provided signing bonuses and initial raises of 17.7 percent, followed by annual raises over the next five years. This means the average captain will make $258,000 a year, and the average first officer, $147,000.

Worldport in Louisville

The UPS hub, on the 550 acres at the Louisville International Airport, is now called "Worldport." It is *massive*—far larger than the nearby passenger terminal—and it is growing. The 4-million-square-foot facility is seventy-five feet high, too big to air condition. Circumnavigating the building's exterior is a five-mile hike. Within are 122 miles of upward, downward, north-, east-, south-, and west-bound conveyor belts, chutes, and ramps—a whole nervous system.

Most of the action—over a million packages a day's worth—takes place between 11 P.M. and 4 A.M. Each night over a hundred planes from all over the world swoop down near the Ohio River—that transportation corridor of yore—to Louisville. Each plane is informed by a marvelous new technology that is making radar obsolete. Yes, UPS, ever striving to enhance efficiency, pioneers aviation technologies. The FAA endorsed a new satellite-based navigation system called Automatic Dependent Surveillance-Broadcast (ADS-B) that will improve safety and streamline aircraft operations. The company has invested $35 million in ADS-B devices over recent years. The ADS-B devices give precise information about where a plane is and where it is headed.

The ADS-B units interface with UPS's information systems, among the most advanced in the world. Among them is UPS Airlines' unique Computerized Operations Monitoring, Planning and Scheduling System (COMPASS). COMPASS not only provides planning, scheduling, and load-handling information, it can plot optimum flight schedules up to six years in advance. Together, such revolutionary new information technologies are improving safety, capacity, and efficiency, saving the company as much as $2 million a year in fuel just by following what the system perceives as the most efficient routes to land in Louisville.

Approximately 5,000 employees come nightly to "the sort." Some unload packages from the planes, making sure to put each package label-side up, onto one of three conveyors. One conveyor is for small parcels like envelopes, which are mostly Next Day Air and 2nd Day Air packages. Another conveyor is for irregularly shaped packages. And the third is for normal six-sided boxes.

Sorters' work isn't complicated, but the label must be pointed upward so the system's infrared image sensor can read the recipient's address, as well as register the parcel's dimensions and weight. Small rubber mallets, called "hockey pucks," line one side of a belt. At a signal from the computer, responding to scanned directions, the pucks push packages onto a belt going a new direction. Scanning, which may occur as many as six times as the parcel courses through Worldport, determines its trajectory. A package that enters Worldport with "smart label" technology can take as little as eight minutes to make its proper journey from inbound to outbound plane.

When labels aren't scannable, employees in the Telecode Office examine the labels electronically. They can almost always rectify the label from their desks. If they can't, they reroute the packages into the "exceptions" circuit where other employees correct the label manually.

Occasionally, package lines jam, which registers as "red" in the computer system. From the approximate thirty mechanics on call, some descend to make repairs. This usually takes less than five minutes. A belt that can't be fixed quickly gets its packages rerouted to others on the matrix, as directed by computer technicians.

Interestingly, most of the night-shift employees are young people, college students, single parents, hard workers trying to get ahead. UPS a hundred years from its inception is an enterprise far beyond the scope of anything Jim Casey could ever have conceived of. Diligent Worldport employees aren't wearing hats with visors and running packages on foot as they were in Seattle. They're a new generation, this century's version of messengers. They're using and aided by the technology that they grew up with, electronics, and they're good at it.

Propelled by all this technology, packages exit Worldport, sorted by automation according to their destinations and placed, also by automation, in "cans." Loaders place the cans in the refueled UPS jets that take off in the early morning darkness for airports all over the world.

A new $1 billion project will expand Worldport to 5.1 million square feet, a 27 percent increase, to the size of 113 football fields and housing a total of 197 miles of belts. Over construction scheduled for the next five years, the expansion will increase sorting capacity by 60 percent, to 487,000 packages per hour. UPS plans to add 1,284 full-time and 3,787 permanent part-time workers, which will swell the UPS Louisville area workforce to almost 23,000, including drivers, ground crews, and supply-chain employees. Louisville International Airport is now the fourth busiest cargo airport in the United States—thanks to UPS.

As it nears its hundredth birthday, UPS owns and operates 268 jet aircraft (including 24 new planes to help cover rapidly growing Asian markets) and charters another 309 to accommodate its transport obligations, making it the world's ninth-largest airline. UPS Airlines' Global Operations Center, in Louisville, employs more than six hundred people whose duties extend from weather tracking, crew scheduling, and maintenance schedules to flight control. The nearby Worldport Freight Facility, which opened this year, handles heavy air freight—packages weighing more than 150 pounds. The facility can sort 1.6 million pounds per hour.

In addition to UPS's ever-pumping heart, Worldport, the company's extensive air network includes international air hubs in Cologne, Taipei, and Miami (to serve Latin America) and an intra-Asia hub in the Philippines. UPS planes land and depart more than 2,000 times each day at some 777 airports across the globe, connecting customers in more than two hundred countries and territories.

In a fitting finale to their decades of acrimony, in June 2006 UPS and the U.S. Postal Service announced a $100 million deal that has UPS carrying U.S. mail on its jets. The three-year contract, with an optional two-year extension, gives UPS the responsibility for carrying mail to and from ninety-eight U.S. cities. The UPS-USPS deal puts "Big Brown" in the driver's seat for an upcoming lucrative $1.3 billion Express and Priority mail contract. Rather than a pact with the devil, the deal exemplifies a rapidly changing world, and one in which UPS is acknowledged as a key player, with air acumen it acquired by testing its wings twice before achieving its meteoric rise.

Continuing its government involvement, in September 2006 UPS was awarded a $119 million contract to provide international delivery services for the U.S. Air Force.

Evert McCabe envisioned and pioneered air deliveries when the company established United Air Express seventy-eight years ago. Even a man of his impressive imagination and energy would marvel at what the future has wrought, a world made smaller by packages in the sky.

10

BROWN AROUND THE GLOBE

Every spring since 1941, top UPS managers have convened for their annual management conference. Along with discussing problems, possible solutions, and company direction, UPSers gather for committee reports and company highlights. The UPS Management Conference in April 1975 was definitely an upbeat, even euphoric occasion. Since the company had finally turned the continental United States brown with forty-eight-state, coast-to-coast coverage, there was a lot of backslapping going on. Unassuming Jim Casey—by then eighty-eight years old—publicly applauded the entire UPS management team, taking no credit for his own incredible contributions.

And then the white-haired, long-faced little man paused, and in his typical visionary manner added this for them to ponder, "But you know, we're only serving 5 percent of the world's population!" Talk about throwing down the gauntlet! The long-awaited coast-to-coast UPS service was barely realized—not even fully in place—and here was Jim Casey already looking beyond the borders of the United States. Casey could've been eleven years old again, staring out over the Puget Sound at an unseen world that was even then delivering goods from far, far away. He wanted UPS not just to have a piece of the action but to *be the action*.

Actually, the first operations outside the United States had already begun (on February 28, 1975), with service within Canada's largest metropolis, Toronto. It was a very modest beginning. You would've thought that Canada would be almost a seamless match with no-nonsense UPS, given the country's reputation for meticulousness and level-headedness. Yet on day one of service, thanks to

Toronto's municipal restrictions of operating only under city licenses, a single Checker cab constituted the entire Canadian fleet. The roomy cab—rendered even more capacious by the absence of its backseat—made a pickup at Toronto's Butterick Fashions Marketing Company and then made deliveries only in the downtown area. UPS's initial Canadian rights did not allow large vehicles. For several years, UPS drivers used only customized regular passenger cars, which did not require the special Canadian transport board's authority.

In 1976, the city of Toronto granted UPS city licenses to serve within the city limits with UPS-type brown vehicles, but drivers in the rest of Ontario continued working out of passenger cars. Then, in 1980, after a three-year regulatory struggle and financial losses, United Parcel Service Canada, Ltd. finally obtained authority to improve its service and operations in the populous province of Ontario. UPS's Ontario service area expanded and the entire fleet became UPS brown. Some three thousand Canadian shippers who were on a waiting list were finally able to take advantage of Big Brown.

Gradually, Canadian service expansions in both ground and air service were extended throughout the country. In 1989, various Canadian regulatory agencies granted UPS additional authority to provide ground service to 90 percent of the population. Today some 7,400 UPS employees work out of fifty-four Canadian facilities and serve every address in the country.

Frustrating and protracted expansions throughout the United States were the UPS management team's specialty. So when Casey offered them the grail of international service at that 1975 meeting, they accepted it, buckled on their multilingual armor, and set off on their next crusade, this time to Europe.

A Lesson in German

As yet, UPS lacked an overall global strategy. It had only a decision to expand to Europe, starting small in a limited area. UPS decided to begin in what was then known as West Germany, a country about the size of Oregon but with a population a quarter that of the

United States. The company selected twenty sharp UPS managers from around the country, some with German language abilities, and in 1976 deployed them to start an operation like the one at home, beginning in Dusseldorf.

Germany, a country known for its punctuality and structure of order, seemed like a perfect location to establish an operation based on UPS's strong values of regimentation and strict service standards. Management was very optimistic, sanguine even. The original U.S.-based management team set off for Düsseldorf a few months in advance of the opening, determined but ill-prepared. Armed with materials printed only in English to "sell" the UPS idea, little understanding of the German employment system, and even less knowledge of the German social fabric, they were little prepared for the challenge of hiring a start-up management team and establishing UPS's first European operations.

Even though they had a basic plan, they had no facilities, no vehicles, and no people. Regardless, they were able to commence operations in a major portion of West Germany on schedule in August 1976 with just over forty employees operating out of twelve rented facilities.

The original group of managers hired were sent to the U.S. for cross-training and proved their value over time, despite the original operational problems. Some reached levels of senior management positions and most were still working for UPS at the thirty-year celebration in 2006.

Full of optimism on opening day, UPS CEO Harold Oberkotter sent an initial congratulatory telegram to the West German team that read (in part), "Despite the vast geographical separation, our service team will be linked by UPS people working together with a common purpose."

Then came the rude awakening.

The work ethic in 1970s Germany was not the fine-tuned Swiss watch the UPS pioneers had anticipated. The country's labor climate was institutionalized by German laws that called for extended vacations, much time off, liberal unlimited sick day policies, short work hours and weeks, and other inflexibilities. The hourly employees listened to the stress and pressure to *get the job done* as if it were Greek. According to Gale Davis, member of the initial start-up team and later the German Region personnel manager, "Most Germans felt that a better way to handle excessive work loads was to hire more and more people." Like most Europeans, the German population didn't even consider the concept of "living to work"; they worked only to live and strived to work as little as possible. You can imagine how this lassitude and lack of commitment struck UPS managers who lived and breathed "brown."

The Type-A American package car driver was an anathema to the available workforce in Germany. Driving was considered a lowly job in Europe, at a lower pay scale than the U.S. standard. As it turned out, the initial group of driver applicants were not German nationals, but rather semiskilled foreigners or "guest workers." Most Germans who sought blue-collar work entered apprenticeships at an early age. That left the lower end of the employee pool for UPS recruiters. Most had minimal education and little driving experience. Theft and absenteeism were both high.

The Germans looked with disdain at features of corporate culture that were much treasured by UPS—in the U.S.—like the security of long-term employment, promotion from within, and overtime. They considered the familiarity of first-name basis and the lack of proper titles insulting. In the German culture, titles are very important, and they preferred to be addressed as "Herr so-and-so"—or "Sir."

The differences were daunting, the challenges unwieldy. UPS management had a hard time making progress, so busy were they overcoming what were becoming blatant missteps in operations. UPS felt the losses company-wide. The 1977 UPS Annual Report announced that new operations in West Germany and Canada caused a reduction of 18 cents per share.

Obviously, the whole world did not march to the same tune heard by a bunch of diligent, hard-working Americans with an eccentric corporate culture. So much for exporting the American dream!

At first the pleas of the American team in West Germany fell on deaf ears. In 1978 the group sent a report to corporate headquarters summarizing their plight. Among other fixes, they requested immediately increasing wages. Corporate denied the request. It got worse. West Germany alone cost the company $59 million in 1979. After four years and a huge financial loss, the company had to stop and assess its situation.

After recognizing the seriousness of oversights in the German start-up, in 1980 UPS assigned a special team of ten managers to delve into the problems. After an investigation, they implemented important culture-sensitive corrections and adjustments, such as granting the aforementioned wage increase, applying better hiring criteria (which resulted in the recruitment of more native Germans), and setting up an assimilation strategy—and even introducing work environment adjustments like adding windows in the hub.

Benefiting from these adjustments, and also enhancing benefits that Germans were used to, the big problems of turnover and absenteeism began to improve. Soon, the German operation became a productive model of a foreign extension of an American company, finally posting a profit in 1981. By 1984, the 2,900-member West German operation delivered 31 million packages. Two years later it was 46 million packages handled by 5,000 UPSers in three German districts and a fleet of 2,800 package cars. The ground operation was so solid that in 1989 domestic air service to Germany commenced. By the thirtieth anniversary in 2006, UPS had 14,000 employees in Germany, by far the greatest concentration of any European country.

UPS learned the hard way that you can't shove everything that works in the United States down the throats of citizens from different cultures. They learned that *adaptability was paramount*. Luckily, the company had taken on only one country, because a multicountry expansion would have been disastrous. As it was, there were still a few lessons to be learned.

End of an Era

As the son of Irish immigrants, Jim Casey no doubt appreciated the way UPS was navigating the new straits in Europe. His family knew a thing or two about hard knocks and grit. But while UPS was practicing its German, the great man who had dared his partners to cross the ocean only eight years before quietly died. Jim Casey's last visit to a UPS facility had been a ninety-fourth-birthday celebration by the Washington district people in 1982. Later that year, he entered a hospital nursing home in Seattle, Washington, and never recovered. On June 6, 1983, James Emmett Casey died at the age of ninety-five.

In announcing Casey's death, CEO and Chairman of the Board George Lamb (1980–1984) remarked, "Jim provided us with our first and most enduring example of the 'Determined Man.' We all tried to live up to his view of this modern leader: 'Determined men make conditions—they do not allow themselves to become victims of them.' We will miss his inspiration and great vision."

Obituaries were innumerable. *Time* magazine summed up its story on Jim Casey with these words, "Casey was a believer in giving executives at every level a say, and a stake, in running the company. As a result of his profit-sharing plan, among the first in American business, U.P.S. is today almost entirely owned by its 12,000 managers and supervisors, their families and heirs."

However, for Casey, UPS wasn't just managers and supervisors. He embraced all employees, down to recent hires and even including those yet to be hired. The following *New York Times* obituary quoted Casey the believer as saying: "Ideals of our company cannot be carried out from the top alone. They must become a part of the makeup of the entire organization. They must be instilled in the minds of all men down through the ranks."

Beyond Germany

Once determined people had put the German operation in the black, and UPS Germany had ranks of its own, UPS decided it was ready to expand in Europe. By the mid-1980s, the European economy was growing. Europeans were beginning to talk of a "European Union." This thinking suggested Europe as an expansion market. It may also have suggested that individual countries had more in common than they really did.

In 1985, UPS began international air service between the United States and six European countries, at first using local ground-delivery companies to deliver the goods. This approach allowed the company to test the waters, to watch the relative efficiency with which different ground couriers worked before developing its own ground operation. Starting two years later, from 1987 to 1992, UPS acquired sixteen different trans-European transportation companies as a way of building a European UPS from the inside out, as the company had done throughout the United States.

Even though this seemed like a prudent approach, again Americans found themselves at loggerheads with what they assumed would be the jubilant recipients of the UPS way of business.

One of the first and largest companies UPS acquired was the Italian delivery company Alimondo. Again, a cadre of top-notch UPS managers arrived to strut their stuff. Everything about them announced, "We know what works." They assumed the Italians would fall over themselves to become part of such a great corporation. According to current UPS International manager David Abney, the U.S. team ignored two critical factors: Italy is not the United States, and Alimondo already had its own successful systems, rules, and processes in place.

If the Germans were different, imagine proud, confident Italian males confronted by a bunch of cocky Americans. They couldn't even eat together. The quick-paced UPS work style did not fly in the relaxed workplace of Italy, where a dinner out with employees takes about three hours.

As Abney wrote, "When in Rome, do as the Romans do—as long as it does not conflict with your core values of honesty or integrity, and safety, or your sense of what's right." The UPS managers had some attitude adjusting to do. They labored to address employees from the Italian point of view. They listened to the Italians and their complaints, no matter how trivial they might have seemed. As a result, they got the locals more involved, and together they became sort of a collaborative team. Turnover improved and the operation became successful.

In France, where UPS extended into ground service in 1985, there were other versions of the Latin male and new twists on the work ethic. French workers knew how to make room for a leisurely lunch with a couple of glasses of wine during each work day, while the UPS managers were more apt to opt for a McHamburger.

Obviously, the company had to prioritize, to separate cultural preferences from policies. Some of the preferences could be accommodated without affecting service. Some couldn't. Longer lunch hours might work, but drinking wouldn't. Adjusting start and finish times to allow for a longer lunch is a cultural fix, but drivers' drinking during the day would be a safety issue and might reduce reliability.

From then on, UPS did its research before making foreign expansion. Teams compared existing cultural and business practices in appealing target countries to the UPS way, then strategized how to cope with them in advance. Operations began to turn around and prosper once UPS began to move forward more cautiously, with respect for the culture into which it was expanding. UPS top leadership made a decision to hire competent management people locally, have American managers train key foreign managers in UPS systems, sometimes rotating them through assignments in the States to give them a better understanding of the UPS corporate culture. They gave them whatever help they needed to get started with acquiring good employees and customers. Then U.S. managers took a backseat, removing themselves from day-to-day operations they might find as discomfiting as a dish of barbecued monkey. Making a decision not to battle any individual country's uniqueness and culture was a new version of UPS humility.

In 1987 UPS expanded to ten more European countries, but it was in the Orient that the company saw its most lucrative future. UPS made its first move there that year when it formed a partnership with Yamato Transport Co., Japan's highly respected and largest package delivery company. The Yamato logo, a yellow cat holding her kitten on a black shield, was the country's most recognizable image. Called UPS/Yamato Express, the new venture covered every address in Japan.

Later that year, UPS established an international air service, using commercial aircraft to move packages between the United States and Japan, and between Japan and West Germany. In 1988 Big Brown added an additional nineteen countries worldwide—Andorra, Australia, Brunei, the People's Republic of China, Greece, Hong Kong, Indonesia, Macau, Malaysia, New Zealand, Papua New Guinea, the Philippines, Portugal, Singapore, South Korea, Spain, Taiwan, Thailand, and Turkey—covering forty-one countries by the year's end. Most of the new countries were in Asia. By that year, those Pacific Rim countries were already growing at twice the growth rate of the U.S. Gross National Product. China, being the largest, was the most tantalizing.

The Chinese Dragon

In the nineties suddenly everything one picked up had a tag that said "Made in China" or "Made in India." Soon "Made in Singapore" and "Made in the Philippines" joined the stacks. For a company whose mission was to "move stuff," clearly Asia was the place to be.

But if Paris seemed foreign to UPS, imagine how exotic Shanghai appeared when the brown brigade set off for the Orient. Visions of brown rickshaws piled with parcels? China represented the biggest cultural challenge the company had ever faced. To start with, China wasn't open. It was even more closed than Texas had been. It was a communist country, with strict controls over everything. Plus the language was daunting. Unlike Europe, where most people speak some English, in China very few people spoke any Western language. And fewer Americans could decipher the writing, much less speak the language. The culture was an enigma and the Chinese seemed to like it that way.

China was on its guard. UPS didn't hail from a communist country. It wasn't from the Soviet Union, for example. No matter how "comradelike" UPS's regimentation and uniforms, the company still wasn't red. It was capitalist and American. The Chinese government decided to let UPS, along with its shipping rival

FedEx, into China, but only under its thumb. FedEx took the early lead in China with its aggressive, high-risk, high-investment approach, while UPS initially followed its typical conservative, low-risk, low-investment approach.

In 1988, UPS initiated an agent partnership with China's biggest freight forwarder, China National Foreign Trade Transportation Group, a state-owned delivery company popularly known as the Sinotrans Group. UPS brought the packages to China and Sinotrans delivered them.

Finally in the late 1990s, the Big Brown bear began to roar in the land of the panda. Despite anti-globalization protests at the 1999 World Trade Organization (WTO) meeting in Seattle, UPS CEO Jim Kelly still maintained, "Globalization is not only good, it's inevitable." He announced that globalization and the rise of the Internet were good news for small business and even better news for the consumer. Obviously, stronger world trade, most notably with China, would accelerate UPS growth too.

Mao's successor Deng Xiaoping and other Chinese leaders had focused on market-oriented economic development. By 2000 Chinese output had quadrupled. For much of the population, living standards improved, personal choices expanded, yet political controls remained tight. Better access to global markets would benefit many Chinese businesses, but China wasn't yet in the WTO that was making the rules. Getting China into the WTO became a top priority, both for China and for UPS.

To that end Kelly aggressively campaigned to get China into the WTO. In his support, he reminded the world, "The simple fact is, today, right now, China plays by nobody's rules." His conviction that legitimate trade with China would bolster the U.S. economy helped pave the way for China's eventual admission to membership in the WTO.

As the largest and mightiest delivery company in the world, UPS now plays a big role in global trade negotiations, known as the "Doha round," after Doha, Qatar, where the negotiations began in the year 2000. The objective behind the ongoing multilateral free-

trade talks is to create new WTO guidelines, to which all or a majority of the member governments will agree. UPS would like customs procedures and other delivery regulations around the world to
be less restricted, or to be more accurate, *unrestricted*. This puts UPS
on the side of multinational corporations who advocate for open
markets, particularly in developing Third World countries.

Ambitious corporations pitted against governments that are
striving to protect their indigenous resources—be they human or
natural—from exploitation is a big part of why the atmosphere
around international trade agreements gets so rowdy. And just add
politics. But UPS wasn't trying to build oil pipelines; it was offering
streamlined shipping that would seem to benefit all countries, developed or not. The term that economists use to describe the tariffs
and regulations that countries use to keep predatory businesses at
bay is "barriers to entry."

When in late 2001 China at last (the accession negotiation,
lasting fifteen years and five months, was the longest in WTO history) joined the World Trade Organization as the 149th member,
many of its "barriers to entry" came down. This unleashed UPS's
economic growth and expansion in trade and investment in China.
Immediately, in 2001, UPS became the first package delivery company to commence direct flights between the United States and
China.

The Chinese government, in the process of implementing its
WTO commitments, finally agreed to allow UPS to operate independently. UPS was then able to purchase its earlier service partners, such as Sinotrans in 2004. In a deal worth $100 million, UPS
assumed direct control of express-delivery services in twenty-three
locations covering two hundred cities and regions throughout
China. That made UPS the only express-delivery service in China
wholly owned by non-Chinese.

To assess the market for American products in China, to tell its
customers which U.S. products are most in demand, and to stay
abreast of Chinese consumer trends, UPS recently sponsored a consumer survey in China. Conducted by Research International, the

survey polled more than 1,140 emerging urban middle-class Chinese consumers. The poll found a distinct preference to "buy American." High-quality personal care toiletries and consumer electronics were the most desired American products, with apparel and fashion accessories and music and videos close behind. The results bolstered the rationale for the UPS presence in China.

A second UPS survey confirmed that China is open for business to U.S. exporters, and again detailed Chinese needs and wants. The Chinese would also like to enjoy Western purchasing options like credit cards and online shopping.

Yet China can still put UPS through hoops. UPS is a key member of Global Express, the express delivery industry's trade association. The group scheduled its 2005 annual meeting to coincide with the Doha round of multilateral free-trade talks in Hong Kong. Global Express—with representatives from UPS and other express mail carriers—is pushing for standardized "customs codes," the numerical identifications assigned to imported goods. Different codes for the same product can hang up a package in ports for days and even weeks while officials determine its contents and tariffs.

While there have been agreements to agree, nothing concrete came out of the December 2005 WTO talks. The pressure is on to conclude the Doha round by 2007 because the U.S. president will lose his special empowerment to negotiate on behalf of his country at the WTO talks after that year.

UPS management is also concerned that China and other new markets will impose limits and taxes on foreign-owned delivery companies. Of China specifically, UPS fears that the national postal service will regulate the entire industry. In fact, there is proposed postal legislation in China that would not only reduce the services UPS will be able to offer there, but also require private operators to contribute 4 percent of gross revenue to fund China Post's operations in rural areas.

In 2006, UPS Asia surveyed more than 1,200 Asian executives from small to midsized businesses in twelve key markets. It focused on this group of firms because they form the backbone of many Asian economies. The survey found that most Asian business leaders—71 percent—are optimistic about the overall state of the Asian economy and expect to see continued growth over the coming year.

UPS has invested over $500 million in China thus far. China is today UPS's fastest-growing market, with shipments up 35 percent from 2005 to 2006. Its new major air hub in Shanghai, at the Pudong International Airport, will open in 2007. In addition, in August 2006 UPS opened its first retail outlets in China by adding two new UPS Express mail centers in Shanghai. Good timing for all this expansion! UPS has been selected as the Official Logistics and Express Delivery Sponsor of the Beijing Olympic Games in 2008. (DHL had beaten out UPS in Athens and Turin, not for the full Olympic Games, but partially.) Under the agreement UPS will develop and execute the logistics operating plan for the games, determining how to best move equipment and people from one venue to another, and also provide express delivery services to all venues during the games. Services will range from movement of time-sensitive film footage and photographic materials to handling and expediting tickets.

Eighteen years after taking on the dragon, UPS still finds that China holds great promise. It is home to 20 percent of the world's population, at 1.3 billion. In the last five years, it has doubled its highway system to 23,000 miles. These ribbons of asphalt, second only to those of the United States in length, welcome UPS package cars to speed delivery and pickup. China is expected to grow from today's sixth-largest gross domestic product to become the world's second-largest economy by 2015. Goldman Sachs estimates it will be the world economic leader by the year 2039.

A World Upside Down

UPS made what seemed like tentative steps into China in 1988, but in 1989 alone—in a series of bold deals—it went from a 41-country base to more than 180 countries worldwide, covering 80 percent of the world's population.

The approach was vintage UPS, an international version of the same method it had used to expand into the Bay Area in 1919. UPS identified existing delivery companies that had rights for one or more countries, set up partnerships with those companies, and later acquired the most of these partners. This round of pioneering thus did not immediately provide the level of service to every address that UPS could offer in the United States, but it established beachheads in the major metropolitan areas in each country.

Early in 1989, the company purchased nine additional European-based transportation companies, eight of them former service partners, like Italy's Alimondo. The ninth was British-based IML Air Services Group Ltd., which served more than a hundred countries. UPS also bought an Asian delivery company that covered much of the western Pacific Rim.

In April the company launched UPS Worldwide Document Service to offer low-cost document delivery to a total of 163 countries. Then, on what UPS celebrates as Founders Day (August 28) in 1989, the company announced the inauguration of international air package and document delivery service to more than 175 countries and territories. It is significant that even with all the posturing around the world that had been going on, UPS did not announce until that date that it was fully committed to worldwide delivery service. The company divided the entire international organization into regions at that time.

In December 1989 UPS established service to major cities in four countries in Eastern Europe: Moscow, USSR; Budapest, Hungary; Berlin, East Germany, and Krakow and Warsaw in Poland. A few months later, early in 1990, UPS bought Cuallado, S.A., Spain's leading package delivery company, which served the entire country.

It took fifteen years to develop a comprehensive, integrated air and ground network in Europe, but by 2005 UPS had established service there much like what is available in the United States and the rest of North America. By purchasing two strong local delivery networks, Stolica Messenger Service in Poland and Lynx Express, Ltd., in the United Kingdom, it further expanded its European customer base. This means that UPS now has the capability to serve any address in either of those two continents.

In addition to Worldport in Kentucky, the company has other air hubs serving UPS international. Cologne, Germany, is the European Union hub. Miami serves the Latin American market. The Philippine hub at Clark Air Force Base in Pampanga takes care of the intra-Asian market. In addition, UPS is in the process of building a 425,000-square-foot distribution and logistics hub at the Singapore Airport, where the Asia Region headquarters is also located. The Shanghai hub, a 53,000-square-foot facility with the right to expand to at least 100,000 square feet, will provide UPS's direct link to Japan—where UPS has acquired a former service partner, UPS Suzuyo Freight Services, and is now serving all key metropolitan areas. UPS is the only foreign delivery company with an air hub in Taiwan (Taipei hub). UPS is currently developing operations in Hong Kong, an important link between China, Europe, and other Asian markets.

Now in Latin America, more than 6,000 UPSers serve fifty countries and territories in the Caribbean area and Central and South America. UPS is the only major express delivery service company offering Monday-Saturday service for Mexico's major cities. UPS has operations across Africa, serving major business centers with branded operations (uniformed drivers and brown vehicles) while UPS partners cover much of the continent.

UPS also has a Middle Eastern presence. The company, in joint ventures with existing delivery services, offers import and export delivery, though not domestic service, to Bahrain, Israel, Jordan, Kuwait, Lebanon, Oman, Qatar, Saudi Arabia, Syria, the United Arab Emirates, and Yemen. To better inform and serve Middle East customers, in 2006 UPS created the company's first-ever Web site in Arabic.

Today, in more than two hundred countries, all of UPS global transportation services combined, which include UPS Supply Chain Services (featured in the next chapter), can reach over four billion people, or about double the portion of the world's population that can be reached by any telephone network. UPS's international segment's 2005 revenue was $6 billion, an increase of 17.2 percent over the year before. It represented 19 percent of the company's revenue. That penciled out as 24 percent of the company's 2005 operating profit. It's an enormous, multilingual version of UPS's earlier nationwide strategy, not "Golden Link" but "Global Link." Don't divide and conquer; consolidate and conquer.

These days, 58,800 UPSers staff locations beyond the U.S. borders, delivering more than 1.5 million packages and documents each day. Whatever happened to those blustering UPS execs who had big ideas about the delivery business but no idea how to hold chopsticks? The company has sloughed the "we know what's best for you" approach to become customer driven. Rather than ship American-born UPSers to China, as an example, UPS uses a new international staffing system that could just as easily be modeled after a benign but fast-moving virus. Today UPS identifies and courts Chinese nationals who are earning their MBAs in the United States. Big Brown teaches them "The UPS Way," often giving them stints at management positions somewhere within the fifty states where they'll learn by doing. Thoroughly indoctrinated, these bilingual professionals can then function as vectors. They can carry the essence of UPS back to Asia and spread it around like a contagion, but using the methods and manners that best suit their own culture.

As a result, fewer than fifty of UPS's international employees are U.S. expatriates—that's less than one-tenth of a percent.

Today, UPS's man in charge of international, Dave Abney, has a map in his office with the southern hemisphere on top. He explained its orientation in an article in *Hemispheres* magazine thus: "People often ask why I have a map configured in that way. I tell them it's to remind me, and anyone who comes into my office, that although the U.S. is one of the world's largest economies and countries, there's a big world out there that doesn't revolve around the U.S. We haven't always felt that way at UPS, but changing our view of the world became one of the secrets of our success."

The view is changed, the lens broader, the methodologies cosmopolitan. Looking at the globe upside down, Abney sees India, Africa, Latin America, even Antarctica. It's a perspective that puts undeveloped nations on top.

Forecasts now indicate that, after China, the huge and heavily populated subcontinent of India is today's plum, anticipated to see the most economic growth. Presently, India receives packages from other inter-Asian hubs and UPS has more than twenty strategically placed delivery centers in India, where the majority of foreign investment occurs.

UPS operates in India through a master license agreement between wholly owned subsidiary Mail Boxes Etc. (The UPS Store) and Jet Air Business Solutions Pvt. Ltd., an India-based service provider.

The UPS Store hung out its first shingle in Bhikaji Cama Place in New Delhi in July 2006. Shortly after that, the company announced it will open 150 new full-service outlets badged as The UPS Store over the next three to five years.

What to do next? UPS has targeted India for future expansion. India has dug in its heels during WTO talks to protect its subsistence farmers from the negative effects of U.S. and European Union farm subsidies and its small industries from obstacles to exportation brought about by rich-country industrial tariffs. You can bet that UPS will be doing everything it can to relieve India's apprehensions.

But in true UPS fashion, *it's not just what you do; it's how you do it.* In March 2006, *Fortune* magazine rated UPS as the "Global Most Admired" company in its industry, far ahead of American, European, and Japanese competitors. UPS was also ranked in the Top Ten among all the companies of the world in eight of the nine categories used to judge corporate reputation. Only four companies out of hundreds surveyed from *any* industry matched or exceeded the 8.38 composite score awarded UPS.

In three decades, UPS has come a long way in its role on the global stage, from a bumbling bit player tripping on the lights to a star bowing to accolades. However, there are still other roles yet unfilled, and, as UPS's unrelenting visionary Jim Casey said way back in 1954, "Our horizon is as distant as our mind's eye wishes it to be."

11

A LEADER IN LOGISTICS

Did Jim Casey turn over in his grave on July 21, 1999? On that day the founder's employee-held company filed a registration statement with the Securities and Exchange Commission (SEC) to do something it hadn't considered since the Curtiss-Wright debacle seventy years before: *sell shares to non-UPSers*. UPS announced it would make an initial public offering (IPO) of 10 percent of its shares by the end of the year.

News of the filing left investors slavering for a piece of one of the most stable, lucrative, and promising businesses in the world. A package-hoisting Atlas in an industry of mere mortals, UPS enjoyed revenues that had swelled an average of 6 percent a year for the past six years. The company generated $24.8 billion in revenues in 1998. Its net earnings increased from $909 million in 1997 to $1.7 billion in 1998.

Plus the shipping giant had its eye on the future. The approaching end of the millennium had marked the beginning of point-and-click online ordering. Brandishing its new "Moving at the Speed of Business" slogan, UPS was already the industry leader in shipping e-commerce. It had the infrastructure and methodologies to deliver electronic commerce solutions to businesses. Its accounts included six of the top ten Internet retailers, including Amazon.com. During the 1998–99 holiday season, UPS delivered over half of all online purchases.

Then there was the matter of employee-ownership. To investors this spelled accountability. Most privately held companies have single owners or small groups of owners (often members of the same family), but by late 1999, over 123,000 people, almost all of them employees, retirees, and family members, owned stock. According to New York banker Harold Tanner, who helped guide UPS through its IPO, "When 50 percent to 100 percent of your net worth is UPS, you really do live and breathe brown." Company employees typically held onto the stock they acquired, which helped increase the reliability of company performance.

The Decision to Go Public

Why would UPS go public? Business was better than good and the company had hardly any debt. The stock price had risen 38 percent in the year prior! Attracted by sky-high valuations of the late nineties, UPS made the decision to sell, perhaps unaware that a lot of the upside that had buoyed so many companies was about to stall. The announced reason was similar to every other bold move the company had ever made—*to stay competitive in a changing world*. It had to be able to offer more negotiable and flexible terms.

An underlying reason not shared with the public was pressure from lawsuits filed by several top-level retirees who claimed that the company had purposely kept the stock price low just when they wanted to cash out. Whether the claims had merit or not, changing to a public company would avoid that type of second-guessing. The conservative company had historically kept its shares underpriced and most shareholders were aware of that. It seems obvious the decision was made to go public well in advance as the Board of Directors began ratcheting the price up all year before the IPO, accounting for the 38 percent increase.

In time, the reasons for possible expansion seemed to loom important. When UPS Chairman and CEO Jim Kelly spoke about the IPO with journalists, he talked about looking to stay ahead and about maintaining UPS leadership in the areas where the company conducted business. Going public would provide additional financial flexibility to pursue strategic alliances and acquisitions. Those acquisitions would contribute to UPS's core business—delivery—

as well as e-commerce business and logistics. It would also help UPS improve service to customers.

UPS was dispersing brown package cars throughout the world at a rapid-fire pace, and that crown jewel—Asia—was within reach, but expensive. A good portion of the expansion wasn't territorial, however, but methodological. Globalization made costly demands— political lobbying, attorneys, customs brokering, tracking technology, delivery technology, aircraft.

Big ideas need capital. A private company has more limited access to external financing, both for debt and equity, than a publicly traded company. Remember that the investment banker in Seattle had turned the UPS founders down back in 1918? As "determined men," they'd had to come up with ingenious alternatives for financing expansion. In 1999, a new generation of UPS strategists made the decision to raise capital by issuing shares of equity to financial markets, but with restraint.

The company wasn't about to make the same mistake as in 1929. It wasn't going to lose control or sell off employee-owned shares. It was only offering 10 percent of its stock, and that 10 percent carried one-tenth the voting rights. UPS announced the intention to create two classes of shares. Class A shares (90 percent of the total), with ten votes per share, would be held by the existing owners of UPS. And Class B shares (10 percent of total outstanding shares), having only one vote per share, would be offered to the public. The Board of Directors approved that plan, and so did the employee-shareholders.

With the customer-first rationale and the majority of the stock still employee-held, Jim Casey might have rested easy in his grave . . . only he wouldn't have wanted to miss what happened next.

The Initial Public Offering

On November 9, 1999, Atlanta-based United Parcel Service of America made financial history when it made what was then the largest U.S. IPO in history—$5.47 billion worth at $50 a share.

Immediately prior to the opening, the stock had split two for one, creating a total 1.1 billion shares. The stock was $3 higher than its previous valuation due to the strong demand from institutional investors.

Many thousands of people immediately made a lot of money, and not just the UPS employees and retirees. James Runde, then a vice-chairman at Morgan Stanley Dean Witter, had made a cold call in 1996 that resulted in his company leading UPS's IPO as an underwriter, that is, lead investment banker. Morgan Stanley put together a syndicate that included Goldman Sachs and Merrill Lynch as senior co-managers. Other co-managers included Credit Suisse, Salomon Smith Barney, and Warburg Dillon Read. The delivery giant quickly sold 109.4 million shares, or 10 percent of its outstanding stock, to the public, infusing the company with more than $5 billion in cash. An overallotment for underwriters pushed the total offering to 120.3 million shares, or $6.015 billion. Called a "Green Shoe," this standard practice provided support for the share price after the offering because Morgan Stanley had to buy back these shares in the open market to replace the short position created by selling more shares than the 109 million UPS offered. The overall underwriter commission was $191,450,000.

The offering was typical of the dot-com decade. Fast and furious, the stock price jumped to $70.1325 from the offering price of $50 a share. At the end of the trading day, UPS shares were trading at $67.25. Based upon this price and the total number of shares outstanding, the market value of UPS was assessed at $80.9 billion.

UPS CEO Jim Kelly saw his own UPS own stock holdings soar to $28.2 million after the offer, and the 123,000 UPS employees and retiree shareholders were jubilant as their stock value went sky high. The year ended with the stock at $69.

People were expecting one or two momentous announcements to follow, but the effects of the remainder of the offering were more subtle. Jim Kelly's announcements about the IPO were hard to interpret: "As a public enterprise, UPS will leverage our financial strength to expand our international business and pursue new opportunities in the movement of goods, information and funds. These opportunities come with the promise of complementing and growing our core package delivery business."

That's what Kelly was saying, but the company also pursued other tacks. As a publicly traded company, UPS now had an additional means of leveraging share value, beyond providing more services. Share buybacks would serve several purposes, the most important being to prevent the dilution of shares of existing shareholders. UPS could effect a balance by covering what was going out. Buying back shares could also make the earnings per share look higher. Six billion dollars was a lot of money, and helped the solvent company actually realize year-end total assets of over $11 billion, up from $5 billion the year before.

In early 2000, the company announced that it would use the majority of its IPO proceeds for a one-time tender offer for Class A shares. It offered to purchase over 100 million Class A shares at $60 per share. The actual number of shares purchased was 68,312,335, which cost the company $4.099 billion. That reduced the number of outstanding Class A shares significantly, with several benefits. It ensured enough shares for future UPS employee programs. Having fewer shares available would also keep the per-share price up. UPS had an expanding share value and expanding footprint. Worldwide, it had accounts with more than 1.6 million corporate customers who got scheduled pickups on a daily basis. Differences brought about by globalization, electronics, and competition had given UPS a broader goal: To become a full-service vendor, offering a wide range of services to manage the flow of information, goods, and funds business to business, retailer to customer, and household to household.

Package Flow

How, then, to press forward to provide easier, faster delivery service globally in a new millennium propelled by electronics? Tracking and moving all these packages (3.28 billion in 1999 alone) was an

IT department's Mount Everest. When Jim Casey defined service as "the sum of many little things done well," he never imagined that the little things would be found within microchips. Yet UPS had invested more than $10 billion in information technology over the five years prior to the IPO and wasn't finished yet.

At the time of this writing, David Barnes is UPS's chief information officer. With a budget of $1 billion a year, he manages 4,700 employees who develop much of the company's software, watch over an Internet site that draws close to 19 million visitors a day, maintain 8,700 servers, and monitor fifteen mainframes capable of processing millions of instructions per second. Barnes's job—just like all the others at UPS—is to exact more efficiency from an already efficient operation that moves an average of 15 million packages a day across the world.

On Barnes's watch, UPS is pushing automation to the summit with "package flow technology." Computerization determines the order in which packages are loaded on a truck and the most efficient route for delivering them, and it makes tracking packages directly available to customers and UPSers. Being phased in companywide, UPS's new $600 million package flow initiative will be fully deployed across the company's 70,000 routes by the end of 2007. UPS expects the system to pay for itself within a year, with $600 million in cost savings.

The flow begins when the customer generates a digital "smart label" on the UPS Web site, or with help from clerks at a UPS shipping outlet, such as The UPS Store. That request transmits customer and package information to a central processing unit, where it is linked with several other systems—including GPS to pinpoint its exact position. The moment that label is generated—say for 123 Main Street, Portland, Oregon—the center that delivers that address is notified when it will arrive. The label, of course, is printed and affixed to the parcel. The parcel is loaded into a feeder (a big rig that transports packages) at the nearest UPS package center, taken to a nearby hub for sorting, and sent on its way.

Information on shipments for every UPS package is stored in databases at a facility in Mahwah, New Jersey, then backed up by a second data center outside Atlanta. Besides allowing UPS to track packages, the databases allow for rerouting as necessary. With enterprise-wide access to the data, each of the 1,100 U.S. delivery centers knows what's coming in, from several days out to the Next Day Air deliveries. At the package center, a scanner validates the smart label and then issues another label, dubbed a Preload Assist Label (PAL), so loaders know how to route the package. The Preload Assist System (PAS) tells the loader where that package should be placed in the package car, in stop-by-stop order. This makes the preloader's job a slam-dunk. (Preloaders are generally part-timers, and the positions have relatively high turnover.) The PAS reduces preloader training from a thirty-day marathon of chart memorizing to a few hours of learning to place the packages in the vehicles. The reduced training time alone should help the PAS pay for itself immediately.

Now, instead of a driver arriving at the center and scanning all the packages in the delivery vehicle and planning the day's route, all that information has already been transmitted to a wireless handheld computer, the Delivery Information Acquisition Device or DIAD. This device is now in its smaller, lighter fourth generation, formally known as the "DIAD IV." (Drivers traded in their coffee smudged, rain-splattered legal pads for the first version of this electronic delivery recorder-transmitter in 1991.) The new DIAD IV system designs delivery routes built from this "inbound package knowledge."

The Enhanced DIAD Download (EDD) system knows exactly what is loaded in each vehicle and will remind drivers if they're forgetting a package or are about to misdeliver one. Say at a large bulk stop, like Wal-Mart or Kmart, the driver unloads eighty-one packages and prepares to get a signature. But the computer says there are eighty-two packages. The driver will be able to retrieve and deliver the missing package rather than backtracking later in the day. The computer will also remind the driver by sounding an alert if the package car stops at the wrong address. It might say "You're on 123 State Street, and the package is for 123 Main Street. Do you still want to make this delivery?" The EDD's GPS system is that precise! The driver can override and say yes, if necessary. EDD also gives UPS dispatchers specific driver location information so they can select the most convenient driver to send for an on-call pickup.

Today's DIAD IV instantly records deliveries and captures signatures, confirming receipt of packages immediately. It can also display critical information about deliveries nationwide, in a specific geographic area, or even to an individual recipient.

At the time of the IPO, UPS already dominated the large business-to-business e-commerce market. It had only to refine the software to capture a large percentage of business-to-household e-commerce. UPS used a chunk of its cash to develop an information network supported by formidable electronics technology, which includes real-time Internet tools—*UPS Online*—to help customers track their goods. Today, information—primarily input from the 96,000 DIAD IVs in use every day—is available to all. Almost 19 million people check out the www.ups.com (online since the mid-nineties) Web site each day, making an average of 10 million tracking requests.

Not only has customer service dramatically improved, but the cost per tracking request has dropped from the $2 it was in 1994 to less than 10 cents. UPS uses its technological advantages and its integrated network of air and ground transport (helped out by machinery that sorts more than 350,000 packages per hour) to keep pace with the home delivery boom created by the Internet and with business-to-business commerce.

Logistics

Thanks to electronics, commerce and tracking could be virtual, but delivery must remain actual. Electronics also had capabilities that could greatly enhance transportation, as UPS was being reminded by competitors FedEx and Roadway Packaging System (later purchased by FedEx) during the 1990s.

UPS had always been operations-oriented, but globalization and competition forced the company to become market-driven. Kent "Oz" Nelson, CEO 1989–1997, came from the company's business development and engineering sectors. Keeping in mind the forward-thinking UPS founder Jim Casey, Nelson and his team had begun steering the mammoth shipping firm into as yet uncharted territory—*logistics*. With that act, the company's focus shifted. In 1995, UPS turned its Roadnet Division into the UPS Logistics Group to help fulfill the needs of individual customers. In 1999 the Logistics Group became UPS Logistics Technologies.

UPS essentially packaged itself, wrapped up what it already did so well—thanks to its armies of efficiency experts—and started selling logistics services to businesses. Electronics gave UPS industrial engineers the tools to reassess and redefine their role and function. So, in addition to auditing, doing time measurements, motion studies, and reports designed for an *internal* audience, the department's efforts could also be reengineered for the customer: looking at customer logistics, customer volume development, and customer satisfaction.

UPS Logistics Technologies takes the kinks out of transportation for businesses like Frito-Lay, Costco, and SYSCO. Its transportation and logistics software—called ROADNET—supports route optimization, territory planning, mobile delivery execution, real-time wireless dispatch and scheduling, and GPS tracking. Other products include daily and territorial route planners, delivery trackers, and loading tools. UPS Logistics Technologies offers significant reduction in transportation, distribution, and inventory costs, as well as predictable and expeditious delivery times.

And we're not just talking parcels. Soon after the IPO, the Ford Motor Company came to UPS asking for help in getting its cars from assembly plants to the showrooms of America. UPS Logistics signed a deal with Ford to optimize the transportation of Ford vehicles from factory to dealer. UPS redesigned everything, the entire delivery network, and even pasted bar codes on windshields. The end result was not only better tracking of each vehicle, but shaving a whopping 40 percent off the time in transit. That added up to big dollars.

Even the Harley-Davidson Motor Company, an American motorcycle manufacturer since 1903, sought the aid of UPS. The company had logistical challenges, primarily inbound transportation and getting parts and accessories to dealerships. Consultation revealed that hundreds of suppliers were shipping components to one of the company's three factories in different states. Then components were stockpiled and consolidated for delivery. UPS helped Harley-Davidson optimize its entire transportation operation by having everything sent to one UPS cross-docking facility and shipped out immediately.

More recently, in mid-2006 European giant Royal Philips Electronics hired UPS to redesign service parts logistics for its medical systems. As a result, customers don't have to wait a day; they get same-day parts replacements for critical medical devices.

Rather than occupying the last rung in the transportation cycle, through UPS Logistics Technologies, UPS now takes care of an earlier phase in the process. That still leaves shipping and keeping track of shipments. And that's where "supply-chain management" comes in. UPS Logistics Technologies is part of UPS Supply Chain Solutions, a business segment of the delivery giant—which is no longer your father's UPS.

Supply Chain Management— Enabling World Commerce

UPS's expanding new world, beyond China, beyond India, beyond any physical location on the Earth, and beyond computer bits and gigs, is *supply-chain management*. This three-word combination means *making multi-phase businesses more efficient and less costly, with as few unnecessary steps as possible*. Sure, UPS has done this since day one with its scampering messenger boys. What has changed since 1907 is, well, practically everything.

By the mid-1990s, many businesses were already outsourcing or offshoring much if not all of their manufacturing to operations in other cities and other countries. If someone in England could get a book delivered to San Clemente, California, faster than another bookstore in Los Angeles, the order went out to the British store. If sweatshops in Manila could make a T-shirt faster than a manufacturer in Philadelphia, the order went out to the Philippines. Physical proximity was no longer an important factor in the supplier-customer equation.

This trend created global supply chains. Outsourcing was cost-effective but presented a rat's nest of challenges for businesses, coupled with the unpredictability inevitable with anything that is out of sight and foreign. Trying to keep track of multisource manufacturing and shipping, foreign currencies, customs duties, and wide distribution can be like trying to juggle a bunch of spinning plates. That's where supply-chain management and solutions kick in.

Think of mountains of cardboard boxes. At suppliers' warehouses, waiting to ship. In customs, waiting to be processed. In airplanes, on ships, on trains headed between warehouses. Perishables stored in containers too long. Or delayed, lost, misrouted, unavailable, while manufacturing waits, while vendors wait. Delivery delays make a big difference. In a competitive marketplace it can be a make-or-break difference.

If cardboard boxes could talk—and UPS labeling technology helps them do so—they would've been saying, "Hey, there's a lot of unnecessary shuffling going on here! Why am I spending so much time in stacks and on shelves? Why am I going from here to there to here, when here to here is so much faster?"

Better supply-chain management and solutions are the answer. As mentioned, the transformation from an operations-oriented company to a market-driven one had already begun. The company decided to position itself at the head of the rapidly growing world commerce by establishing UPS Supply Chain Solutions (SCS). In 1996, UPS SCS went into the business of *synchronizing commerce*.

To support SCS, UPS was strategically buying companies in the late 1990s, and even creating them if they did not exist. Under CEO Oz Nelson and then Jim Kelly, the enterprise was determined to grow in uncharted territory by managing the movement of goods, the accompanying flow of information, and even providing the financing if necessary. UPS Supply Chain Solutions assists customers with logistics, global freight, mail services, consulting, and financial services. The new mantra at UPS would be the heady and ambitious catchphrase "Enable World Commerce."

The world shrank, most noticeably for information, but for goods and services as well. Demanding consumers were no longer willing to wait for "backorders" to materialize, especially when a competitor can, and will, deliver the same commodity within days. Each company's entire supply chain now competes with the competition's supply chain. The UPS Supply Chain Solutions is a plethora of services that, either singly or collectively, helps companies beat their competitors to market.

UPS SERVICES

UPS Airlines	UPS Exchange Collect
UPS SonicAir Service	The UPS Store/Mail Boxes Etc.
UPS Worldwide Express	UPS Customhouse Brokerage
UPS Worldwide Express Plus	UPS Cargo
UPS Worldwide Expedited	UPS Capital
UPS Standard Service	UPS Consulting
UPS Imports	UPS Freight
UPS Worldease	UPS Logistics Technologies
UPS TradeAbility	UPS Supply Chain Services
UPS Trade Direct	UPS Mail Innovations

Let's look at an example. Nikon, the world leader in precision optics, wanted to help retailers meet customer demand for the new, high-tech digital cameras. It called on UPS Supply Chain Solutions to help streamline the distribution process. UPS coordinated Nikon's manufacturing centers in Japan, Indonesia, and Korea with air and ocean freight and customs brokerage. It designed everything to go to Louisville, Kentucky, where Nikon-related tasks joined those of hundreds of other companies at UPS Supply Chain Solutions Logistics Center. There UPS employees prepare Nikon kits, adding accessories like batteries and chargers, then repackage them and send them on their way to thousands of retailers throughout the United States, Latin America, and the Caribbean. UPS SCS participation significantly shortened Nikon's supply chain, increased the speed of product to market, and created a higher level of service to the retailers.

At the time of the IPO in 1999, UPS had been marketing its supply chain management systems to corporate customers for three years. SCS was all about reducing inventories, optimizing just-in-time manufacturing processes, and getting those antsy cardboard boxes to quiet down and hustle along. Say you have customers in Massachusetts whose products are manufactured in China. After these products are manufactured, they need to be distributed, but maybe sending them back to Massachusetts is an unnecessary middle step. That is where "integrated delivery" comes in. Supply-chain management helps businesses by eliminating unnecessary shipping steps.

UPS ramped up for this new kind of expansion, which in a broad sense was a matter of the commercialization of micromanaging. Remember, we're talking about an outfit that tells drivers which hand should hold the keys! It wasn't for nothing that the company had paid industrial engineers and efficiency experts millions of dollars over the decades. Before 1999, UPS already had the insights and the will to create a supply-chain revolution. It only needed the means.

In 2001, the newly appointed CEO, Mike Eskew, remarked,

> Our strategy is focused on complementing and growing our core package delivery business with new, innovative supply-chain solutions.

We'll accomplish that by inserting our unmatched capabilities in managing the flow of goods, information and funds across our customers' supply chains. Over the past year, our strategy has been manifested by the launch or acquisition of new logistics, freight forwarding, customs brokerage, financial services, mail, and consulting businesses that expand the scope and power of our distribution and supply chain solutions.

The synchronized commerce that has resulted since 2001 is precise and unified across the supply chain so that goods, information, and funds move quickly and efficiently, keeping the wheels of commerce turning. The company continued to broaden its reach and added freight transportation like Overnite Freight (now called UPS Freight) to its growing services.

As an "integrated carrier," the new UPS offers shipping products and services to streamline the distribution process. Take Timex. Timex began in Waterbury, Connecticut, in the nineteenth century, and that's where its headquarters still are. Yet 7,500 Timex employees—in Connecticut and Arkansas, as well as Brazil, France, Germany, the People's Republic of China, Israel, India, and the Philippines—contribute to the end product. This means shipping goods between one continent and another. The various components converge in Cebu, Philippines, where 80 percent of the watches are assembled. There, Timex's Global Distribution Center daily distributes 170,000 watches, shelf-ready with pricing and security measures already in place, not to Waterbury, but to their retail customers.

Who helps Timex "be there now"? UPS. Steve Garrett, vice president of global supply chain and logistics for Timex, says, "We are jointly working on a trade direct air model for small package delivery that will allow Timex to complete U.S. retail store door deliveries from a ship point over 8,000 miles away."

Timex is gigantic. What about smaller manufacturing operations? A *World Trade* magazine article told how UPS was helping Neil Pryde Sails, another Connecticut-based business, which designs and sells approximately 4,000 boat sails a year. Neil Pryde designs in Connecticut, manufactures in Shenzhen, China, and ships finished sails to customers around the globe, customers who want their sails "yesterday."

Neil Pryde Sails uses UPS OnLine WorldShip software. The time-saving database provides automated shipping forms for tracking and tracing. UPS Worldwide Express guarantees the pickup, drop-off, and in-transit times for all Neil Pryde Sails shipments from Hong Kong, and ensures door-to-door deliveries internationally. UPS Customhouse Brokerage makes sure that products clear customs quickly and reduces duties by billing all customers in their local currency. UPS Imports allows the company easy-to-follow billing in U.S. dollars. So much shipping can be handled online that Neil Pryde Sails no longer needs to warehouse products, because UPS is providing what it refers to as a "warehouse in motion."

UPS has become a multitasker *par excellence*. Now UPS not only sorts and delivers business clients' products, it may, through UPS Supply Chain Solutions, help assemble, repair, and store them. UPS employees can be found servicing broken computers, mixing pet food, quality checking sports footwear, troubleshooting and repairing cameras, gathering and consolidating motorcycle components, and even custom-dressing teddy bears for shipment . . . all as services to other businesses. Businesses then achieve a better turnaround time and better customer service. UPS can even interact with businesses' customers in place of the businesses' own staffs.

Sometimes supply-chain solutions eliminate extra transportation steps. UPS has minimized the transport in the repair industry. Say your Toshiba laptop goes on the fritz. You call Toshiba's 1-800 number. Either you take it to The UPS Store or your UPS driver shows up at your door to whisk away the laptop, padded box in hand. The box flies to the Louisville hub and from there, not to Japan, but two miles down the road to another UPS building where UPS employees—not Toshiba employees—fix it.

Yup, it's UPS people who are doing the actual repairing. Specially trained and certified by Toshiba, UPSers clad in powder blue factory smocks are a far cry from the men in brown shorts hustling packages to your door. Within three days, your Toshiba is back at your house in tiptop shape. When it turned to UPS Supply Chain Solutions, Toshiba saw its customer complaints instantly drop.

Toshiba is but one of several hundred companies that enjoy the benefits of UPS service centers positioned just outside the Louisville International Airport in Kentucky, the site of Worldport, the main UPS Air hub. UPS has become such a presence in Kentucky's largest city that Louisville has the largest concentration of UPS employees anywhere—more than 20,000 UPSers, with another 5,000 planned in imminent expansions. (Of these, approximately 7,500 work not at SCS but at Worldport.)

Two more happy consequences of UPS Supply Chain Solutions: less fuel expended, more American workers at work. Interestingly, in this era of outsourcing, UPS is *insourcing* by staffing logistics services with Americans in the United States. This multitasking isn't just in Louisville. UPS operates supply chains for companies of every size in 186 countries and territories, with about 35 million square feet of distribution space and over 1,000 facilities worldwide.

Nike, the original footwear icon, has UPS providing a lot of bounce. Nike's products are synchronized to be delivered directly from Asian factories to UPS Kentucky facilities. They don't go to a Nike warehouse; they stay with Big Brown. Orders from Nike are dispatched directly to UPS throughout the day. UPS personnel fill the orders, check the orders, package the orders, and send them to the nearby Louisville airport. UPS brown-tails "swoosh" them off to their destinations. Not only is the turnaround time drastically shortened, Nike can focus on what it does best—design and market shoes.

The goal is to make it as easy for a business to ship across the world as it is for an individual to send a gift across the state. Larry Darrow, UPS vice president for international business, was quoted in *World Trade* as saying, "We have developed international services that are time-definite, small package express or a combination of both. Our subsidiaries can provide brokerage service, warehousing, even pick, pack and ship so that shippers don't have to have a presence in all the countries where they're doing business, although the perception would be that they are a local player."

If you have that special something—say 750 metric tons of Beaujolais that you want to move from France to Japan or the hundreds of fresh lobsters author John McPhee tracked in his book *Uncommon Carriers*—UPS's supply-chain managers can help you.

And what about a grandmother wanting to send her favorite grandchild a care package of goodies? To keep the household-to-household business, UPS toyed with a network of UPS Pack and Ship stores across the country, but instead it finally joined forces with Mail Boxes Etc. in 2001, buying the parent company out from the brink of bankruptcy, for $191 million cash. In 2003, Mail Boxes Etc. franchises began rebranding as The UPS Store, although 278 franchises (of the 4,409 in the United States) decided to keep the Mail Boxes Etc. name. There are presently more than 5,600 franchises in forty countries around the world.

Customers can access UPS from home too. When you order merchandise online, it triggers a supply-chain algorithm that may click several times across the globe. In a likely scenario, the item you ordered from a U.S. company is sourced from a Chinese warehouse, routed to the Hong Kong hub, and voilà!—three business days later the UPS driver stands at your door, merchandise in hand. And when The UPS Store processes that box you just left there, the hubs and destination center "feel" its presence electronically, triggering seamless physical actions that further it along its journey.

To recap this mind-blowing global enterprise, UPS has built a comprehensive electronic network and has applied this to its massive international transportation network, facilitated by what may be the largest technological infrastructure in commercial history. This incredible infrastructure, plus the global staff that supports it, constitutes UPS's innovative supply-chain and logistics services.

Domestic and international delivery are still the largest segments of UPS's current business, but its Supply Chain Solutions segment is the fastest-growing, and, together with UPS Freight, reflects 14 percent of the company's revenue, or approximately $6 billion a year. Over the past decade, UPS has undergone a radical transformation, from its long-hallowed "Tightest ship in the shipping business," and "What can Brown do for you?" to the forward-thinking twenty-first-century mantra "Enabling global commerce."

12

THE LEGACY OF JIM CASEY

Jim Casey would be bowled over by the scope of what UPS has become. Anyone would. UPS vehicles are more common than buses. The company is edging toward a half a million employees. It's racking up $4 billion profit a year. It delivers almost 15 million packages every day, serving 7.9 million regular customers.

Still, there probably isn't a UPS package center, hub, or logistics center in the world that doesn't reflect the spirit of Jim Casey. Even in Montevideo, Uruguay, even in Yantai, China, UPS's self-effacing founder would be fascinated and thrilled. He would find much to learn and much to teach.

Remember how Jim Casey delighted over the tactile aspect of packages being wrapped in department stores? He cried out, "Deft fingers! Deft fingers wrapping thousands of bundles. Neatly tied! Neatly addressed! Stuffed with soft tissue paper! What a treat!" His beguiling exclamation, "Ah, packages!" became the title of the *New Yorker*'s 1947 feature story on him.

How about today's young UPSers (many of whom are working their way through college), their fingers flying over keyboards as they track and move packages? Talk about deft! Or UPSer hands assembling and repairing customer goods, more effectively and less expensively than manufacturers can do it themselves. Casey would be ecstatic.

The scale of goods UPS moves between continents is many, many times the volume that moved off the Seattle wharves in 1907. Yet that cargo is what inspired Jim Casey to urge his company on. He would be boggled but thrilled over the *tons* UPS now moves daily.

Picture that eager little man at Worldport, in Louisville. The new Worldport, with its nearly two hundred miles of package super-highways, would be Casey's kind of heaven.

Meanwhile, what of the personal values of Jim Casey and his partners, which became those of the company? That the founders' legacy has endured is a tribute to how ingrained it is. Some of these principles are just as strong as ever—promotion from within, poli-cies that emphasize care for people, good grooming, hard work, service, and safety to name a few. (The company even received *Workforce Management* magazine's 2005 Optimus Award for its com-prehensive safety program, which has reduced workplace accidents 62 percent since 1996.) Yet some of the culture and ideals that have survived the better part of a century are being challenged on several fronts as UPS reaches its one-hundred-year mark.

Humility in the Twenty-First Century

Casey used to say, "I'm just the president. The boys operate the busi-ness. I'm just a spoke in the wheel." He might have seen himself that way then, but his enduring legacy proves that he was actually more like the compass. The culture Casey and his associates created functions as a touchstone, a test through which to vet new objec-tives and solutions.

His closely guarded nature hid news of the company's moves and countermoves while he was at the helm. The brown UPS pack-age cars were the company's only advertising. An occasional news-paper article was the only publicity. Contrast that approach with the thousands of UPSers whose job it now is to promote Big Brown.

The unassuming founder might have found their buzz-making efforts anathema, even though he would have applauded their knack for getting media attention. Just two days ago, as I was writing this book, UPS was featured in the *Wall Street Journal, USA Today, US News & World Report,* a flotilla of smaller publications, and all over the Internet. All that publicity on view the same week! Even if broadcasting UPS's business would seem less than humble to Casey, and the mass distribution of facts and figures highly unwise, the *industriousness* that led to these feature stories is vintage Jim.

The media minions are a necessary outgrowth, a response to stiff competition and a now-public company. Customers need to hear what UPS does better than FedEx, better than DHL, better than the U.S. Postal Service. Investors need to have confidence that UPS will keep doing it. Potential new markets need to hear the singing of UPS praises so that they too will welcome Big Brown across their borders. It's all good news, all the time. Otherwise investors, employees, retirees, and the company lose money when the stock value dips . . . dips not because UPS isn't outstanding, but perhaps because of a compression of the Price/Earnings ratio, or because of possible negative interpretations from financial analysts.

Yet, despite the P.R., despite the articles, despite UPS's much increased advertising budget, despite the company's presence on the NASCAR circuit, despite the 19 million hits on www.ups.com daily, UPS still isn't flashy. Big Brown, though ubiquitous, still *feels* "under the radar." The thousands of package cars, the tractor trailers, and the brown-tailed jets aren't head-turners. They're not painted with attention-getting advertising or splashy prints.

And the drivers—as quickly and modestly as the drivers arrive, the drivers depart. They're not too stylish. They don't put on airs. They're *utilitarian*. Jim Casey would be proud. Inconspicuous, sedulous, the company serves the engine of commerce by keeping people and goods connected. The world over, UPS just keeps on truckin'.

Spreading the Wealth

UPS has been successful largely because dedicated people have made it so. Unfortunately, those same dedicated people have caused the company's biggest mistakes over its first hundred years. Smugness derived from success sometimes blinded UPSers, leading to costly errors: ignoring FedEx, forgetting cultural differences abroad, underestimating a Teamsters leader, and more recently, ignoring proper protocol in addressing Wall Street analysts.

When Jim Casey passed away in 1983, the *Los Angeles Times* reported, "Casey is credited with developing efficient package handling equipment and starting one of the first profit-sharing programs by an American business." Casey took great pride in that profit-sharing, in employee ownership. He saw partnership as the heart of the company. When, in 1929, the merger deprived UPSers of their stock, he labored inexorably to get it back.

For years, shareholders talked about how much more the stock would be worth if they went public. This was mostly fanciful speculation. UPSers were stunned when it actually happened.

Jim Kelly, who led the IPO in 1999, reflects, "We agonized about whether we could go public and maintain our corporate culture. If we couldn't reconcile the two, we wouldn't have done it." UPS feels that it honored Jim Casey's commitment to individuals and to customers. But did it?

Casey probably would have commended the stated purpose of the IPO—that of vastly increased flexibility for future purchases and expansion. After all, he learned creative financing and flexibility early on and knew you had to be ready to take advantage of a situation. With the IPO, the stage was set. Purchasing and acquisition options were widely increased, and remain so.

Would Casey have approved of the safeguards, the 10 percent Class B shares with their diminished voting rights? Would he have celebrated UPS's ability to offer such valuable stock, not just to UPSers but to the public? No one knows whether Casey would have felt that the upsides of going public were worth the downsides. While it was genius to offer limited voting shares, it seems UPS underestimated the powerful ramifications of publicly held shares, regardless of the number. Most shares were snapped up by institutional investors who did not have UPSers' intimacy with the company. And the company has had a difficult time placating them. Unfortunately, often heard in the financial community is this refrain, "UPS? Great company, but blah stock."

UPS now has the placate the public too. Outside the acknowledged voting power, will the company continue to treat all shareholders the same, offering the same dividends and value to both "A" and "B" shares? While it's important to maintain the culture and dedication of employee-shareholders, it's also important to realize that outside shareholders have faith in the company and do not want to be treated in a less than equal manner.

Casey would have boiled over the perturbations visited on his company's stock through the New York Stock Exchange. Previously, the board of directors did not allow outside speculation or daily market tics to influence the stock value. Hence they could more exactly project where the company was going, thus allowing them to ensure that the stock was priced for the long term. As mentioned, they often kept it somewhat underpriced. That's all over now.

Management doesn't determine stock value four times a year any more, as it had since 1927. Going public gave UPS stock a market valuation. The first day was great. Stock went from $46 a share before the offering to $67 right after. Then in 2000 the stock fluctuated and languished, closing the year at $58.75. It flattened further in 2002–2003, when the stock market as a whole took a beating.

Many retirees and employees, unaccustomed to seeing the stock value decline, were aghast. It was hard for us to realize that 10 percent of the shareholders, and (horrors) nonemployees yet, were, by succumbing to the whims of the market, dictating what our nest eggs were worth. Instead of complaining, though, we should have appreciated all the money we'd made up front. In November 1998, UPS stock had been valued at $20. To have it hovering around $60 in a year tripled our money. The stock has yo-yoed ever since, most of the time in the $65 –$83 range. Not a great five-year return, and it would have been much higher except there has been a continuing compression of the Price/Earnings ratio of UPS stock.

Because of an operating margin nearly three times the industry average (and 50 percent higher than FedEx's over the past five years), one would think the company deserved its higher (24-30) P/E. But the bluntness displayed by UPS executives on Wall Street resulted in the P/E dropping below 20. While profits surged forward, the stock price remained stagnant.

CEOs and CFOs adhering to age-old company refrains like "Not promising more than you can deliver" actually hurt the company's stock price several times after it went public. UPS leaders were not accustomed to sugar-coating reality in quarterly reports for the fickle denizens of Wall Street. UPS still hasn't learned financial finesse and typical UPS quarterly announcements often do not endear the company to analysts. In blunt UPS fashion, announcements come across sounding to others like, "This is how good we are. Take it or leave it."

UPS has been slow to learn that a good profit is not enough—you must meet the expectations of the analysts and convince them that you will continue to do so. Therein lies one of the company's greatest present struggles, that of pacifying Wall Street while maintaining the honesty and reliability that are the core of the corporate culture. Meanwhile, the shift from private to public company has had other negative ramifications in a kind of ripple effect.

Business building, to Casey, depended on the hard work and loyalty that the stock ownership inspired. In 1955 Jim Casey said, "The basic principle which I believe has contributed more than any other to the building of our business as it is today, is the ownership of our company by the people employed in it." The vast majority of UPSers carry that torch every day. Still, the vicissitudes of the stock market have introduced a sort of intemperance into a company that was notoriously careful. Shareholder intemperance.

After the IPO, the company made a few formula changes to its Management Incentive Plan. Based for years on the most recent quarterly price, it had to accommodate a fluctuating stock price. Also, decision makers were concerned over newer management members selling shares right away, so in 2005 they revised the plan to ensure continued management ownership. Half of the shares presented were restricted to vest over a five-year period, increasing in value each year much like a U.S. Savings Bond. A supervisor who wished to do so could sell half right away, but would pay a big penalty for selling the other half before its maturity. As numbers of shares and their values increase, young supervisors too are enjoying the ownership and partnership in a company that is their own. By vesting those shares, UPS could also spread the cost over a five-year period.

UPS still uses stock as incentive—to drive both hard work and loyalty—but the public ownership has weakened that incentive. Now, when employees or retirees transfer or sell their Class A shares, they can convert them to Class B shares if they want, although there are brokerage fees for so doing, but their flexibility for diversifying their portfolio on a moment's notice increases. And once the stock is Class B they can sell their shares to anyone, not just to the company. This means that not just investors but also employees can contribute to stock-market fluctuations by selling off shares. Without the instant gratification of constantly rising stock, new shareholders sometimes prefer to cash out. As a result, the carrot beckoning hard work and loyalty has lost a little of its appeal.

Integrity

Integrity was the number one word looked up on Merriam-Webster's online dictionary in 2005. Seems as if others are striving to learn the meaning of what has long been of prime concern at UPS. Jim Casey said in 1957, "We have become known to all who deal with us as people of integrity, and that priceless asset is more valuable than anything else we possess."

As mentioned earlier in the book, back when UPS was expanding nationwide and filing over a hundred applications for delivery rights, some wags suggested greasing a few palms to expedite matters. That it didn't happen honored the proud, proprietary feeling management had toward the company, even though it took over twenty-three years to get all the rights.

George Lamb, CEO and Chairman of the Board from 1980 to 1984, told a memorable story about integrity. He described a CEO leadership development class he'd attended at Harvard. Participants took turns talking about ethical challenges they had faced in business. The examples didn't necessarily have to involve illegality. They were looking for incidents that conflicted with their own personal values—maybe not reporting something to the SEC, a corner cut here or there, or a report that omitted embarrassing information.

When George Lamb's turn came, he had to apologize. He had racked his brain for examples of how running UPS had pushed him to the ethical edge, but he'd come up with nothing. What he could remember were the times when UPS principles, principles published in the *UPS Policy Book*, had saved him from moral lapse.

George Lamb left a lasting impression on UPS and the company's employees. His sense of integrity was without compromise. It is not surprising that after he died of cancer in 2001 his widow, two sons, and two daughters created the George C. Lamb, Jr. University Professorship at Duke University. It is intended for scholars who unite graduate business studies and ethics.

Jack Rogers, who succeeded George Lamb as CEO, was also a leader of high integrity, with a strong sense of business ethics. He once said, "None of us could be proud of our business achievements if results were obtained in anything but an 'above board' manner."

Current CEO Mike Eskew echoed the attitudes of his antecedents when he said, "We care as much about how we get results as we do about getting the results. Getting results at the cost of violations of laws or through unscrupulous dealings do more than violate our standards—they challenge our ability to grow our business and undermine our reputation."

UPS remains sensitive to business ethics and is keen to avoid any kind of breach that could lead to litigation. The rigid *UPS Policy Book*, which is reviewed regularly, and other specialized programs, publications, and classes continue to remind UPSers to do the right thing. It becomes a sort of self-governing paradigm, a religion with or without divine inspiration.

Here's an example. A few months ago three employees of Coca-Cola (based in Atlanta like UPS) presented PepsiCo with the opportunity to buy Coca-Cola's highly guarded trade secret, its beverage formula. When this incident occurred, a UPS spokesman said,

"If someone tried to sell us something from FedEx, we'd contact FedEx and contact authorities. We don't play those games."

UPS relies on its insular corporate culture to protect information around such subjects as mergers and acquisitions and technology. Information is on a "need to know" basis. Since managers typically are promoted from within and stay at the company their entire working lives, they have a vested interest in protecting the company and maintaining its high integrity.

Yet employees face many temptations to forgo integrity in the stressful, pressure-packed world of UPS. Supervisors work such long hours that many hourly employees decline to become supervisors. The company, in an attempt to control excessive hours, generated a form that identifies supervisors who work more than fifty hours a week. It's possible that list is not comprehensive. Supervisors may not report their actual hours, because they might not want to look bad, or fear reprisals. Worse are the bosses who might suspect an omission but turn a blind eye. To maintain itself as an industry leader in integrity, UPS needs to address these types of challenges.

As it is, consumers ranked UPS as the second-most-trustworthy company in the United States, with Johnson & Johnson garnering the top spot with the highest percentage of positive rankings for ethical standards in the 2005 Corporate Reputation Survey. The top two companies switched places in the same survey's results for Sincerity of Corporate Communications, with UPS number one.

Politics

To many people, the words *politics* and *integrity* just don't fit in the same sentence. Today's UPSers are expected to meld the two. Under Jim Casey, UPS was relatively nonpolitical. Politics didn't play as huge a role in business as it has in recent years, and most contact with politicians was directed toward extending delivery nationwide. The company, as you've read, also used lobbyists to prevent the U.S. Postal Service from undermining UPS growth and service. Learning from those experiences, UPS formed its Public Affairs department in the 1960s.

Among numerous activities through the years, the UPS Public Affairs department has coordinated all activities pertaining to politics and is unique in that it has a grassroots program that has been in place since 1976. Called the UPS Congressional Awareness Program, it involves having someone in each district who is responsible for cultivating a relationship with each legislator in that district, regardless of political bent. UPS representatives visit the members of both houses of Congress, invite them to address UPSers at the center, and even have them ride with drivers if they wish. And many don the required browns and do just that. In 2005, there were 226 facility visits and thirty on-car rides nationwide.

With global commerce at stake and over $35 billion dollars' worth of assets to oversee, UPS finds it very much in its own best interest to keep careful tabs on and continue to maintain good relations with the government decision makers who could so greatly affect the company's future.

Since the average single congressional campaign costs in excess of $4 million, legislators need and solicit donations from every possible quarter. Of course, donors hope to be looked on favorably by those legislators in the future.

Campaign finance laws that passed in the seventies led to the creation of political action committees (PACs), which add another source for solicitation, in addition to official corporate donations to candidates. With so many interests competing for congressional attention, Congress members tend to respond to lobbyists who most bend their ear and donors who contribute most to their ongoing profession—staying elected.

UPS's political action committee (UPSPAC) solicits soft money from employees and doles it out to selected politicians. The PAC money is different from official UPS corporate donations. Setting a good example, Mike Eskew donated $18,856 in campaign contributions from 1990 to 2005, about $1,250 a year. Eskew's example is working. According to Federal Election Commission records, UPSPAC has been the most generous contributor to federal candidates for every election since 1992, donating a total of $14 million through December 31, 2005.

UPS's contributions are bipartisan, but tilted toward the majority party and legislators who serve on committees that affect the transportation industry. In 2005, 66 percent of UPSPAC funds went to Republicans, and 34 percent went to Democrats.

Since UPS is largely employee-owned, it makes sense that the employee shareholders would want Congress on their side. During the 2004 election cycle, UPS's was the largest corporate PAC, taking in $2.8 million in donations. Written material is sent annually to each management member recommending a commensurate donation based on job responsibility. Few don't contribute. While there is a certain amount of quiet pressure, donation is not mandatory. In 1998 the Federal Election Commission (FEC), however, ruled that UPS failed to make that point clear and fined the company a token $9,000. That was the first time the FEC has levied such a penalty; UPS paid the fine and agreed to inform employees that all PAC contributions are strictly voluntary. It appears the zeal to involve everyone was at odds with "doing the right thing." My bet is that, despite the FEC's ruling, donations will continue to grow as long as the managers envision the company as their own. In 2005, over 80 percent of eligible UPSers supported UPSPAC.

UPS ranks twenty-first on the All Time Political Donor Profile, which has tracked contributions since 1989. From 1989 to 2006, UPS has given $19,721,745 to political campaigns. This is less than its biggest competitor, FedEx, which ranks fifteenth and gave $22,171,015 in the same time span.

Lobbyists are another piece of the political puzzle. Way back when, only a few dozen lobbyists for all companies worked the congressional committees and the press rooms. Every once in a while, a corporate suit would fly into Washington from headquarters to help out.

That was then. Growing federal regulation during the seventies triggered the first major increase in lobbyist numbers. The professional hound dogs worked defensively. Lobbyists, once primarily former lawyers, then appeared with diverse expertise. Their numbers include public relations specialists, engineers, accountants, and consultants of every stripe. All engage in a multitude of activities, from raising money for election campaigns to conducting and presenting studies, with the objective of influencing the course of legislation and government decision making. UPS too added sophistication and depth to its Public Affairs department.

The importance of lobbyists continues to grow. According to the *Washington Post*, the number of registered lobbyists in Washington has more than doubled since 2000 to more than 34,750, and the number of companies with registered lobbyists is up 58 percent in the same period. This makes sense when you consider that federal spending is up 39 percent—another $640 billion a year for which enterprising companies compete.

Corporations with interests that range as widely as UPS's need people in Washington to keep track of everything that's going on. This is particularly true for UPS now that its business is more than transportation-related; it takes constant effort to mitigate bad legislation and to press for advantages. This isn't just for the company. It's for its customers! The *Open Secrets' Lobbying Spending Database* reports that UPS spent $2,817,640 on lobbyists in the year 2005. The organization names nine lobbyist firms that help keep UPS priorities—by now far-reaching—in front of legislators.

Contributions, lobbyists, and especially the Congressional Awareness program staff from each UPS district keep representatives and senators aware of UPS priorities. Happily, with UPS everywhere in the United States, all states and congressional districts rely deeply upon the company and most senators and representatives are willing to help when they can. For example, after 368 of the 535 members of the House and Senate wrote in support, the Transportation Department approved the UPS request to begin deliveries to Beijing and Shanghai in 2001.

Today the UPS lobbying team, led by Public Affairs, is involved on several fronts. For one, they are working hard to have legislators create a public-private partnership to fund sorely needed railroad infrastructure improvements. As the nation's largest corporate customer of the six major North American railroads, UPS stands to lose valuable time-in-transit when railway breakdowns occur.

Another lobbying hot button for UPS is improving workers' compensation. The company spends $1.2 million *per day* on workers' compensation cases and obviously would like to see that figure trimmed, while at the same time continuing to provide the very best medical care to UPSers.

Eager to expand to the southern half of the world, which Dave Abney keeps pointing up on his desk-top globe, UPS spent $1.3 million lobbying for the Central American Free Trade Agreement and legislation that provided more highway funds in 2005.

The unregulated, untaxed U.S. Postal Service has always been a thorn in UPS's side. In 2002, the two companies working hardest to defeat postal reform legislation were UPS and FedEx, the USPS's biggest competitors and also two of the country's largest political spenders. In the form of individual, UPSPAC, and soft money contributions to candidates and parties in the 2002 election cycle, UPS distributed more than $1.3 million (FedEx distributed $1.1 million) according to figures from the Center for Responsive Politics, a Washington-based research group that tracks campaign donations.

USPS isn't the only competitor that UPS is keeping its eye on. FedEx and UPS have both for years fought the powerful Deutsche Post, Germany's monopoly mail provider, which has used every tactic it could to prevent private companies from entering or expanding in the German delivery market. To gain a presence in America, Deutsche Post bought DHL Worldwide Express in 2002, but UPS and FedEx were not placated, arguing that DHL did not meet foreign ownership requirements for U.S. air carriers.

In support of UPS and FedEx, in 2003 Senator Roy Blunt (R-Missouri) inserted into the Senate version of the wartime supplemental appropriations bill (S 762) language that could effectively bar DHL from winning Pentagon airlift contracts in postwar Iraq. The provision also called for an administrative law judge to rule on a petition by UPS and FedEx, in which they charged a subsidiary of German-owned DHL was operating illegally in the United States.

Long an advocate of the American carriers, Senator Blunt was on the receiving end of both companies' PACs. Since 1999, UPS has contributed $96,200 in cash and in-kind services to Senator Blunt while FedEx contributed $32,499.

Despite opposition from the White House and Florida (where DHL has headquarters), the measure was adopted and approved, barring DHL from military contracts. But after DHL's acquisition of Airborne Express in late November 2003, the petition was rejected; a federal administrative law judge in December 2003 ruled in favor of DHL.

The multiemployer pension fund mess addressed in Chapter Six is another area that has pressed lobbyists into overtime. UPS joined a coalition that worked hard to champion reform and made sure legislators understood just how serious the problem was. Included in the coalition with UPS were several other large other companies, numerous unions, and associations including the American Trucking Association, Motor Freight Carriers, the Newspaper Association of America, and the U.S. Chamber of Commerce.

Their collective influence worked; on July 28, 2006, Congress passed HR 4, the Pension Protection Act of 2006, by a vote of 279–131. In essence, this first major overhaul of pension laws in nearly thirty years is expected to provide important reforms and strengthen the pension system through a proposed balanced approach.

The new act allegedly will make sure that employers properly and adequately fund their worker pension plans, protect taxpayers from costly bailouts by the Pension Benefit Guarantee Corporation (PBGC), require companies to provide more information to workers about the status of their pension plans, and make commonsense modifications to defined contribution laws to encourage greater personal savings for retirement. How this will exactly affect UPS is hard to determine at this writing. But the lobbying proved an effective means of getting legislator support.

Various affected parties, the companies, the unions, the plans, and the retirees might have solved the problem differently. Everyone, however, agrees that a fix has been needed, and this act may well be the first step. Jim Casey would be furious if he thought the welfare of his employees might be threatened. That would have been his first thought and he would have battled fiercely to ensure pension continuity.

Companies have to protect their own interests, now more than ever in this competitive global economy. UPSers, reared in an atmosphere of integrity, have to balance good business sense with what outsiders might construe as unsavory political tactics. In the big scheme of things, cultivating good political partners through PACs and frequent legislator contact benefits the company, but the frequently abused political arena will continue to challenge UPS's hard-won legacy of integrity.

Respect for the Individual and Decentralization

Jim Casey believed in people. He wanted them to share in profits, but he also trusted them to do a job, gave them the latitude to do it, and respected their opinions. Top managers reflected on their experiences with Jim Casey in a company pamphlet called *Inspired Management*. One manager remarked, "I have been so impressed— as it is not the case in many other companies—with the recognition that our people are not just hired for their hands, arms or legs. When you employ a person, according to Jim, you have the entire person with all his strengths and flaws. Develop the strengths and you not only build a good employee, but you build a bigger person. He has clearly shown, by repeated emphasis, that he recognizes these same needs are in all, whatever kind of work they do." Another commented, "Jim has never ordered or driven people. Instead he gets people so inspired that they drive themselves."

The U.S. Department of Labor inducted Jim Casey into its Hall of Fame in 2002, saying, "Jim Casey, the founder of United Parcel Service, proved that employers and employees could work together to build a strong company. He showed how good management and motivated workers can contribute to the economy, compete in the global marketplace, and make a good living for everyone in the company. Jim Casey achieved the American dream."

Close connections and communications in the company have always been a paramount component of UPS's "people" orientation, and in many ways electronic technology has made this easier as it has grown ever more pervasive. Physical proximity is no longer an important factor, not for communication among UPS employees nor between UPS and customers.

Everyone can stay in touch, all the time. Everyone can know where any UPS employee is and get in touch with that employee, no matter the location. Along with vastly improved efficiency, major cost savings, and curtailed energy use, real-time support is a big upside of an omniscient "Big Brother" at the Atlanta headquarters eyeing a driver in Milliken, Colorado, or Tupelo, Mississippi. A downside for some drivers might be the disappearing independence, the loss of the ridin'-the-range autonomy of the strong-forearmed UPS driver.

The new package flow technology UPS is now introducing— which tells drivers where to go, what to pick up, and even when they've erred—initially had some drivers feeling threatened, feeling that their self-determination was being taken away. However, drivers often complain about any type of change, especially one that is technical in nature. You should have heard them when the initial DIAD came out in 1991, replacing the drivers' familiar clipboards. They howled. Yet try to take DIAD away from them now.

As with any new system there are initial bugs to work out. Those glitches feed complainers who now—thanks paradoxically to technology—can vent their complaints on the Internet. Package centers hold several meetings to explain the new system. Supervisors encourage drivers to coordinate with them about overriding the delivery routing based on ongoing situations, like new streets, construction, closed gates, and so on. Those coordination meetings can adjust future routing. In addition, drivers retain the autonomy to make daily changes too; they can override the sequence for whatever reason, including specific customer needs.

As always, each new innovation is a learning process for management too, not only understanding how the system works best, but how to best sell it to the drivers. One Great Basin District manager told me, "We've found that it is much easier to get the drivers behind [the new EDD] when we just start a few drivers at a time on the system versus the entire center."

My guess, as a veteran UPSer, is that as loaders and drivers get used to the system, they will discover that they will still make the choices to better serve their customers. One Kansas City driver said, "It's just a lot easier to plan my day." He added, "My truck is loaded the same way, so when I'm on vacation, another driver knows exactly where to go."

Electronic technology has made UPS far more efficient. Casey would have loved the idea of the Teflon driver, one who no longer gets stuck in traffic snarl-ups or delayed by unexpected circumstances. The new technology has made UPSers more nearly infallible. Yet electronics—particularly the new package flow technology—has also partially centralized operations, working against one core UPS policy—decentralization.

With a company as vast as UPS, the surprise is that decentralization has remained as generally intact as it has. However, many of its attributes have been eroded over the years. Districts complain that the "region" makes them do this and that. Regions, which theoretically help implement policies, complain that "corporate" is coming up with one program after another.

Center managers today have to abide by so many rules and methods that trickle down from division managers, from all the staff departments, and from newly implemented corporate policies, some might feel that they are just minding the store. But managers still have authority; it's just cloaked in a web of regulations. Drivers, too, can still use their good sense, personalities, and charisma to better serve their customers. They just have a lot more operating decisions laid out for them.

Service

Jim Casey, who prided himself on his company's reputation for service, would nonetheless be flabbergasted by the great lengths UPS now goes for its customers. A world where customers can make their own labels in a few clicks. A means of getting a parcel tens of thousands of miles away in a few hours. Handy retail UPS Stores. Freight services. Custom brokerage. Electronics repair. Dog-food mixing. Banking. The list goes on and on.

"Our ambition is not just to get things from here to there, but to enable commerce," CEO Mike Eskew is quoted as saying. "And enabling commerce can encompass an awful lot." UPS's can-do attitude seemingly has no bounds. In the last ten years, it has pushed the company to phenomenal achievements and diversifications, every one of which has direct benefits to customers.

To usher in the current and modern UPS, the company rebranded itself again in 2003. The forty-two-year-old "package with strings" shield, which reflected Jim Casey's obsession, was no longer a comprehensive expression of UPS's twenty-first-century "synchronized commerce." In its place came a new logo. Brown still dominates as a symbol of the company's heritage of quiet confidence and humility. Gold also remains as a part of UPS's identity, representing excellence and the quality of UPS service. The shield shape symbolizes UPS strengths of operational excellence, innovation, intelligence, and human spirit. The image's depth and dimension give it a feeling of energy. The big change is the new dynamic curve across the top, which suggests movement and points to UPS as a global business.

UPS has expanded beyond its traditional role as a delivery service into operations partnerships with its business customers. This has at times challenged traditional corporate precepts, pushing the company to evolve carefully in order to hold on to its treasured, and indeed critical, corporate culture.

The old UPS was egalitarian. It charged all accounts the same rates, regardless of volume shipped or type of delivery. It wanted to avoid charges of customer favoritism, notwithstanding that it cost less to move packages to businesses than to residences. This practice may have benefited the mom-and-pop operations, but big shippers felt slighted and UPS lost business to competitors. Customers clamored for heavier weight limits, discounts for multiple packages going to the same location, and much more.

The new UPS is customer-tailored, with numerous billing options. It has the ability not only to react to each customer's individual situation but even to guide customers so they make the best decisions, to expedite *their* getting *their* products to *their* consumers. Individuals and small businesses don't suffer, but bigger shippers really benefit. Having additional customers allows UPS more opportunities like those born of its early consolidation practices. The company can capitalize on economies of scale using its vast global network of planes, delivery vehicles, computers, and warehouses. Customers can trust their distribution to the expert—UPS. This is working well for all UPS business customers, of every size and nationality.

The proof that service is still the primary motivator is evident in management wages. Compare Mike Eskew's 2005 salary of $3,151,762, including bonuses, with other CEOs of America's top companies. Eskew was at number 216, listed with the CEOs of much smaller companies. Many salaries are much higher. In fact, each of the forty highest-paid CEOs made *more than $25 million!*

Core Values and Progress

Though only a handful of today's employees ever knew Jim Casey personally, his legacy persists. His sayings, ideals, and management style live on, and—through employees who pass them on to their children—even to future generations. Employees who enjoy being part of Big Brown almost always credit Jim Casey for the legacy they have inherited.

It's almost like Jim Casey saw the IPO coming back in 1945 when he said, "Ideals and dollars don't mix. However, we have found that if we really have ideals, and live up to them, the reward will be paid in dollars." Progress and growth are inevitable. Core values are not. All UPSers must work to maintain them, and to identify which ones need to be refortified to meet future occasions. Management shoulders the responsibility for passing the legacies from leader to leader, to encourage the priorities that permeate the entire workforce. Keep the culture; keep the integrity, and hopefully everything will fall into place.

In 2004, Mike Eskew gave a speech to an outside group in which he compared Jim Casey with former President Ronald Reagan.

> Like the president, Jim Casey preached a doctrine of enduring values. He told us that while times and conditions will—and indeed should—cause us to change our strategies, mission and even our purpose—the one thing that must never change is our core values. One might think that holding on to nearly century-old values may be restrictive. But let me assure you it's just the opposite—it's liberating. At UPS, we're not as interested in the next quarter as we are in the next quarter century.

If anything today buffets those core values, it's simply the nature of the modern world, the wave of progress, with the perils and opportunities that progress delivers. It's a wave Jim Casey rode his entire life. He was a natural master at scrutinizing its changing character, at assessing its dangers, and at remaining on top. The hope—and certainly the evidence—is that Casey's style, his code of business as instilled in generations of UPSers over the decades and in the corporate culture, will continue to carry the United Parcel Service of America, Incorporated, forward as unfailingly as your ever-reliable, ever-cheery UPS driver delivers your packages.

> Transition seldom comes easily. Of course, we cannot clearly see all of the steps ahead. It is always easier to see difficulties than to develop methods of solving them. But first, let us take sight of a goal. The difficulties will be solved in ways we cannot now see.

First is the dream, then development, followed by
improvement until the dream becomes a reality.
Later a new dream makes the products of an earlier
one obsolete. This has been the course of industrial
history, and in its path have been the victims and the
victors of progress.

—Jim Casey (1888–1983)

Appendix A
UPS Glossary of Terms

Big Brown: Nickname for UPS.

Browns: Term used to describe driver's uniform.

Bulk: Larger packages that don't fit on regular shelves.

Call Tag: A slip of paper that requests a driver to stop at a consignee's residence or place of business and pick up a package being returned to sender.

Center: The local UPS facility where packages are loaded into UPS vehicles for delivery to consignees. Center manager and supervisors coordinate the area's drivers (10–80, depending on population density).

DIAD: Delivery Information Acquisition Device. The UPS driver's handheld computer, onto which the consignee affixes a signature to confirm delivery. The fourth generation is in use today, known as DIAD IV.

EDD: Enhanced DIAD Download. New technology for DIAD IV, wherein package delivery information is already downloaded by the time UPS drivers report to work. The computer organizes delivery stops by its knowledge of incoming parcels.

Feeder: The UPS term for a tractor-trailer, semi, or big rig, which was coined for the same reason as "package car." So named because packages are "fed" hub-to-hub or to outlying centers. There are feeder vehicles, feeder equipment, and even a Feeder Department.

Hub: Larger UPS facility, with sorting capabilities and generally several package centers. Each metropolitan area has at least one hub.

Package Car: A UPS delivery vehicle, which is never called "a truck." Early on UPS wanted to be known as a delivery company, not a trucking company, so some interesting terminology developed.

PAL: Preload Assist Label. The "smart" label that (when filled out at point of origin) lets the system know what's arriving at a delivery center.

PAS: Preload Assist System. The computerized plan that tells the pre-loader the stop-for-stop order of all parcels loaded into a delivery car.

PCM: Prework Communications Meeting. Brief meeting held by the UPS supervisor or manager at the beginning of each workday to inform UPS employees of important events or other informa-tion they need to know.

Pickup: Refers to regular shipping accounts UPSers stop at daily; also refers to the packages picked up, taken to center, loaded onto feeder, and sent to hub.

Preload: Packages that arrive in the center are sorted and loaded onto package cars. A preloader is the UPS employee who loads the package car during the preload operation.

Service Provider: The official employee description for UPS drivers.

UPS Brown: Official UPS color, originally was Pullman brown—named after the color of George Pullman's railroad sleeper cars—but slightly modified. The exact shade of brown is trademarked.

UPSer: What UPS employees are called.

Worldport: The 4-million-square-foot heart of the UPS Air Operation in Louisville, Kentucky. Equipped with the latest technology, it has 17,000 conveyors that stretch for over 122 miles, is capable of sorting 304,000 packages per hour, and is home to 5,000 UPSers. Even so, this largest-ever UPS facility is currently being expanded by about one-third.

Appendix B
Fact Sheet of
UPS Operations

Worldwide Facts

Founded: August 28, 1907, in Seattle, Washington, USA
World Headquarters: Atlanta, Georgia, USA
World Wide Web Address: www.ups.com
Chairman & CEO: Michael L. Eskew
2005 Revenue: $42.6 billion
Employees: 407,200 Worldwide (348,400 U.S.; 58,800
    International)

Package Operations

2005 Revenue: $36.6 billion
2005 Delivery Volume: 3.75 billion packages and documents
Daily Delivery Volume: 14.8 million packages and documents
Daily U.S. Air Volume: 2.2 million packages and documents
Daily International Volume: 1.5 million packages and
    documents
Service Area: More than 200 countries and territories; every
    address in North America and Europe
Customers: 7.9 million daily (1.8 million pickup, 6.1 million
    delivery)
UPS.com: Average 10 million daily online tracking requests
Retail Access: The UPS Store, 4,400; Mail Boxes Etc., 1,300;
    UPS
Customer Centers, 1,000; Authorized outlets, 17,000; UPS
    Drop Boxes, 40,000
Operating Facilities: 1,788

Delivery Fleet: 91,700 package cars, vans, tractors, motorcycles
UPS Jet Aircraft Fleet: 268
Chartered Aircraft: 309
Daily Flight Segments: Domestic—1,071; International—767
Airports Served: Domestic—400; International—377
Air Hubs:

- United States: Louisville, Kentucky (Main US Air Hub); Philadelphia, Pennsylvania; Dallas, Texas; Ontario, California; Rockford, Illinois; Columbia, South Carolina; Hartford, Connecticut
- Europe: Cologne/Bonn, Germany
- Asia Pacific: Taipei, Taiwan; Pampanga, Philippines; Hong Kong; Singapore
- Latin America and Caribbean: Miami, Florida, USA
- Canada: Hamilton, Ontario

Supply Chain and Freight

2005 Revenue: $6 billion

UPS Supply Chain Solutions

Key Services: Logistics and distribution; transportation and freight (air, sea, ground, rail); freight forwarding; international trade management; customs brokerage
Specialty Services: Service parts logistics; technical repair and configuration; supply chain design and planning; returns management; urgent parts delivery
Facilities: 1,000+ facilities in more than 120 countries; 35 million square feet

UPS Freight

Key Services: Leading provider of less-than-truckload services coast-to-coast
Delivery Fleet: 6,700 tractors; 22,100 trailers
Facilities: 200+ service centers

Bibliography

"100 Best Corporate Citizens 2006." *Business Ethics*, Spring 2006.

"Adapt and Deliver: Interview with UPS's David Abney." *Hemispheres Magazine*, May 25, 2006.

Albright, Horace Marden. *Creating the National Park Service*. Norman: University of Oklahoma Press, 1999.

"Alliances." *DC Velocity*, February 2003. Available online: www.dcvelocity.com/articles/february2003/newsworthy04.cfm. Access date: September 4, 2006.

"America's Most Admired Companies." *Fortune*, March 17, 2005.

"An Illustrated History of the Big Bend Country, Embracing Lincoln, Douglas, Adams and Franklin Counties, State of Washington." Western Historical, 1904. Available online: http://freepages.genealogy.rootsweb.com/~heeyjude/Douglas/sheehantw.html. Access date: September 4, 2006.

"Aviation Comes of Age." Century of Flight, n.d. Available online: www.century-of-flight.net/Aviation%20history/coming%20of%20age/splash.htm. Access date: September 4, 2006.

Barnum, John W. "What Prompted Airline Deregulation 20 Years Ago?" McGuire Woods, September 15, 1998. Available online: http://library.findlaw.com/1988/Sep/1/129304.html. Access date: July 4, 2006.

Bertauche, Ruth McCabe. *Evert McCabe and the Founding of United Parcel Service*. Seattle: University of Washington Press, 1983.

Bird, Jerry W. "Yukon Memories and the Klondike Gold Rush." Adventures in Travel Expo, 2005. Available online: www.airhighways.com/klondike.htm. Access date: September 4, 2006.

Birla, Madan. *FedEx Delivers*. Hoboken, N.J.: Wiley, 2005.

Birnbaum, Jeffrey H. "The Road to Riches Is Called K Street: Lobbying Firms Hire More, Pay More, Charge More to Influence Government." *Washington Post*, June 22, 2005, p. AO1. Available online: www.washingtonpost.com/wp-dyn/content/article/2005/06/21/AR2005062101632.html. Access date: September 4, 2006.

Bowman, Robert J. "100 Great Supply Chain Partners Readers Recognize: Providers Who Improve Efficiency." *Choice Logistics*, August 25, 2004.

Available online: www.realtimefreight.com/site/media22.htm. Access date: September 4, 2006.

"Brown Goes Green for Power." Knight Ridder/Tribune Business News. March 30, 2005. Published online: www.hoovers.com/free/co/news/detail. xhtml?COID=40483&ArticleID=NR2005033. The story is no longer available at that site; inquiries may be addressed to www.hoovers.com.

Brown, William H. "A Letter from William H. Brown, III." U.S. Equal Employment Opportunity Commission, n.d. Available online: www.eeoc.gov/abouteeoc/35th/voices/brown.html. Access date: September 7, 2006.

Buckley, Chris. "U.P.S. Buys Chinese Delivery Service, a Former Partner." Company News. *New York Times*, December 3, 2004.

Buckley, Dan. "The Messenger Company That Became United Parcel Service." *Portage Magazine*, 3(3), Summer 1982.

Cabardo, Roberto M. "PGMA Inaugurates New Timex Facility." PIA Information Service, August 11, 2005. Available online: www.pia.gov.ph/news.asp?fi=p050811.htm&no=5. Access date: September 6, 2006.

"Candelaria." Online Highways, n.d. Available online: www.nvohwy.com/c/candghos.htm. Access date: September 4, 2006.

"Candelaria and Mettalic [sic] City." Ghost Towns.com, November 14, 2003. Available online: www.ghosttowns.com/states/nv/candelaria.html. Access date: September 4, 2006.

Cappelli, Peter. "A Market-Driven Approach to Retaining Employees: Rethinking Employee Retention in a Competitive Economy." Harvard Business School Working Knowledge, March 28, 2000. Available online: http://hbswk.hbs.edu/item.jhtml?id=1422&t=organizations. Access date: September 4, 2006.

Carey, Bill. "Two Titans of the Tracking Industry Are Sizing Up Each Other." *Traffic World*, June 12, 2006.

Carey, Nick. "U.S. Railroads, Under Pressure from Customers over Network Congestion." Reuters, May 23, 2006.

Casey, J. E. "Letter Offering Shares to Employees." New York: UPS, May 27, 1935.

Casey, J. E. *J.E. Casey: Our Partnership Legacy*. Greenwich, Conn.: United Parcel Service, 1985.

Casey, J. E., McCabe, Evert, Casey, George, and Soderstrom, C. W. "Letter Offering Shares to Employees." Los Angeles: UPS, December 20, 1927.

Cassidy, William B. "After Fighting Bitterly for Decades to Organize Overnite Transportation, Now UPS Freight, the Teamsters Finally Scent the Possibility of Success." *Traffic World*, June 12, 2006.

Census Microfilm Records: Montana, Nevada, Oregon, Washington, 1900. Washington, King County, Roll 1745.

Chabrow, Eric. "Oil Companies Aren't the Only Ones Using IT." *Information Week*, June 5, 2006.

Chang, Yi Hsin. "UPS Makes Wish Come True." *Motley Fool*, July 22, 1999. Available online: www.fool.com/EveningNews/foth/1999/foth990722. htm. Access date: September 4, 2006.

Chao, Elaine L., Secretary of Labor. "14th Annual Labor Hall of Fame Induction Ceremony." U.S. Department of Labor, October 10, 2002. Available online: www.dol.gov/_sec/media/speeches/20021010_ HallofFame.htm. Access date: September 4, 2006.

"Charity, Volunteerism Highlight UPS Efforts in China." US-China Archives, October 2005, Week 2, #1, second part of file. Available online: http://lists.state.gov/SCRIPTS/WA-USIAINFO.EXE?A2=ind0510b &L=us-china&H=1&O=D&P=76. Access date: September 5, 2006.

Chinagate. "UPS Hopes to Spread Its Wings in China." *China Daily*, February 17, 2004. Available online: www.chinadaily.com.cn/chinagate/doc/ 2004–02/17/content_306886.htm. Access date: September 5, 2006.

Cohen, Don, and Prusak, Laurence. *In Good Company*. Boston: Harvard Business School Press, 2001.

Common Dreams Newswire. "Shipping Companies: Blunt Pushed an Anti-Competitive Measure for UPS and Federal Express." *Public Citizen*, January 2006, p. 30.

Conover, Ted. "Capitalist Roaders." *New York Times Magazine*, July 2, 2006. Available online: http://travel2.nytimes.com/2006/07/02/magazine/ 02china.html. Access date: September 5, 2006.

Cornwell, Susan. "Republican Leaders Push for Pension Reform Bill." Reuters, June 13, 2006.

CousinConnect.com: County Galway Genealogy Queries. "Casey Genealogy Queries." Available online: www.cousinconnect.com/p/a/1105/s/ CASEY/; click "Submit Query." Access date: September 5, 2006.

"Curtiss-Wright." PilotFriend, n.d. Available online: http://www.pilotfriend. com/acft_manu/Curtiss_Wright.htm. Access date: September 6, 2006.

Dade, Corey. "Moving Ahead: How UPS Went from Low-Tech to an IT Power— and Where It's Headed Next." *Wall Street Journal*, July 24, 2006.

Darren Barefoot. "In Praise of My UPS Shirt" (blog entry), August 30, 2004. Available online: www.darrenbarefoot.com/archives/001081.html. Access date: September 5, 2006.

Davis, Preston W. *1907: A Memorable Year*. New York: Self-published, 1982.

Deal, Terrence E., and Kennedy, Allan A. *Corporate Cultures: The Rites and Rituals of Corporate Life*. Cambridge, Mass.: Perseus Publishing, 2000.

Decker, Kathi, Engleman, Shara, Petrucci, Tony, and Robinson, Shirley. "United Parcel Service and the Management of Change." Harvard Business School: Working Knowledge, February 28, 2006. Available online: http://inside.cbpa.louisville.edu/bruce/cases/ups/htm/ups.htm. Access date: September 5, 2006.

Dillon, Tim. "UPS' Pay, Perks Make It a Destination Job for Many." *USA Today*, October 14, 2003.

Donnelly, Sally B. "Out of the Box." *Time* (Inside Business), November 1, 2004. Available online: www.time.com/time/insidebiz/printout/ 0,8816,749420,00.html. Access date: April 18, 2006.

Edsall, Thomas B. "House Majority Whip Exerts Influence by Way of K Street." *Washington Post*, May 17, 2005. Available online: www.washington-post.com/wp-dyn/content/article/2005/05/16/AR2005051601334_ pf.html. Access date: September 5, 2006.

"Educating Future Business Leaders: A Broad Approach." *BenchMark*, May 26, 2005. Available online: http://152.3.224.76/campaign/benchmark/ bench16/CampDuke.html. Access date: September 5, 2006.

Encyclopaedia Britannica Online. "Dale Carnegie," n.d. Available online: www.britannica.com/eb/article?tocId=9020403. Access date: September 5, 2006.

Federal Election Commission. "Campaign Contribution Search." News Meat, constantly updated. Available online: www.newsmeat.com/ceo_ political_donations/Michael_Eskew.php. Access date July 30, 2006.

Foust, Dean. "Big Brown's New Bag." *BusinessWeek* Online, July 19, 2004. Available online: www.businessweek.com/print/magazine/content/04_ 29/b3892102_mz017.htm?chan=. Access date: September 4, 2006.

Frank, Robert. "UPS Men Deliver More Than Packages." In Ken Wells (Ed.), *Floating off the Page: The Best Stories from the Wall Street Journal's 'Middle Column.'* New York: Simon & Schuster, 2002.

"Freight Congestion Prompts Worries of Shipment Delays." C F Rail, March 31, 2004. Available online: http://www.cfrail.com/newsevents.asp? type=news&id=2#Article. Access date: September 5, 2006.

Friedman, Thomas L. *The World Is Flat.* New York: Farrar, Straus & Giroux, 2005.

Garrett, Wilbur E. (Ed.) *Ireland and Northern Ireland: A Visitors Guide.* Washington, D.C.: National Geographic Society, 1981.

Geisel, Jerry. "Tentative Deal Reached on Pension Reform Bill." Business Insurance, July 19, 2006. Available online: www.businessinsurance.com/ cgi-bin/news.pl?newsId=8055. Access date: September 5, 2006.

Ghost Town Explorers. "Candelaria, Nevada," November 14, 2003. Available online: http://www.ghosttownexplorers.org/nevada/candelar/candelar. htm. Access date: September 5, 2006.

Gorlick, Adam. "'Integrity' Most Looked-up Word." Associated Press, December 12, 2005. Available online: http://www.merriam-webster.com/info/ pr/2005-words-of-year.htm. Access date: October 18, 2006.

Green, Ed. "Local Contractors Await Chance for More UPS Work." *Business First*, May 19, 2006.

Green, Frank. "County's Big Grocers Are Finding That Web Offers Growth Market." *San Diego Union Tribune*, July 2, 2006. Available online:

www.signonsandiego.com/news/business/20060702-9999-lz1b2online.
html. Access date: September 5, 2006.

Gunther, Marc. *Faith and Fortune: The Quiet Revolution to Reform American Business*. New York: Crown, 2004.

Gunther, Marc. "How UPS, Starbucks, Disney Do Good." *Fortune*, February 27, 2006. Available online: http://money.cnn.com/2006/02/23/news/companies/mostadmired_fortune_responsible/index.htm. Access date: September 5, 2006.

Hamburger, Philip. "Ah, Packages!" *New Yorker*, May 10, 1947.

Hamburger, Philip. *Mayor Watching and Other Pleasures*. New York: Rinehart, 1958.

Hardesty, Greg. "$50 Million Donation to Hospital an Easy Call." *Orange County Register*, April 14, 2005. Available online: http://nl.newsbank.com/nlsearch.asp (search on title). Access date: September 5, 2006.

Hargis, Michael. "95 Years of Revolutionary Industrial Unionism." *Anarcho Syndicalist Review*, # 27 and #28. Available online: www.iww.org (search on "Hargis"). Access date: September 5, 2006.

Hays, Constance L. *The Real Thing: Truth and Power at the Coca-Cola Company*. New York: Random House, 2004.

Hine, Lewis W. "Child Labor in America, 1908–1912." The History Place, 1998. Available online: www.historyplace.com/unitedstates/childlabor/about.htm]. Access date: April 26, 2005.

"History of the US Postal Service." U.S. Postal Service, n.d. Available online: www.usps.com/history/his3.htm. Access date: June 16, 2006.

Hitt, Greg, and Miller, Scott. "In Trade Talks, Western Farmers Hold Their Ground." *Wall Street Journal*, December 13, 2005.

Hogan, Con (Senior Consultant, Annie E. Casey Foundation). "Con Hogan Speaks in Hartford." State of Connecticut: Commission on Children, March 26, 2003.

Holly, Susan. "Taking the High Road." *Warfield's* (Baltimore County), November 1989.

Hudson, Zack. "Sixteen of Georgia's Fortune 50 Companies Received High Marks." *Atlanta Southern Voice*, July 7, 2006.

Hughes, John. "U.S. Aviation Regulators Said They Will Deploy a Satellite-based Navigation System." Bloomberg, May 2, 2006.

"Industry Rushes to Katrina Victims." *DC Velocity*, October 2005. Available online: www.dcvelocity.com/articles/20051001/news.cfm. Access date: September 5, 2006.

Institute of Chartered Financial Analysis. "FedEx & UPS—Competing in China." Available online: http://icmr.icfai.org/casestudies/catalogue/Marketing/MKTG069.htm. Access date: July 12, 2006.

International Boxing Hall of Fame. "Enshrinees: Battling Nelson." Excerpt from James B. Roberts and Alexander G. Scutt, *The Boxing Register*.

Ithaca, N.Y.: McBooks, 1999. Available online: www.ibhof.com/bnelson.htm. Access date: September 15, 2006.

International Boxing Hall of Fame. "Enshrinees: Joe Gans." Excerpt from James B. Roberts and Alexander G. Scutt, *The Boxing Register*. Ithaca, N.Y.: McBooks, 1999. Available online: www.ibhof.com/gans.htm. Access date: September 5, 2006.

"James E. Casey: Labor Hall of Fame 2002 Honoree," U.S. Department of Labor, November 14, 2003. Available online: www.dol.gov/oasam/programs/laborhall/jec.htm. Access date: September 5, 2006.

Janetzko, Andreas. "Setting Up the Supply Chain in China: Challenges and Changes." Report of Eyefortransport: Second European 3PL Summit, November 25, 2004. Available online: www.eyefortransport.com/europe3pl/presentations/europe3pl2004/UPS_Supply_Chain_China.pdf. Access date: September 5, 2006.

Jeffords, Sarah. "United Parcel Service Inc.'s Decision to Add 5,000 Positions." *Business First*, May 28, 2006.

"Jim Casey Is Dead at 95." *New York Times*, June 7, 1983.

"Jim Casey Obituary." *Los Angeles Times*, June 7, 1983.

"Jim Casey Obituary." *Time*, June 20, 1983.

Karman, John R., III, and Adams, Brent. "Close Ties Among UPS, Government and Development Officials Helped Expansion Package Come Together Quickly." *Business First of Louisville*, May 19, 2006.

Keller, Michelle. "Bringing Gen Y Aboard for the Long Haul: Integrating the Roaming 'Entitlement Generation' into the Workplace Is Often a Challenge." *Los Angeles Times*, July 10, 2006.

Kelly, James P. "Postal Service Stacks Deck." *Journal of Commerce*, April 5, 1999.

Kempner, Matt. "Ingenuity Delivered." *Atlanta Journal Constitution*, July 6, 2005.

"Klondike Gold Rush: Yukon Territory 1897." Quest Connect, n.d. Available online: www.questconnect.org/ak_klondike.htm. Access date: September 5, 2006.

LaGesse, David. "UPS Is Betting on Tech to Deliver a Competitive Edge." *US News and World Report*, July 23, 2006.

LeDuc, Doug. "International Hybrid Improves Fuel Economy." *Business Weekly* (Fort Wayne, Indiana), Technology Column, June 27, 2006.

Levin, Alan. "The Government Is Endorsing a New Concept for the Future of Guiding Planes." *USA Today*, May 2, 2006.

"Louisville International Ranked 4th Busiest Cargo Airport in the U.S." Louisville Regional Airport Authority, April 3, 2006. Available online: www.flylouisville.com/upload/202.pdf. Access date: September 5, 2006.

Lukas, Paul, and Overfelt, Maggie. "UPS United Parcel Service James Casey Transformed a Tiny Messenger Service into the World's Largest Shipper by Getting All Wrapped Up in the Details of Package Delivery."

Fortune, April 1, 2003. Available online: http://money.cnn.com/ magazines/fsb/fsb_archive/2003/04/01/341024/index.htm. Access date: September 5, 2006.

Lundberg, Murray. "Maritime Ghosts of the Klondike." Seattle: Explore North, 2001. Available online: www.explorenorth.com/library/yafeatures/ bl-ghost.htm. Access date: September 5, 2006.

Lynch, David J. "Thanks to Its CEO, UPS Doesn't Just Deliver." *USA Today*, July 23, 2006.

Maney, Kevin. *The Maverick and His Machine: Thomas Watson Sr. and the Making of IBM*. New York: Wiley, 2003.

Maranjian, Selena. "America's Biggest Employers." January 28, 2004. Available online: www.fool.com/News/mft/2004/mft04012801.htm. Access date: October 18, 2006.

"Market Wars. How Postal Service Rivals Are Clambering for Position in the US." *Uni Global Union*, March 5, 2000. Available online: www. union-network.org/unipostal.nsf/4fe7c562be09acf3c1256da5004960d0/ 90d5f977eb9ed006c12568d4004a9934?OpenDocument. Access date: September 5, 2006.

Marshall, John. "Drivers for Rival UPS and FedEx Prefer Joshing to Jousting." *Seattle Post-Intelligencer*, June 18, 2003. Available online: http:// seattlepi.nwsource.com/local/127014_ups18.asp. Access date: September 5, 2006.

McNamee, Mike. "1999: The Triumphs and Turkeys." Business Week Online, December 27, 1999. Available online: www.businessweek.com/1999/ 99_52/b3661048.htm. Access date: September 4, 2006.

McPhee, John. "Out in the Sort." *New Yorker*, April 18, 2005, pp. 160–173.

McPhee, John. *Uncommon Carriers*. New York: Farrar, Strauss & Giroux, 2006.

"Messenger Boy's Murder Willful and Deliberate. *Goldfield Review* (Goldfield, Nev.), September 20, 1906.

Moreno, Richard. "City of Gold Is Now Just a Ghost." Nevada Commission on Tourism, November 14, 2003. Available online: www.travelnevada. com/story.asp?sid=25. Access date: September 5, 2006.

Murawski, John. "CEO Describes How UPS Weathers Storms." *Raleigh News & Observer*, June 8, 2006.

National Association of Social Workers. "Second Annual Social Work Month Gala," March 13, 2003. Available online: www.naswfoundation.org/ events/swm_gala_2003/GalaProgram.pdf. Access date: September 5, 2006.

National Park Service. "Klondike Gold Rush: Seattle Unit," n.d. Available online: www.nps.gov/klse/. Access date: September 6, 2006.

National Park Service. "Seattle: A National Register of Historic Places Travel Itinerary: Pioneer Square—Skid Road Historic District," n.d.

Available online: www.cr.nps.gov/nr/travel/seattle/s28.htm. Access date: September 6, 2006.

Natl. Parcel v. *J.B. Hunt Logistics*. U.S. 8th Circuit Court of Appeals, August 10, 1998. Available online: http://caselaw.lp.findlaw.com/scripts/printer_friendly.pl?page=8th/974284p.html. Access date: September 7, 2006.

New York University/Leonard N. Stern School of Business. "From Private to Publicly Traded Firm: The Initial Public Offering," n.d. Available online: http://pages.stern.nyu.edu/~adamodar/New_Home_Page/invfables/ipo.htm. Access date: July 16, 2006.

"Not Protective but . . . Restrictive": ERA Advocates Oppose Protective Legislation for Women. History Matters. December 30, 2004.

Paher, Stanley W. *Goldfield: Boom Town of Nevada*. Las Vegas: Nevada Publications, 1977.

Paher, Stanley W. *Nevada Ghost Towns and Mining Camps*. Las Vegas: Nevada Publications, 1993.

"Parcel Carriers Offer Musical." *New York Times*, April 12, 1942, p. 46.

"Philips Medical Selects UPS to Run Global Logistics Network." *Money Magazine*, May 30, 2006.

"Pioneer Hall of Fame." Women in Aviation International, n.d. Available online: www.wai.org/resources/pioneers.cfm. Access date: July 3, 2006.

Preston, Edmund. "The Government Role in Civil Aviation: An Overview." U.S. Centennial of Flight Commission, n.d. Available online: www.centennialofflight.gov/essay/Government_Role/POL-OV.htm. Access date: June 10, 2006.

Putnam, Robert D., and Feldstein, Lewis M. *Better Together: Restoring the American Community*. New York: Simon & Schuster, 2003.

Raines, Laura. "Want to Know What Makes a Company a Great Place to Work?" *Atlanta Journal-Constitution*, March 19, 2006.

Rauch, Jonathan. "Suckers! Washington's Parasite Class Keeps Growing and Growing and Growing and . . . " *Reason Magazine*, July 24, 2006. Available online: http://reason.com/9405/fe.rauch.9405.shtml. Access date: September 5, 2006.

Reason, Tim. "Office Politics: Banned from Making Political Contributions, Companies Harvest Them from Employees Instead. *CFO Magazine*, July 1, 2004. Available online: www.cfo.com/article.cfm/3014831/c_3046615?f=insidecfo. Access date: September 7, 2006.

Rivas, Teresa. "Remember That Embarrassing Nickname?" *Wall Street Journal*, May 30, 2006.

Rumerman, Judy. "The Curtiss-Wright Corporation." U.S. Centennial of Flight Commission, n.d. Available online: www.centennialofflight.gov/essay/Aerospace/Curtiss_wright/Aero9.htm. Access date: July 27, 2005.

"Rumors of War: Uniform Behavior." Snopes, Urban Legends Reference Pages, April 2003. Available online: www.snopes.com/rumors/ups.asp. Access date: September 6, 2006.

Salant, Jonathan D., and Newton-Small, Jay. "UPS Uses Political Clout to Press for Cuts in Pension Benefits." Bloomberg.com, March 20, 2006. Available online: www.bloomberg.com/apps/news?pid=10000103& sid=aZ4baobjLWaQ&refer=us. Access date: September 5, 2006.

Schenck, Marian Albright. *National Park Service: The First 75 Years*. Washington, D.C.: National Park Service.

Schlangenstein, Mary. "United Parcel Service Inc. Workers Represented by the Teamsters Want Early Contract Talks." *Bloomberg News*, June 5, 2006.

Sheehey, Katherine Summers. "UPS Founder Grew Up on Goldfield Streets." *Nevadan*, January 8, 1984.

"Shot Dead by Wife in Tudor City Home: Evert McCabe, Executive, Slain by Woman Believed Crazed by Death of Son." *New York Times*, January 13, 1933, p. 36.

Silbermann, Paul. "Clement Melville Keys Papers." National Air and Space Museum Archives. Washington, D.C.: Smithsonian Institution, 1995 & 2003.

"Slayer of Dead Husband Freed: Mrs. McCabe, Confined in Hospital Since 1933, Wins Discharge." *New York Times*, July 28, 1936, p. 11.

Smith, George D. *Our Partnership Legacy*. Greenwich, Conn.: United Parcel Service, 1970.

Snyder, Jodie. "United Parcel Service to Buy, Expand SonicAir." High Beam Research. Knight Ridder/Tribune Business News, January 4, 1995.

Sonnenfeld, Jeffrey. *United Parcel Service*. Boston: Harvard Business School (Report A), 1987.

Sonnenfeld, Jeffrey. *United Parcel Service*. Boston: Harvard Business School (Report B), 1987.

Spears, Sarah David. "CEO Survey Names UPS America's Top Brand." *Business First of Louisville*, May 15, 2006.

"Special Report: Executive Compensation." *USA Today*, April 10, 2006.

Starr, Kevin. *Endangered Dreams: The Great Depression in California*. New York: Oxford University Press, 1996.

Stein, Alan J. "Dave Beck Forms the Western Conference of Teamsters in 1937." Online Encyclopedia of Washington State History, June 26, 2005. Available online: www.historylink.org/essays/output.cfm?file_id=7359. Access date: April 18, 2006.

"Teamsters Seeking Early Negotiations with UPS." *Transport Topics*, June 5, 2006.

The National Center for Public Policy Research. "UPS Fined for Involuntary Atmosphere of PAC Involvement." *Political Money Monitor*, 7, January 16, 1998. Available online: www.nationalcenter.org/PMM7.html. Access date: September 6, 2006.

"The Uniform Approach to High Fashion." (South Florida) *Sun Sentinel*, May 17, 2006.

"The U.S. Environmental Protection Agency (EPA) Has Unveiled the First-Ever Series Hydraulic Hybrid Diesel Urban Delivery Vehicle." *Wall Street Journal*, June 22, 2006.

"The Waldorf in History." *Desert Sun*, January 18, 2006.

"The Young and the Restless: Victoria Rowell." CBS.com, n.d. Available online: www.cbs.com/daytime/yr/about/bios/vrowell.shtml. Access date: June 24, 2006.

Thuermer, Karen E. "Small Package Delivery Goes Global Like the Big Boys." *World Trade Magazine*, July 1, 2004. Available online: www.world-trademag.com/CDA/Articles/Small_Package_and_Express/3178938c89af7010VgnVCM100000f932a8c0. Access date: September 6, 2006.

"Tracking Consumers' Company Recall." *Wall Street Journal*, December 5, 2005.

"Travels in the American Southwest: Goldfield." CmmdrMark dot Com, n.d. Available online: www.cmdrmark.com/goldfield.html. Access date: September 7, 2006.

Trimble, Vance H. *Sam Walton, Founder of Wal-Mart*. New York: Penguin Books, 1990.

United Parcel Service. *Big Idea*. Numerous issues. Los Angeles, New York, Greenwich: United Parcel Service, 1924–1995.

United Parcel Service. *Call Red Arrow*. Los Angeles: United Parcel Service, 1930.

United Parcel Service. *Manual of Instructions for Drivers and Helpers*. New York: United Parcel Service, 1948.

United Parcel Service. *UPS Song Book*. Los Angeles: United Parcel Service, 1950.

United Parcel Service. *United Parcel Service 50th Anniversary Program*. New York: United Parcel Service, 1957.

United Parcel Service. *New Southern California Plant of United Parcel Service*. Los Angeles: United Parcel Service, 1958.

United Parcel Service. *UPS Annual Reports*. 1968–2005. New York, Greenwich, Atlanta: United Parcel Service, 1968–2005.

United Parcel Service. *United Parcel Service 75th Anniversary Program*. Greenwich, Conn.: United Parcel Service, 1982.

United Parcel Service. *Inside UPS*. Numerous issues. New York, Greenwich, Atlanta: United Parcel Service, 1990–2005.

United Parcel Service. *UPS Policy Book*. Greenwich, Conn.: United Parcel Service, 1992.

United Parcel Service. "UPS Breaks United Way Record for a Fifth Consecutive Year" (Press Release), March 16, 2005.

United Parcel Service. "UPS's 'Circle of Honor' for Safe Drivers Grows to 3,956; 354 Honorees Added This Year; 87 Pass 35-Year Mark" (Press Release), October 4, 2005. Available online: www.socialfunds.com/news/release.cgi?sfArticleId=4506. Access date: September 7, 2006.

University of Washington. *Klondike Gold Rush, Yukon Territory, 1897*. Seattle: University of Washington Archives, 2005.

"U.P.S. and FedEx in New Air Services." *New York Times*, April 12, 1995.

"UPS and the Beijing Organizing Committee for the Olympic Games (BOCOG) today signed a Memorandum of Understanding." June 6, 2006. Available online: www.ups.com/content/cn/en/about/news/press_releases/06_06_2006_cn.html. Access date: October 18, 2006.

"UPS Drivers Avoid Blue-Collar Union Blues." Reuters, February 21, 2006. Available online: www.msnbc.nsn.com/id/11486765/from/ET/print/1/displaymode/1098/ Access date: September 7, 2006.

"UPS Environment-Friendly Trucks Reach Milestone." Spotlighting News, June 13, 2006. Available online: www.spotlightingnews.com/article.php?news=2436. Access date: September 7, 2006.

"UPS Expands in China." Franchiseek China, n.d. Available online: www.franchiseek.com/China/Franchise_UPS_China_News.htm. Access date: July 12, 2006.

"UPS' Green Fleet Clocks Up 100 Million Miles." Just Auto editorial team, June 19, 2006. Available online: www.just-auto.com/article.aspx?id=88103&lk=s. Access date: September 7, 2006.

"UPS Is Buying 50 Hybrid Electric Delivery Vehicles." *Consumer Affairs*, February 24, 2006.

"UPS Unveils Hybrid Truck." *Journal of Commerce*, June 22, 2006.

VandeHei, Jim. "GOP Whip Quietly Tried to Aid Big Donor." *Washington Post*, June 11, 2003.

Villiers-Tuthill, Kathleen. *History of Clifden, 1810–1860*. Dublin, Ireland: Dublin Press, 1981.

Walsh, Mary Williams. "Congress to Weigh Easing U.P.S. Role on Pension Funds." *New York Times*, December 13, 2006.

Ward, Karla. "UPS Air Hub Features 122 Miles of Conveyor System." *Lexington Herald-Leader*, July 24, 2006.

Western Historical Publishing Co. *An Illustrated History of the Big Bend Country, Embracing Lincoln, Douglas, Adams and Franklin Counties, State of Washington*. Western Historical, 1904.

Winter, Greg. "George C. Lamb, Jr., Ex-Chief of United Parcel, Dies at 75." *Motley Fool*, April 7, 2001.

Witt, Clyde E. "Four Years After Opening the Most Technologically Advanced Air Package Sorting Hub." *Material Handling Management*, May 24, 2006.

Acknowledgments

The remarkable founder of UPS, Jim Casey, in a way wrote this book. Stories about him and by him inspired me, as they inspired all UPSers. I quote him often and his ideals are hereby promulgated. I thank several surviving members of the Casey family, especially Paul Casey, Jim's nephew, who assisted with background for *Big Brown*. Shirley (Casey) Miller was an integral part of my decision to attempt this book. Tim Casey, a grandnephew, also provided input.

I gleaned information from notes, letters, and personal conversations from some UPS pioneers including Ruth McCabe Bertauche (daughter of founder Evert McCabe), Frank McCabe (Evert's brother), Russel Havighorst (first UPS engineer), and Ray McCue (first five-year safe driver).

All UPSers over the years served as an inspiration for this book. Numerous retirees fed me information for which I am grateful, including Gale Davis, Mike Grennan, John McHale, and Alda Williamson (who assisted Jim Casey with clerical duties). Steve Maxwell was especially helpful, answering questions and suggesting direction. Current UPSers Steve Goodrich and Gene Reilly also added anecdotal input. It was a collective effort; typical of the way UPS has done business over the past hundred years.

Special thanks to my agent Sally van Haitsma of the Castiglia Literary Agency, who has gone far beyond what an agent normally does. She embraced this project with fervor and has helped edit, rewrite, refine, revamp, and nurture *Big Brown* from concept to completion. Julie Castiglia has also been very supportive and attentive.

This book's final shape is largely due to Tershia d'Elgin, a talented and diligent writer/editor, who worked very closely with me to help ensure the *Big Brown* story has been told in a fascinating and engaging manner. Thanks to everyone at the Jossey-Bass/Wiley team, especially editor Neal Maillet who really went to bat to make this book happen and energized the whole JB team with his enthusiasm.

Others edited early drafts and offered numerous suggestions: Anne Batty and Shirley Miller, first draft editors, and Ed Robertson, who helped with a second draft. I appreciate their input. I often sought advice from editor Jennifer Redmond of Sunbelt Publications.

Numerous museums, archivists, newspapers, and universities were helpful, from answering a simple question to more detailed research. I especially thank the University of Washington, the Washington State Museum of History and Industry, the Esmeralda County Courthouse in Goldfield, Nevada, and the Goldfield Historical Society.

And finally, and most important, my grateful appreciation to my wife, Leila, who had to weave our social obligations and travels around my constant attention to this supposedly retirement project.

About the Author

Greg Niemann holds a B.A. in journalism from Cal State University, Los Angeles, and was a publications editor with United Parcel Service before he retired in January 1995 with over thirty-four years service. He has personally known every UPS CEO from founder Jim Casey to today's Mike Eskew.

He was president of both the Los Angeles and Orange County chapters of the International Association of Business Communicators and was named Communicator of the Year by that organization. He has also served on the Board of Directors of the Outdoor Writers Association of California.

He contributes regularly to several publications and is presently on the staff of the *San Clemente Journal*.

Niemann's Baja California books (*Baja Fever*, published by Mountain N' Air Books of La Crescenta, and *Baja Legends*, published by Sunbelt Publications of San Diego) are very popular in Southern California and Mexico. *Baja Legends* also won an award from the Outdoor Writers Association of California.

His historical book, *Palm Springs Legends: Creation of a Desert Oasis*, published by Sunbelt Publications, has been a best-seller at several Southern California bookstores.

Niemann worked for UPS as a teenager in 1957–58, spent two years in the U.S. Army, and returned in 1961 as a delivery driver in Hollywood, California. Getting his education at night, he was promoted into management in Los Angeles, where he edited the company magazine, the *Big Idea*, in Southern California for years and later coordinated the editing of numerous company publications as the West Coast manager of the Corporate Communications department.

Niemann and his wife, Leila, reside in Southern California.

Index